11+ Maths

For the CEM test – ages 10-11

Passing the 11+ is no mean feat, but luckily this CGP book is the ultimate way to prepare for CEM Maths. It's a one-way ticket to 11+ success!

With pages of study notes and step-by-step worked examples, it'll help you understand every topic. Then there are plenty of questions to put what you've learned into practice.

And if that's not enough, we've also included some mixed tests and two test-style papers with answers, so you're as ready as possible for the big day.

―――― How to access your free Online Edition ――――

This book includes a free Online Edition to read on your PC, Mac or tablet.
You'll just need to go to **cgpbooks.co.uk/extras** and enter this code:

0393 0659 8862 9952

By the way, this code only works for one person. If somebody else has used this book before you, they might have already claimed the Online Edition.

Complete
Revision & Practice

Everything you need to pass the test!

Contents

About the 11+

What's in the 11+ 2
What's in the Maths Part of the 11+ Test 3
How to Prepare for the 11+ 4

Section One — Working with Numbers

Place Value 5
Rounding Up and Down 7
Addition 9
Subtraction 11
Multiplying and Dividing by 10, 100 and 1000 13
Multiplication 15
Division 18
Mixed Calculations 21
Practice Questions 23

Section Two — Number Knowledge

Types of Number 27
Factors, Multiples and Primes 29
Fractions 32
Ratio and Proportion 35
Percentages, Fractions and Decimals 37
Practice Questions 40

Section Three — Number Problems

Algebra 43
Number Sequences 47
Word Problems 50
Practice Questions 54

Section Four — Data Handling

Data Tables 57
Displaying Data 59
Analysing Data 63
Misleading Data 65
Practice Questions 67

Section Five — Shape and Space

Angles 71
2D Shapes 73
2D Shapes — Area and Perimeter 77
Symmetry 81
3D Shapes 83
Shape Problems 87
Coordinates 90
Transformations 92
Practice Questions 94

Section Six — Units and Measures

Units...100
Time 103
Practice Questions 106

Section Seven — Mixed Problems

Mixed Problems..108
Practice Questions 112

Mixed Practice Tests...114
Test-Style Paper 1 122
Test-Style Paper 2 133

Glossary 144
Answers..145
Index 158

Published by CGP

Editors:
Sarah George, Sean McParland, Caley Simpson

With thanks to Sammy El-Bahrawy and Shaun Harrogate for the proofreading.
With thanks to Lottie Edwards for the copyright research.

Please note that CGP is not associated with CEM in any way.
This book does not include any official questions and is not endorsed by CEM.

ISBN: 978 1 78908 596 9

Printed by Elanders Ltd, Newcastle upon Tyne.
Clipart from Corel®

Based on the classic CGP style created by Richard Parsons.
Text, design, layout and original illustrations © Coordination Group Publications Ltd. (CGP) 2020
All rights reserved.

Photocopying more than one section of this book is not permitted, even if you have a CLA licence.
Extra copies are available from CGP with next day delivery • 0800 1712 712 • www.cgpbooks.co.uk

About the 11+

What's in the 11+

Make sure you've got your head around the basics of the 11+ before you begin.

The 11+ is an Admissions Test

1) The 11+ is a test used by some schools to help with their selection process.
2) You'll usually take it when you're in Year 6, at some point during the autumn term.
3) Schools use the results to decide who to accept. They might also use other things to help make up their mind, like information about where you live.

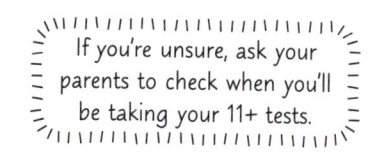

If you're unsure, ask your parents to check when you'll be taking your 11+ tests.

You'll be tested on a Mixture of Subjects

1) In your 11+, you'll be tested on these subjects:

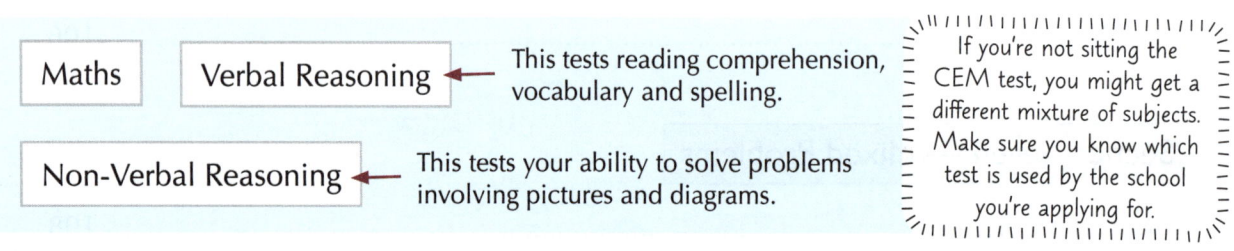

- Maths
- Verbal Reasoning — This tests reading comprehension, vocabulary and spelling.
- Non-Verbal Reasoning — This tests your ability to solve problems involving pictures and diagrams.

If you're not sitting the CEM test, you might get a different mixture of subjects. Make sure you know which test is used by the school you're applying for.

2) You'll probably sit two 45 minute tests, each made up of a mixture of subjects.
3) This book will help you with the Maths bit — it's called Numerical Reasoning in the test.

Get to Know what Kinds of Questions you might get

The questions in your test could be either multiple choice or ones where you have to write the answer yourself.

Look out for the tips at the end of each topic — they'll give you practical advice about the test, plus revision tips and extra hints to help you crack 11+ Maths.

Multiple-Choice

1) For each question you'll be given some options — either on the question paper, or on a separate answer sheet.
2) You should draw a clear pencil line in the box next to the option that you think is correct.

Fill in the Blanks

To answer these questions, you'll have to write numbers in boxes. These will either be on the question paper, or on a separate answer sheet. Here's an example:

What is 34 × 40? | 1 | 3 | 6 | 0 | |

Just write the numbers neatly inside the boxes — you might not need to use them all.

About the 11+

What's in the Maths Part of the 11+ Test

Here's a bit about the sorts of things you'll need to know for the Maths part of the test.

Maths involves Solving Number Problems

1) You should have covered most of the Maths topics that will be on the test at school. However, you may not have learnt about all of them yet, and the test might contain some types of question that are unfamiliar to you.

2) We've grouped the topics that usually come up into seven sections in this book.

Working with Numbers

You might not be tested on questions from every topic in the real test.

You'll need to use addition, subtraction, multiplication or division to answer these questions (or all four to solve some mixed calculations). You'll need to use place value and rounding to solve number problems.

Number Knowledge

You'll need to be able to work with fractions, percentages and decimals and you'll need to understand ratio, proportion and a bit about different types of numbers.

Number Problems

You'll need to look for number patterns as well as use formulas and algebraic expressions. You could be given word problems where you need to use information in the question to find the answer.

Data Handling

Some questions use data in tables and graphs. You'll need to be able to find information in a table and know how to read different types of graphs. You also need to be able to find the mean of a data set.

Shape and Space

You may be tested on the names and properties of 2D and 3D shapes. Other questions may ask about symmetry, coordinates, transformations, volume, area and perimeter. You might also have to imagine shapes being rotated to solve shape problems.

Units and Measures

You may be tested on units and time. You'll need to be able to read scales and convert between different units (e.g. mm and cm).

Mixed Problems

There might also be questions that cover more than one topic. For example, you may be given a question where you have to read a graph and do some calculations.

About the 11+

How to Prepare for the 11+

Give yourself a head start with your Maths revision — be organised and plan ahead.

Divide your Preparation into Stages

1) You should find a way to prepare for the 11+ that suits you. This may depend on how much time you have before the test. Here's a good way to plan your Maths revision:

> Use this book to revise strategies for answering different question types. Read through the study notes and follow the worked examples carefully — make sure you understand the method used at each step.
>
> ↓
>
> Do plenty of practice questions, concentrating on the question types you find tricky.
>
> ↓
>
> Sit some practice papers to prepare you for the real test. We've included two test-style Maths papers at the back of this book to get you started.

2) When you first start answering 11+ Maths questions, try to solve the questions without making any mistakes, rather than working quickly.

3) Once you feel confident about the questions, then you can build up your speed.

4) You can do this by asking an adult to time you as you answer a set of questions, or by seeing how many questions you can answer in a certain amount of time, e.g. 5 minutes. You can then try to beat your time or score.

5) As you get closer to the test day, work on getting a balance between speed and accuracy — that's what you're aiming for when you sit the real test.

There are Many Ways to Practise the Skills you Need

The best way to tackle 11+ Maths is to do lots of revision and practice. This isn't the only thing that will help though — there are other ways you can build up the skills you need for the test:

1) Practise your times tables with a friend by taking it in turns to test each other.
2) Divide up a cake, a pizza or a pie between a certain number of people. Work out what fraction each person is given.
3) Try drawing different shapes on a piece of paper. Use a small mirror to find lines of symmetry and work out what the shapes look like when they've been reflected.
4) Play games that involve counting like darts or Monopoly® to help you practise number calculations. You could also do activities like sudoku to help you to develop your problem solving skills, and play Battleships to practise using coordinates.

About the 11+

Section One — Working with Numbers

Place Value

Place value is about knowing the value of all the digits in a number.
You can use place value to compare numbers and work out which is biggest or smallest.

The **Value** of a **Digit** depends on its **Place** in a **Number**

Each Digit in a **Whole Number** has a different **Value**

1) This example shows you what each digit is worth in a 7-digit number — **1 256 297**.

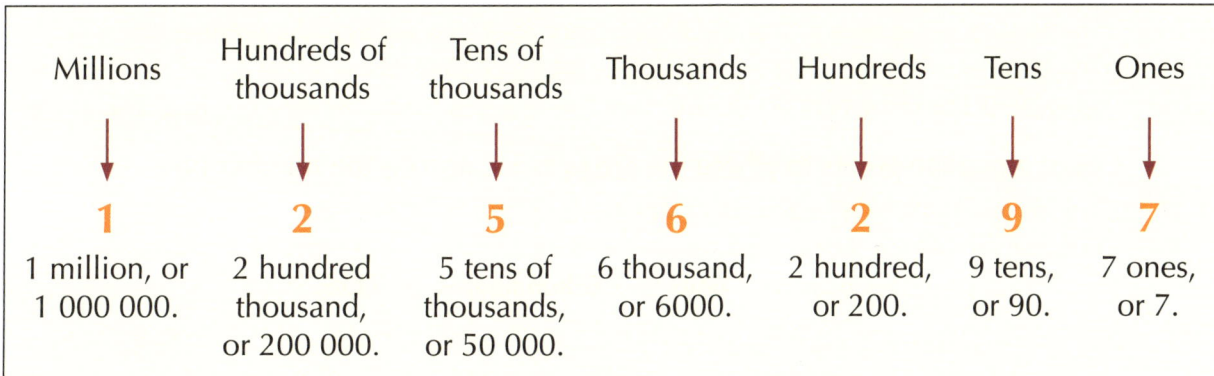

2) Each digit has the same value as 10 lots of the digit
   to its right, e.g. 1 hundred is equal to 10 tens.

3) Whole numbers have a greater value when there are more digits,
   e.g. 1 256 297 has a greater value than 256 297 because it has a millions digit.

4) When comparing whole numbers that have the same number of digits,
   you need to look at the value of each digit. For example, 254 is greater than 249.
   They have the same number in the hundreds column, but 254 has a greater number
   in the tens column than 249.

Each Digit in a **Decimal Number** has a different **Value**

1) This example shows you what each digit is worth in a decimal number — **1.365**.

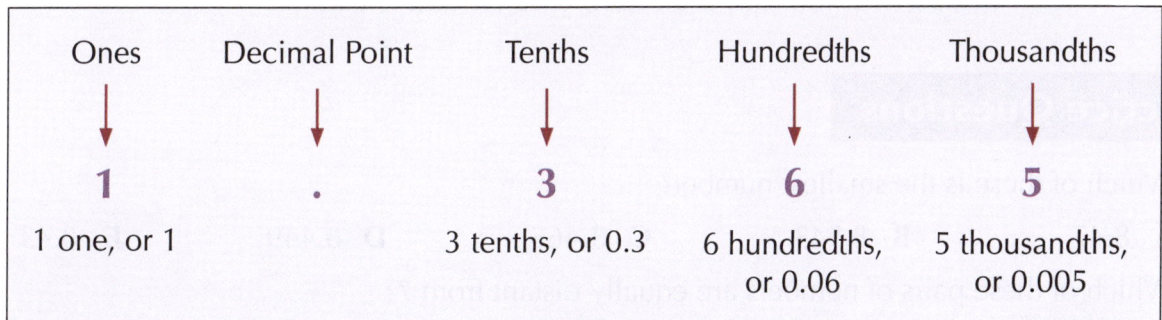

2) Each digit has the same value as 10 lots of the digit
   to its right, e.g. 1 tenth is equal to 10 hundredths.

3) When comparing decimal numbers you need to look at each digit in turn. For example,
   0.56 is greater than 0.53. They have the same number in the tenths column, but 0.56
   has a greater number in the hundredths column than 0.53.

Section One — Working with Numbers

Place Value

 **What number is the arrow pointing to on this number line?**

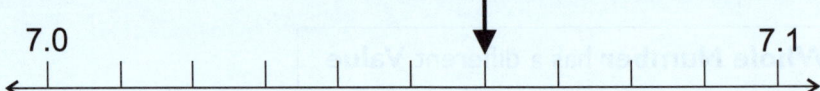

1) Look at the <u>numbers</u> given and <u>how many points</u> there are on the number line.

   The answer is between 7.0 and 7.1, and there are ten points on the number line.
   The difference between 7.0 and 7.1 is one tenth, or 0.1. 0.1 is made up of ten hundredths, so each of the ten points on the number line is equal to one hundredth, or 0.01.

2) Count along the points to <u>where</u> the <u>arrow</u> is located on the number line.

   The arrow is pointing to the 6th point to the right of 7.0 on the number line, which means that this point is equal to 6 hundredths or 0.06.
   So the value of this point is 7 units and 6 hundredths, or **7.06**.

EXAMPLE: Luca, Steve, Flo, Sue and Tom all drove one lap around a go-kart track. They put their results in a table.

Name	Luca	Steve	Flo	Sue	Tom
Time (seconds)	49.7	49.65	49.92	49.84	50.1

Who drove the quickest?

1) To find out who drove the <u>quickest</u> you need to find the <u>shortest time</u>, which means that you're looking for the <u>lowest value number</u>.

   Look at the tens and the units of each driver's time. Tom's time is the slowest because 50 (which has 5 tens) is greater than 49 (which has 4 tens).

2) <u>Luca</u>, <u>Steve</u>, <u>Flo</u> and <u>Sue</u> all have the <u>same number</u> of <u>tens</u> and <u>units</u> in their time, <u>49</u>. So you then need to look at the <u>first decimal number</u> of their times.

   They each have a different value for the first decimal place. **Steve** has a lower number of tenths than the others, 6, so his time is **quickest**.

Practice Questions

1) Which of these is the smallest number?

   A 8.47   B 8.543   C 8.465   D 8.449   E 8.43

2) Which of these pairs of numbers are equally distant from 7?

   A 6.97 and 7.3   B 6.89 and 7.11   C 6.8 and 7.02
   D 6.94 and 7.1   E 6.9 and 7.19

Check the place value of each digit...

When you're putting numbers in order, look at each digit of the numbers one by one. If they have the same digit in the same place value column, look at the next digit to the right instead.

Rounding Up and Down

You guessed it — you can round numbers up or down to give an estimated value.

The **Number 5** is **Important** when you're **Rounding Numbers**

1) To round any number you need to follow a simple rule:

   - If the digit to the right of the one you're rounding is less than 5 then you round down.
   - If the digit to the right of the one you're rounding is 5 or more then you round up.

   For example, to round 17 872 to the nearest 100, you need to round the digit in the hundreds column.

   When rounding down, the digit you're rounding stays the same.

   17 **8**72 — The digit in the hundreds column is 8.

   Now look at the digit to its right, in the tens column, to see whether you need to round up or down.

   17 **8**72 — The digit in the tens column is 7, so you round up 17 872 to 17 **9**00.

2) You can use this method for rounding decimals too. For example, to round 1.428 to one decimal place (or the nearest tenth), you need to round the digit in the tenths column.

   Rounding to two decimal places means rounding to the nearest hundredth. Three decimal places means to the nearest thousandth.

   1.**4**28 — The digit in the tenths column is 4.

3) To work out whether to round this digit up or down you need to look at the digit to its right — in the hundredths column.

   1.**4**28 — The digit in the hundredths column is 2, so you round down 1.428 to 1.4.

11+ Example Questions

EXAMPLE: What is 46.98 rounded to one decimal place?

1) Work out which digit you need to round.

   One decimal place is the first digit after the decimal point — 46.**9**8.

2) Look at the digit to the right of the digit you need to round and work out whether you need to round up or round down.

   The digit to the right of the digit you need to round is 8 — 46.9**8**.

   8 is more than 5 so you need to round up. Rounding up 9 tenths will give you 10 tenths, which is equal to 1 unit. This will increase the digit in the units column from 6 to 7 and leave 0 tenths. So 46.98 rounded to one decimal place is 47.0, or 47.

Section One — Working with Numbers

Rounding Up and Down

More 11+ Example Questions

 **Which of these is 1500?**

A 1508 to the nearest 10   B 1448 to the nearest 100
C 1562 to the nearest 100   D 1498 to the nearest 10
E 1504 to the nearest 1000

1) Look at each option one by one.
   A 1508: 0 is being rounded, 8 is more than 5 — 1508 rounds up to 1510 not 1500.
   B 1448: 4 is being rounded, 4 is less than 5 — 1448 rounds down to 1400 not 1500.
   C 1562: 5 is being rounded, 6 is more than 5 — 1562 rounds up to 1600 not 1500.
   D 1498: 9 is being rounded, 8 is more than 5 — 1498 rounds up to 1500.
   So the answer is D.

2) If you have time you can check your answer by looking at the last option.
   E 1504: 1 is being rounded, 5 is 5 or more —
      1504 rounds up to 2000 not 1500.

 **Round 43.389 kg to the nearest 10 grams.**

A 50 kg   B 43.4 kg
C 43 kg   D 40 kg
E 43.39 kg

1) You need to find 43.389 kg to the nearest 10 grams —
   it'll be easier to round this figure if you convert it into grams.
   One kilogram is the same as 1000 grams, so
   multiply 43.389 by 1000. 43.389 kg is 43 389 g.

2) Work out which digit is in the tens column and look at the digit to its
   right (in the ones column) to see whether you need to round up or down.
   43 389: 8 is being rounded, 9 is more than 5 so 43 389 rounds up to 43 390.
   To convert this back into kilograms you just need to divide 43 390 by 1000.
   The answer is 43.39 kg.

Practice Question

1) Round 174 782 to the nearest ten thousand.

   A 174 800   B 180 000   C 170 800   D 170 000   E 175 000

 **You can use rounding to estimate answers...**

For example, to check your answer to 4988 + 507, round the numbers to 5000 and 500.
5000 + 500 = 5500, so make sure your answer to 4988 + 507 is pretty close to 5500.

Section One — Working with Numbers

Addition

You've been adding numbers together for years. Here are a few examples of the sorts of questions you could get in the test, and some methods you could use to answer them.

11+ Example Questions

 **Eva buys an apple for 48p and an orange for 55p. How much does she spend in pounds?**

1) You need to find the exact answer to this question.
2) Add the numbers together to find the answer in pence.

   48p + 55p = 103p

3) Convert this answer to pounds to find the amount Eva spends.

   103p = £1.03, so Eva spends £1.03.

 **Marco has £4.13, Kenny has £3.42 and Janet has £8.70. How much money do they have in total?**

A £15.95   B £18.25   C £17.85   D £16.25   E £14.25

Quick Method

1) You can estimate the answer to the question by rounding the numbers to the nearest pound to make more manageable numbers.

   £4.13 is rounded down to £4.00   £3.42 is rounded down to £3.00
   £8.70 is rounded up to £9.00

2) Add the rounded numbers together to estimate the answer.

   £4.00 + £3.00 + £9.00 = £16.00

3) The answer is around £16.00. Looking at the options, the answer could be A or D.

4) As you rounded down by 55p (13p + 42p) and you rounded up by 30p, your estimate will be lower than the actual answer.
   So, the actual answer must be £16.25 — option D.

Written Method

1) An alternative method is to add the three values together in columns.

   ```
       4 . 1 3
       3 . 4 2
     + 8 . 7 0
     ─────────
     1 6 . 2 5
             1
   ```

   Remember to carry the digit over if the answer is more than 9.

   Add together the numbers in each column starting from the right.

   Make sure that you line up the place value columns and the decimal points.

2) This method gives you the exact answer, £16.25.

Section One — Working with Numbers

Addition

Another 11+ Example Question

EXAMPLE: The table shows the amount of juice in litres sold by Cathy on her market stall over 8 weeks.

Work out the total amount of juice Cathy sold from week 3 to week 6.

Week	Amount of juice sold (l)	Week	Amount of juice sold (l)
1	43.71	5	46.30
2	46.18	6	59.12
3	82.63	7	21.14
4	34.18	8	63.94

1) For this question there are no options to choose from. So you need to find the exact answer — you can't use rounding.

2) The question is asking for the total sales from week 3 to week 6, so find the data you need in the table.

Week 3 = 82.63 litres   Week 5 = 46.30 litres
Week 4 = 34.18 litres   Week 6 = 59.12 litres

3) Arrange the four weekly values into columns. Add together the numbers in each column starting from the right.

```
    8 2 . 6 3
    3 4 . 1 8
    4 6 . 3 0
  + 5 9 . 1 2
  ─────────────
    2 2 2 . 2 3
      2 1   1
```

Use the column method to find the exact answer.

4) The total amount of juice sold from week 3 to week 6 by Cathy is 222.23 litres.

Practice Questions

1) Katie buys a cycling helmet for £13.89, a bell for £3.35 and some gloves for £12.30. How much money does she spend?

   A £31.96   B £29.54   C £32.14   D £28.76   E £26.89

2) Rafid, Freia, Martin and John take part in a relay race. Rafid's leg took 12.37 seconds, Freia's leg took 11.88 seconds, Martin's leg took 13.24 seconds and John's leg took 10.94 seconds. What was their total time for the race?

Think about whether your answer makes sense...

When you've worked out an exact answer, you could check that your answer is sensible by using the rounding method to do a quick estimate. Your answer shouldn't be too far from the estimate.

Section One — Working with Numbers

Subtraction

Subtraction can get a bit tricky. All the more reason to get in lots of practice...

11+ Example Questions

EXAMPLE: Emma has £13.10. She donates £2.21 to charity. How much money does Emma have left?

A £10.89   B £11.81   C £9.89   D £11.79   E £10.79

Method 1

1) <u>Partition</u> the number that you are subtracting into its <u>ones</u>, <u>tenths</u> and <u>hundredths</u>:

   £2.21 splits up into £2 + £0.20 + £0.01
   ones   tenths   hundredths

2) <u>Subtract</u> each number <u>one at a time</u>:

   £13.10 − £2.00 = £11.10
   £11.10 − £0.20 = £10.90 ← Be careful here — you're changing the value in the ones column as well as the tenths.
   £10.90 − £0.01 = £10.89

   Your answer is £10.89 — option A.

Method 2

1) You can also subtract numbers by writing them in <u>columns</u>.
2) Write the <u>number you're subtracting from first</u>. Make sure the decimal points <u>line up</u>.

   Subtract the numbers in each column starting from the right.

   ```
     1 ²ʒ ¹0̸ ¹1̸ 0
   −    2 . 2 1
   ─────────────
     1 0 . 8 9
   ```

   If you have to subtract a bigger number from a smaller number, make an exchange from the next place value column.

EXAMPLE: A bag of three apples weighs 450 g. Two of the apples weigh 183 g and 144 g. How much does the third apple weigh?

1) <u>Add up</u> the weights of the two apples.   Add each part one at a time.

   144 splits up into 100 + 40 + 4.
   183 + 100 = 283, then 283 + 40 = 323, and 323 + 4 = 327.
   So the two apples weigh 327 g.

   You could also subtract each weight separately instead.

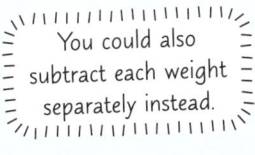

2) Work out how much the third apple weighs by <u>subtracting</u> this from the <u>total weight</u>.

   327 splits up into 300 + 20 + 7.
   450 − 300 = 150, then 150 − 20 = 130, and 130 − 7 = 123.
   So the third apple weighs 123 g.

Section One — Working with Numbers

Subtraction

EXAMPLE: Three people ran two 200 m races. Their times for race 1 are shown in the table. All three ran faster in race 2.

Vanessa ran 1.8 seconds faster.
Rajpal ran 0.9 seconds faster.
Stacey ran 2.5 seconds faster.

Who had the fastest time in race 2?

Name	Race 1 (s)
Vanessa	25.3
Rajpal	24.2
Stacey	26.2

1) For each person, you need to take the time they ran in race 1, and subtract the amount of time that they ran faster by.

2) You could use the counting back method. Start with each person's time for race 1 and count back in easy steps to get their time for race 2.

You could use a written method to work out the difference in time for each person, but it would take more time.

First subtract the whole number. Vanessa ran 1.8 seconds faster in race 2, so subtract 1 second.

Then remove the decimal part. After subtracting 1, Vanessa's time is 24.3 seconds and there are still 0.8 seconds to subtract. Take away 0.3 to get 24.0 seconds.

Vanessa:
25.3 − 1 = 24.3
24.3 − 0.3 = 24.0
24.0 − 0.5 = 23.5

Rajpal:
24.2 − 0.2 = 24.0
24.0 − 0.7 = 23.3

Stacey:
26.2 − 2 = 24.2
24.2 − 0.2 = 24.0
24.0 − 0.3 = 23.7

That leaves 0.5 still to subtract. Take this away to get her time for race 2.

3) Rajpal has the fastest time in race 2 (23.3 seconds).

You could also round the number you're subtracting to the nearest whole number, subtract it, then count on or back by the amount you rounded by. E.g. for Rajpal, 24.2 − 1 = 23.2, then count on by 0.1 to get 23.3.

Practice Questions

1) Gavin's bath holds 75.63 litres of water when it is full. Gavin pours 48.28 litres of water into the bath. How many more litres of water would he need to fill the bath?

   A 27.45   B 27.75   C 26.95   D 28.15   E 27.35

2) The table shows the results of five students in two tests. Which student had the greatest increase in score between test 1 and test 2?

Name	Test 1 (%)	Test 2 (%)
Joe	57.6	61.5
Holly	60.2	63.8
Lucille	62.7	63.0
Dave	64.1	59.9
Anita	59.8	64.7

Be extra careful when the numbers have different numbers of digits...

Make sure you always line up the numbers using the place value columns or decimal points. Add zeros to the end of decimal numbers to make them have matching numbers of digits.

Section One — Working with Numbers

Multiplying and Dividing by 10, 100 and 1000

When you multiply or divide any number by 10, 100 or 1000, you just move the digits left or right.

Move digits **Left** to **Multiply** by **10, 100** or **1000**

1) If you're multiplying a number by 10, move the digits one place to the left.

   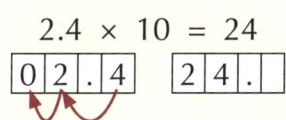

2) If you're multiplying a number by 100, move the digits two places to the left.

   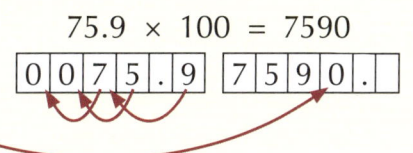

   Put a zero here to fill in the gap before the decimal point.

3) If you're multiplying a number by 1000, move the digits three places to the left.

   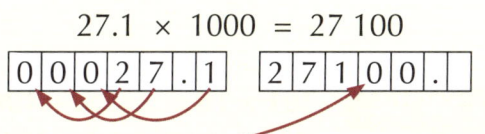

   This time you need to put two zeros before the decimal point.

Move digits **Right** to **Divide** by **10, 100** or **1000**

1) If you're dividing a number by 10, move the digits one place to the right.

   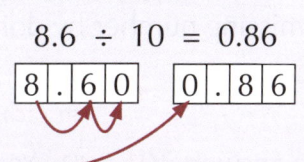

   Put a zero before the decimal point to fill in the gap.

2) If you're dividing a number by 100, move the digits two places to the right.

   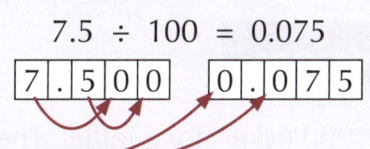

   Put one zero before the decimal point and one zero after to fill in the gaps.

3) If you're dividing a number by 1000, move the digits three places to the right.

   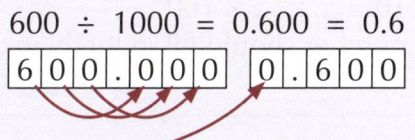

   Put a zero before the decimal point to fill in the gap.

Section One — Working with Numbers

Multiplying and Dividing by 10, 100 and 1000

 11+ Example Questions

EXAMPLE: Which of these calculations equals 843?

A 84 300 ÷ 10   B 0.843 × 1000
C 84 300 ÷ 1000   D 0.0843 × 1000
E 0.843 × 100

You can draw out the place value columns to help you if you're finding these calculations tricky.

1) Work out the answer to each calculation:
   A Move each digit one place to the right: 84 300 ÷ 10 = 8430
   B Move each digit three places to the left: 0.843 × 1000 = 843
   C Move each digit three places to the right: 84 300 ÷ 1000 = 84.3
   D Move each digit three places to the left: 0.0843 × 1000 = 84.3
   E Move each digit two places to the left: 0.843 × 100 = 84.3

2) The correct answer is 0.843 × 1000 — option B.

EXAMPLE: 301 × 10 = ... ÷ 100
Which number should fill in the blank?

1) Multiply 301 by 10 to work out the first part of the calculation.

   301 × 10 = 3010   ← *To multiply by ten, move each digit one place to the left.*

2) The second part of the calculation must also equal 3010.
3) When you divide the missing number by 100, it will equal 3010.
   So, calculate the missing number by doing the inverse operation — multiplying by 100.

   3010 × 100 = 301 000   ← *This time you are multiplying by 100, so each digit moves two places to the left.*

4) That gives you the answer: 301 000. You can check it's correct by dividing 301 000 by 100. It should equal 3010.

 Practice Questions

1) Mark has sold 1000 tickets for a raffle. The tickets were sold in books of ten.
   In total, Mark collected £375 for all 1000 tickets. How much did one book cost?

   A £0.37   B £3.75   C £3.57   D £7.35   E £37.50

2) 4.2 ÷ 10 = ... × 100
   What number should fill in the blank?

 **Make sure to move the digits in the correct direction...**
The options for a multiple-choice question might include the answer you would find if you were to mix up the rules for multiplying and dividing by 10, 100 or 1000.

Section One — Working with Numbers

Multiplication

There are a few ways that multiplication can be tested — these pages will show you the sorts of things that might come up, and how to tackle them.

11+ Example Questions

EXAMPLE: A DVD costs £3.99. How much will nine DVDs cost?

A £35.91   B £36.00   C £36.04   D £35.97   E £36.09

Quick Method

1) Round the cost of each DVD to the nearest whole number. Then multiply by nine.

   £3.99 rounds up to £4.00. £4.00 × 9 = £36.00

   You added 1 penny for each DVD, and there were nine DVDs.

2) £36.00 is not the exact answer though. You added nine pence to this answer when you rounded the price of the DVDs. You need to subtract nine pence to reach the final answer.

   £36.00 − £0.09 = £35.91

   Your answer is £35.91 — option A.

Written Method

1) You can multiply the numbers together in columns.
2) Make sure you line up the decimal point and the place value columns in your answer.

   ```
       3 . 9 9
   ×         9
   ─────────────
     3 5 . 9 1
         8 8
   ```

   Starting from the right, multiply the hundredths, tenths and ones by 9.

   9 × 9 = 81. If the answer is more than 9, the left-hand digit is carried to the next column.

   In the final column, the carried digit goes here. (9 × 3) + 8 = 35.

   The carried digit gets added to the answer of the next column. Here, (9 × 9) + 8 = 89.

EXAMPLE: What is 400 × 70?

1) Start with a similar calculation that is easier to work out.

   4 × 7 = 28

2) Now work out how much larger the numbers in the question are than the numbers you used in the simple calculation.

   400 is 100 times larger than 4, and 70 is 10 times larger than 7.
   So the answer to 400 × 70 is 100 × 10 = 1000 times larger than 28.

3) Multiply to find the final answer.

   28 × 1000 = 28 000

Section One — Working with Numbers

Multiplication

More 11+ Example Questions

EXAMPLE: What is 12.4 × 6.3?

A 0.7812   B 7.812   C 78.12   D 781.2   E 7812

1) In each option, the numbers are the same, but the decimal point is in a different place.
2) This means you can estimate the answer by rounding the two numbers in the calculation to the nearest whole number, then multiplying them together.

   12.4 is rounded down to 12.   6.3 is rounded down to 6.   12 × 6 = 72

3) The estimated answer is 72. The only option that is near to 72 is 78.12 — option C. 78.12 must be the exact answer.

EXAMPLE: 526 × 24 = 12 624   ← This is a number fact.

What is 526 × 12?

Quick Method

1) Use the number fact to help you work out the answer to the question.
2) 12 is half of 24. So the answer to 526 × 12 will be half of the answer to 526 × 24.

   12 624 ÷ 2 = 6312 ⟶ 526 × 12 = 6312

Written Method

1) An alternative method would be to use long multiplication.
2) Line the numbers up in columns and put the bigger number on top.
3) Multiply each digit in the bigger number (starting from the right) with the ones and tens of the smaller number:

   Multiply each digit by 2.
       5 2 6
   ×   1 2
     1 0 5₁2
   Write the answer here.

   Then, multiply each number by 10.
       5 2 6
   ×   1 2
     1 0 5₁2
     5 2 6 0
   Write the answer on the line below.

4) Add your two answers together to get the final answer.

       5 2 6
   ×   1 2
     1 0 5₁2
   + 5 2 6 0
     6 3 1 2
       1

   You may have been taught a different method for written multiplication. That's fine — just use whichever one works best for you.

Section One — Working with Numbers

Multiplication

 **What is 47 × 30?**

Method 1

There's more about how to multiply by 10, 100 or 1000 on page 13.

1) 30 is a <u>multiple of 10</u>. So multiply 47 by 10 to start off with.

   47 × 10 = 470

2) 30 is the <u>same</u> as 3 × 10, so <u>add together</u> 3 lots of 470.

   470 + 470 + 470 = 1410

   You could do this quickly in your head by rounding 470 up to 500, adding the numbers together, then subtracting 90.

Method 2

1) 30 is the <u>same</u> as 3 × 10, so first multiply 47 by <u>3</u>.

   47 × 3 = 141

   You could do this quickly in your head by rounding 47 up to 50, doing the multiplication, then subtracting 9.

2) Then multiply the result by 10.

   141 × 10 = 1410

Practice Questions

1) 3.5 × 7.9 = 27.65
   What is 350 × 79?

2) A toy robot costs £5.49. How much will six toy robots cost?
   A £32.94   **B** £30.30   **C** £33.00   **D** £31.94   **E** £32.96

3) What is 6.9 × 8.2?
   A 64.40   **B** 48.18   **C** 45.95   **D** 56.58   **E** 72.52

4) Each bookshelf in a library can hold 18 books.
   How many books can be held on 53 bookshelves?

 **Use a number fact to make things easier for yourself...**

If a question gives you a number fact, it's a pretty big clue that there's a quick way to work out the answer. Look closely at how the numbers in the number fact are related to the numbers in the question. This will help you save precious time in the test.

Section One — Working with Numbers

Division

Division is the opposite of multiplication — you're splitting a number into groups.

11+ Example Questions

 **Each guinea pig cage holds 3 guinea pigs. How many cages would 124 guinea pigs need?**

Quick Method

1) You need to <u>divide</u> 124 by 3, but 3 isn't a <u>factor</u> of 124.
2) <u>Partition</u> 124 into two numbers that are <u>easier</u> to work with. You need to find a number that's close to 124 and is a multiple of 3. You could split 124 into <u>120</u> and <u>4</u>.
3) Start by working out how many cages you'd need for <u>120 guinea pigs</u>.

   Using your 3 times table, you know that $12 \div 3 = 4$.
   120 is 10 times bigger than 12, so $120 \div 3 = 40$.

4) Next, work out how many cages you'd need for the <u>remaining 4 guinea pigs</u>. Then <u>add</u> your two answers <u>together</u>.

   $4 \div 3 = 1$ remainder 1 $40 + 1$ remainder $1 = 41$ remainder 1

5) You still have a <u>remainder of 1</u> — so if you just have 41 cages there will be 1 poor guinea pig <u>without</u> a cage. You need 42 cages so that every guinea pig has a cage.

Written Method

1) You can also use a written method to divide 124 by 3.

   ```
        0  4  1 remainder 1
      3 ⟌ 1 ¹2  4
   ```
   Starting with the hundreds, divide each number by 3.
   If you have a remainder, put it as a ten in front of the next digit — so 2 becomes 12.
   Write down any remainders you have left at the end.

2) 41 cages will leave <u>one extra guinea pig</u> without a cage, so the answer must be 42.

 **Libby divides a number by a smaller number. Her answer has a remainder of 7. Which of these numbers could Libby have divided by?**

   A 8   B 4   C 6   D 5   E 7

There's <u>no clear method</u> to follow here — you need to think about it logically:

To get a remainder of 7, Libby can't have divided by a number less than 7, otherwise it could've been divided again. E.g. 4 would go into 7 once, giving a remainder of 3.

If Libby had divided by 7, then there wouldn't have been a remainder at all (because $7 \div 7 = 1$).

Libby must have divided by a number greater than 7. So the answer must be 8 — option A.

Section One — Working with Numbers

Division

 **Talia ran for a distance of 2726 metres. It took her 11 minutes. To the nearest whole metre, how many metres did she run per minute?**

1) You need to <u>divide</u> the <u>total distance</u> Talia ran by the <u>length of time</u> it took her. <u>Long division</u> is often worth doing when you're dividing by a two-digit number.

```
        0 2 4 7  remainder 9
    11 | 2 7 2 6
        -2 2 ↓
           5 2
          -4 4 ↓
             8 6
            -7 7
               9
```

<u>Step 1</u>:
11 doesn't go into 2, so look at the <u>next digit</u>. It goes into 27 <u>two times</u>, so put a 2 above the 7. 2 × 11 = 22, so <u>subtract 22</u> from 27 and write the answer underneath.

<u>Step 2</u>:
Carry the <u>next digit</u> down — here it's 2. <u>52</u> is the new number to divide into. 11 goes into 52 <u>four times</u>, so put 4 in the answer above the 2. 4 × 11 = 44, so <u>subtract 44</u> from 52 and write the answer underneath.

<u>Step 3</u>:
Carry the <u>6</u> down. <u>86</u> is the new number to divide into. 11 goes into 86 <u>seven times</u>, so put 7 in the answer above the 6. 7 × 11 = 77, so <u>subtract 77</u> from 86.

9 is the remainder.

2) The question asks for the answer to the <u>nearest whole number</u>. So, 247 remainder 9 should be <u>rounded up</u> to 248 metres.

If the remainder is greater than half of the number you're dividing by, it should be rounded up. If it's less, it should be rounded down.

 **What is 12.5 divided by 5?**

1) First, <u>convert</u> the decimal number into a <u>whole number</u> — this makes it <u>easier</u> to divide.

   Multiply 12.5 by 10 to make a whole number. 12.5 × 10 = 125.

2) Then, find the <u>answer</u> to the <u>division</u>.

   Find 125 ÷ 5. Partition 125 into 100 + 25 and divide each bit separately.
   100 ÷ 5 = 20, 25 ÷ 5 = 5. So 125 ÷ 5 = 20 + 5 = 25.

3) Because you <u>multiplied 12.5 by 10</u> at the start, you've got to <u>divide</u> your answer <u>by 10</u>.

   25 ÷ 10 = 2.5, so 12.5 divided by 5 = 2.5

Section One — Working with Numbers

Division

 $3150 ÷ 9 = 350$

What is 9450 ÷ 9?

This is similar to the method you used to answer the number fact question on page 16.

Quick Method

1) Use the number fact to help you work out the answer to the question.

2) See if you can spot how the numbers in the two calculations are related to each other. 9450 is three times larger than 3150. So, the answer to 9450 ÷ 9 will be three times larger than 350.

You could work this out by doing 300 × 3 and then 50 × 3. Then add the answers together. → $350 × 3 = 1050$ → $9450 ÷ 9 = 1050$

Written Method

1) You could use a written method to divide 9450 by 9.

2) Write out the division and divide each number in 9450 by 9:

$$\begin{array}{r} 1\ 0\ 5\ 0 \\ 9\overline{)9\ 4\ ^45\ 0} \end{array}$$

← The answer is 1050.

Divide each number by 9.

Practice Questions

1) What is 8.8 ÷ 4?

2) A soft toy costs £1.30. How many soft toys can you buy with £14.50?

3) 19 200 ÷ 16 = 1200. What is 19 200 ÷ 4?

   A 600   B 2400   C 4800   D 7200   E 9600

4) Each level on a computer game takes 8 minutes to complete. If Jamil spent 264 minutes playing the computer game, how many levels did he complete?

5) Glenda has £1680 in her bank account. She divides it equally between her 15 grandchildren. How much does each child get?

Don't panic if you can't see how to start a division question...

It's not always obvious how you should work out the answer to division questions. Think carefully about what the question is asking you to do — sometimes you'll need to partition a larger number into smaller chunks that are easier to work with.

Mixed Calculations

Mixed calculation questions will test all of your adding, subtracting, multiplying and dividing skills. But don't worry — there are some handy tricks you can learn to make them much easier.

BODMAS is Really Important

Operations are things like ×, ÷, + and −.

1) BODMAS tells you the order in which operations should be done in a mixed calculation.

BODMAS = Brackets, Other, Division, Multiplication, Addition, Subtraction

'Other' is things like square numbers.

2) Work out anything in Brackets first, then Other things like square numbers, then Divide / Multiply groups of numbers before Adding or Subtracting them.

11+ Example Questions

EXAMPLE: What is $7 + 12 ÷ (9 − 7) + 4^2$?

Take a look at page 27 if you're unsure about square numbers.

You need to follow BODMAS to make sure you do the calculations in the correct order.

1) Do the bit in brackets first. $7 + 12 ÷ 2 + 4^2$ ← $9 − 7 = 2$

2) Then work out the square number. $7 + 12 ÷ 2 + 16$ ← $4^2 = 4 × 4 = 16$

3) Next work out the division. $7 + 6 + 16$ ← $12 ÷ 2 = 6$

4) Then add all the remaining numbers together: $7 + 6 + 16 = 29$

EXAMPLE: What is $2 × 15 ÷ (2 + 3) × 7$?

Multiplication and division are as important as each other, so once you've worked out the bit in brackets, you do the rest of the calculations from left to right.

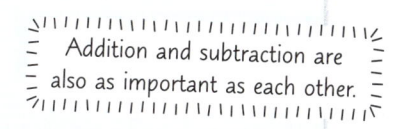

Addition and subtraction are also as important as each other.

1) Do the bit in brackets first. $2 × 15 ÷ 5 × 7$ ← $2 + 3 = 5$

2) Then work out the first multiplication. $30 ÷ 5 × 7$ ← $2 × 15 = 30$

3) Next work out the division. $6 × 7$ ← $30 ÷ 5 = 6$

4) Then do the last multiplication. $6 × 7 = 42$

Section One — Working with Numbers

Mixed Calculations

More 11+ Example Questions

 What is $\dfrac{360}{40 \times 1.5}$?

Treat the top and bottom of a fraction as if they have brackets round them — so you do the calculations before you divide the top by the bottom.

1) The calculation is displayed as a fraction, which means that you need to divide 360 by the product of 40 × 1.5.

2) First calculate 40 × 1.5. You could partition 1.5 into 1 and 0.5, then add together the products of the multiplications.

   40 × 1 = 40
   40 × 0.5 = 20 ← Multiplying by 0.5 is the same as halving a number.
   40 + 20 = 60

3) Then divide 360 by 60.

   360 ÷ 60 = 6 ← If you divide both 360 and 60 by 10, this is the same as 36 ÷ 6 = 6.

 42 × 603 + 58 × 603 =

A 1206   B 34 974   C 60 300
D 25 326   E 54 270

You could also use a written method or estimation to work out each of the steps of this calculation — but it would take a lot more time.

Following the BODMAS rule you do each multiplication before adding.
But 42 and 58 are both multiplied by the same number, 603.
You can just add 42 and 58 and multiply this number by 603 to find the answer.

42 + 58 = 100. So 42 × 603 + 58 × 603 simplifies to 100 × 603.
100 × 603 = 60 300 — so the correct answer is option C.

Practice Questions

1) What is $6 + 4 \times 3^2 \div (16 - 13)$?

2) What is $1450 \times 1.7 + 1450 \times 8.3 + 110$?

Make sure you're very comfortable with BODMAS...

You have to follow BODMAS when you're doing a question with mixed calculations. To make sure you don't forget about it, you could write 'BODMAS' at the top of some scrap paper.

Section One — Working with Numbers

Practice Questions

Once you're done with the Working with Numbers section, find out how much you've learned by having a go at these Practice Questions.

1. Theo wrote down the distance he walked in metres on four hikes. What is the distance of his longest hike? Circle the correct answer.

   A 14 320 m   B 13 987 m   C 14 354 m   D 14 263 m

2. What number is the arrow pointing to on the number line below?

   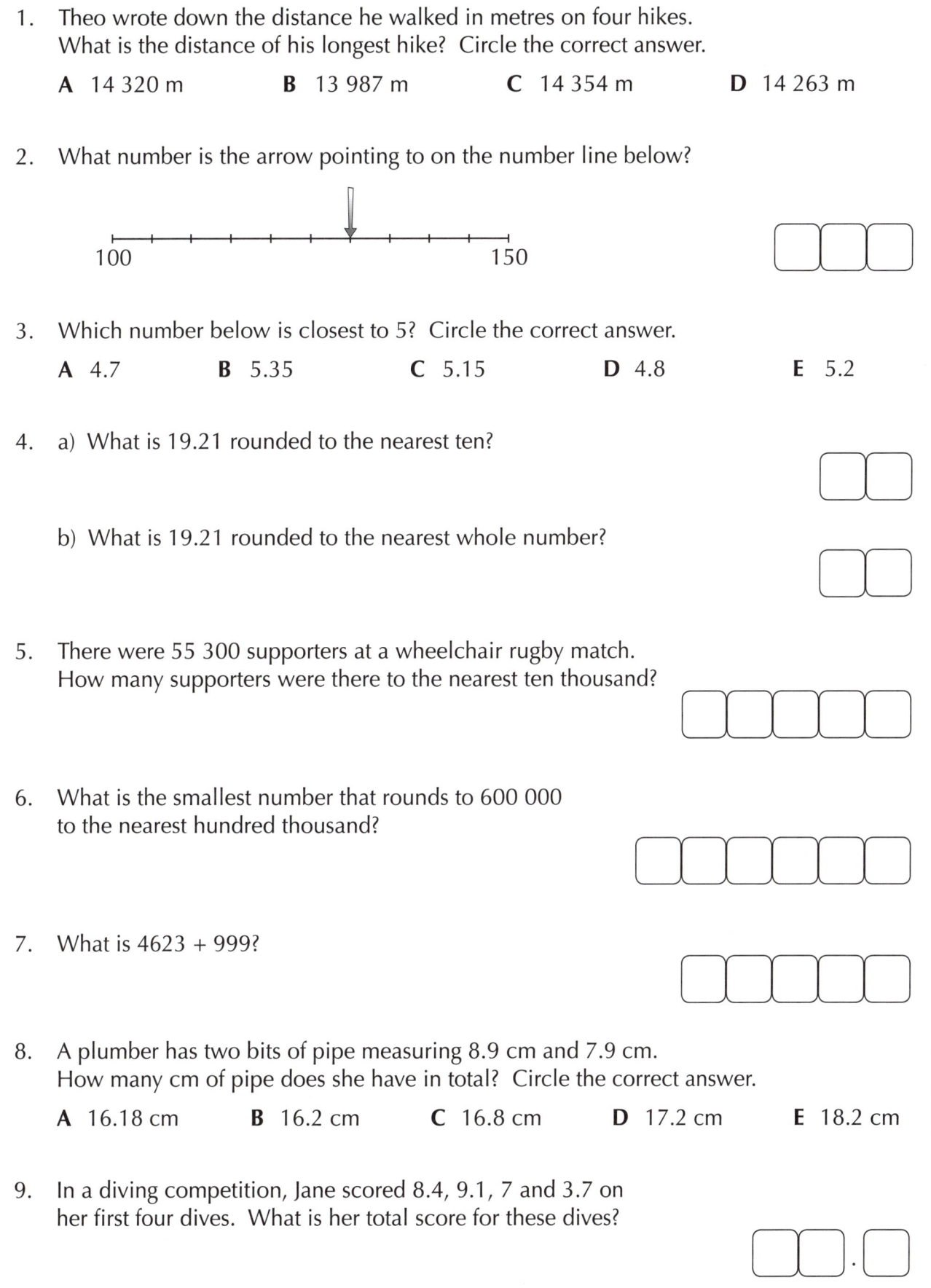

3. Which number below is closest to 5? Circle the correct answer.

   A 4.7   B 5.35   C 5.15   D 4.8   E 5.2

4. a) What is 19.21 rounded to the nearest ten?

   b) What is 19.21 rounded to the nearest whole number?

5. There were 55 300 supporters at a wheelchair rugby match. How many supporters were there to the nearest ten thousand?

6. What is the smallest number that rounds to 600 000 to the nearest hundred thousand?

7. What is 4623 + 999?

8. A plumber has two bits of pipe measuring 8.9 cm and 7.9 cm. How many cm of pipe does she have in total? Circle the correct answer.

   A 16.18 cm   B 16.2 cm   C 16.8 cm   D 17.2 cm   E 18.2 cm

9. In a diving competition, Jane scored 8.4, 9.1, 7 and 3.7 on her first four dives. What is her total score for these dives?

Section One — Working with Numbers

Practice Questions

10. What is 90 − 6.78? Circle the correct answer.

    A 82.32   B 83.22   C 83.32   D 84.22   E 84.32

11. What is 7450 − 2120?

12. Isobel has £2.18, Josh has £4.65 and Tammy has £3.22.

    a) How much do they have in total? Circle the correct answer.

    A £10.05   B £10.95   C £9.95   D £11.05   E £9.90

    b) How much more does Josh have than Tammy?

    £ ☐.☐☐

13. Monib had £50. He bought some headphones for £22.99 and a microphone for £20.50. How much does Monib have left?

    £ ☐☐.☐☐

14. The table shows the number of tickets sold for four shows at a theatre.

    a) How many tickets were sold for shows 1 and 3 in total?

	Number of tickets sold
Show 1	4578
Show 2	2018
Show 3	3444
Show 4	6475

    b) How many more tickets were sold for show 4 than for shows 2 and 3 combined?

15. What is 1468 ÷ 100?

    A 146.8   B 1.468   C 14 680   D 14.68   E 146 800

16. Circle the number that is missing from this calculation: 1000 × ___ = 57 840

    A 0.5784   B 5.784   C 57.84   D 578.4   E 5784

17. Justin buys 100 bars of soap for £1.27 each. How much does he spend in total?

    £ ☐☐☐.☐☐

Section One — Working with Numbers

Practice Questions

18. Paul has three piles of rocks. The first pile is 100 times heavier than the second. The second pile is 10 times lighter than the third. How many times lighter is the third pile than the first?

    A 10 **B** 100 **C** 0.1 **D** 1000 **E** 1

19. There are 12 marbles in a bag. Mr Fayed buys 100 bags and shares the marbles equally between 10 boxes. How many marbles are in each box?

20. There are six penguins in a zoo. They each eat 4 fish a day. How many fish do they eat in total in a week?

21. Which calculation gives the smallest answer? Circle the correct answer.

    A 54.3 × 79 **B** 5.43 × 79 **C** 5.43 × 7.9 **D** 54.3 × 7.9

22. A hot air balloon rises 1.5 metres every second. How high will the hot air balloon rise in 200 seconds?

    ___ m

23. Circle the number that is missing from this calculation: 120 × 9 = 3 × ____

    A 40 **B** 60 **C** 240 **D** 360 **E** 720

24. Izzy runs 140 km each month. How many km does she run in a year? Circle the correct answer.

    A 1400 km **B** 1540 km **C** 1680 km **D** 1740 km **E** 1780 km

25. Padma has 28 pencils. Amy has 5 times as many as Padma. Una has 4 times as many as Amy. How many pencils does Una have?

26. Circle the number that is missing from this calculation: 182 ÷ ____ = 26

    A 5 **B** 6 **C** 7 **D** 8 **E** 9

27. A 480 cm long plank of wood is chopped into 4 equal lengths. How long is each piece?

    ___ cm

Section One — Working with Numbers

Practice Questions

28. 4865 ÷ 7 = 695. What is 48.65 ÷ 7?

    A 69.5   B 6950   C 69 500   D 0.695   E 6.95

29. Kay shares 4325 ants equally between five ant farms.
How many ants are in each ant farm?

30. Oli bought 5 pastries for £3.20. How much was each pastry?

31. A caretaker is putting chairs out for assembly. If he uses all the chairs he can either make 11 or 12 rows. Which of these could be the total number of chairs?
Circle the correct answer.

    A 168   B 176   C 209   D 264   E 308

32. Leon has between 200 and 210 comic books. If he puts them into 9 equal piles there are 7 left over. How many comic books does he have?

33. What is 42 ÷ 3 − (1 + 4)?

34. Which of these expressions has the answer 7.5?
Circle the correct answer.

    A 14 ÷ 2 + 3 − 1   B 9 − 3 + 5 ÷ 2   C 3 ÷ 2 + 3 × 2
    D (8 − 6) ÷ 2 + 5   E 3 × 1 + 12 − 9

35. What is 28 × 38 + 72 × 38?

36. Which of these expressions has the smallest answer?
Circle the correct answer.

    A 90 + 30 ÷ 15 − 5   B 90 − 30 ÷ 15 + 5   C 90 ÷ 30 + 15 − 5
    D 90 + 30 − 15 ÷ 5   E 90 − 30 + 15 ÷ 5

37. What is 6000 ÷ (80 × 2.5)?

Section One — Working with Numbers

Section Two — Number Knowledge

Types of Number

It's really useful to know a few facts about different types of numbers.

Negative Numbers are Numbers Below 0

1) You can use number lines to compare the values of negative numbers. The numbers on the number line increase from left to right. So –1 is greater than –6.

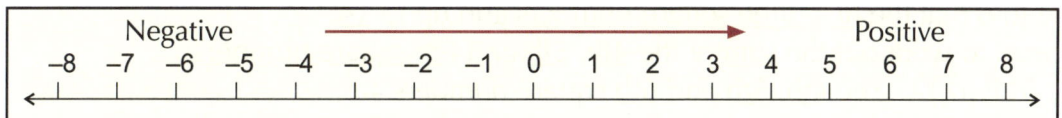

2) Number lines can be used to help you with calculations that involve negative numbers. For example to work out 2 – 9, just count back 9 places from 2 along the number line:

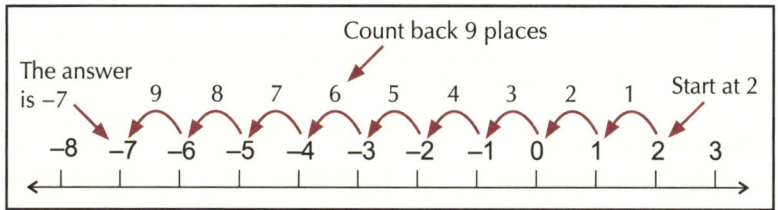

3) You can use these two symbols to show whether one number is bigger or smaller than another:

< means 'is less than'. For example, –3 is less than 2 or **–3 < 2**.
> means 'is greater than'. For example, 7 is greater than 5 or **7 > 5**.

Whole Numbers are either Odd or Even

1) An even number is any whole number that can be exactly divided by two to give another whole number. For example, 6 is an even number because 6 ÷ 2 = 3.
2) An odd number is any whole number that can't be divided by two to give another whole number. For example, 5 is an odd number because 5 ÷ 2 = 2.5.

Multiply a Whole Number by Itself to give a Square or Cube Number

1) For example, if you multiply 4 by itself (4 × 4) you get 16 — a square number. Or, if you multiply 4 by itself twice (4 × 4 × 4) you get 64 — a cube number.
2) You can show a number is squared or cubed using a small 2 or 3, e.g. 5 × 5 = 5^2, 1 × 1 × 1 = 1^3.
3) The first 5 square numbers are: $1^2 = 1$ $2^2 = 4$ $3^2 = 9$ $4^2 = 16$ $5^2 = 25$
4) The first 5 cube numbers are: $1^3 = 1$ $2^3 = 8$ $3^3 = 27$ $4^3 = 64$ $5^3 = 125$

Roman Numerals are Letters which represent Numbers

1) There are letters to represent the numbers in the box — all other numbers are written as a combination of these numbers.

1	5	10	50	100	500	1000
I	V	X	L	C	D	M

2) To write most numbers, find the biggest numbers from the box that add up to make your number, and write the matching letters. For example, 13 = 10 + 1 + 1 + 1, which is XIII.
3) 4s and 9s are a bit trickier. For these, you write them as subtractions. The number you take away goes before the number you take it away from, e.g. 4 = 5 – 1 so it's IV.

Types of Number

11+ Example Questions

EXAMPLE: The sum of the first three square numbers is 14. What is the sum of the first 6 square numbers?

1) You're told that the first three square numbers add up to 14. You need to work out the sum of the 4th, 5th and 6th square numbers and add it to 14. The 4th, 5th and 6th square numbers are:

   $4^2 = 4 \times 4 = 16$ $5^2 = 5 \times 5 = 25$ $6^2 = 6 \times 6 = 36$

2) Now add 14 to the sum of the 4th, 5th and 6th square numbers:

   $16 + 25 + 36 = 77$ $14 + 77 = 91$

EXAMPLE: Which of these numbers will go into the shaded section of the Venn diagram?

A 8   B 9   C 27
D 64   E 85

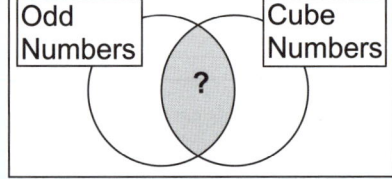

1) Data that's put into a Venn diagram must match its labels. Odd numbers must go in the left-hand circle of this Venn diagram, and cube numbers can only go in the right-hand circle. Where the circles overlap, the data must match both labels — so numbers in this section must be both odd and cube. Data that doesn't match any of the labels must go in the box outside the circles.

2) Numbers that are both odd and cube must go in the shaded section. Start off by working out which of the options are cube numbers.

   8, 27 and 64 are all cube numbers: $8 = 2 \times 2 \times 2$, $27 = 3 \times 3 \times 3$, $64 = 4 \times 4 \times 4$.

3) Then, work out which of 8, 27 and 64 is an odd number.

   8 and 64 are even because they're divisible by 2.

   27 is odd because it isn't divisible by 2 — C is the answer.

Practice Question

1) The table shows which floor of a tall building different people work on.

   How many floors higher is the person who works on the highest floor than the person who works on the lowest floor?

Person	Floor
Sheila	13
Heather	15
Rohit	−1
Ji-woo	5
Archie	−4

Keep an eye out for the order of Roman numerals...

When a numeral is smaller than the one after it, you need to subtract (e.g. IX = 10 − 1 = 9).

Factors, Multiples and Primes

Factors, multiples and primes are more types of number you need to know about.

Factors of a number are Whole Numbers that divide Exactly into it

1) The factors of a number are all the whole numbers that divide into that number exactly (so there's no remainder). For example the factors of 9 are 1, 3 and 9:

$$9 \div 1 = 9$$
$$9 \div 3 = 3$$
$$9 \div 9 = 1$$

2) If a question asks for the common factors of some numbers, you need to find the factors that the numbers all share. Here's how to find the common factors of 12, 24 and 36:

> Find the factors of each number, then work out which factors are the same for all three numbers.
>
> The factors of 12 are: 1, 2, 3, 4, 6 and 12.
> The factors of 24 are: 1, 2, 3, 4, 6, 8, 12 and 24.
> The factors of 36 are: 1, 2, 3, 4, 6, 9, 12, 18 and 36.
>
> 1, 2, 3, 4, 6 and 12 are all common factors of 12, 24 and 36.

Remember to include the number itself in the list of factors.

3) The highest common factor (HCF) is just the biggest number that will divide into all the numbers in the question. In the example above, the HCF of 12, 24 and 36 is 12.

A Multiple is the Result of Multiplying one Whole Number by another

1) The multiples of a number are just the times table for that number, e.g. multiples of 4 are 4, 8, 12, 16 etc.

2) If a question asks for some common multiples of some numbers, you need to find multiples that the numbers all share. Here's how to find some common multiples of 4 and 6:

> Find the first few multiples of each number and check if any of them are the same.
>
> If not, work out a few more multiples, then try again.
>
> The first six multiples of 4 are: 4, 8, 12, 16, 20 and 24.
> The first five multiples of 6 are: 6, 12, 18, 24, 30.
>
> So the first two common multiples of 4 and 6 are 12 and 24.

3) The lowest common multiple (LCM) is just the smallest multiple that the numbers in the question share. In the example above, the LCM of 4 and 6 is 12.

Section Two — Number Knowledge

Factors, Multiples and Primes

Prime Numbers only have Two Factors

1) A prime number is a number with exactly two factors — the number itself and one. For example, 23 is a prime number — the only factors of 23 are 1 and 23.
2) 1 is NOT a prime number — it doesn't have exactly two factors.
3) Apart from 2 and 5, all prime numbers end in 1, 3, 7 or 9 (but not all numbers ending in 1, 3, 7 or 9 are prime numbers).
4) The only even prime number is 2.

> The first ten prime numbers are: 2, 3, 5, 7, 11, 13, 17, 19, 23 and 29.

5) Whole numbers that aren't prime are made up of prime numbers multiplied together — these prime numbers are called prime factors. Here's how to find the prime factors of 40:

Write down any factor pair of 40, then keep splitting the factors until they are all prime numbers:

40 = 5 × 8

5 is a prime number. It is a prime factor of 40.

8 isn't a prime number, so split this into a factor pair:
40 = 5 × 2 × 4

2 is a prime number. It is a prime factor of 40.

4 isn't a prime number, so split this into a factor pair:
40 = 5 × 2 × 2 × 2

You can use a factor tree to quickly find prime factors.

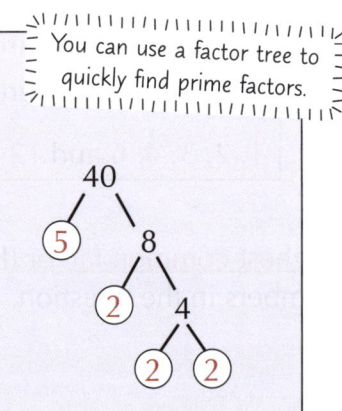

11+ Example Questions

EXAMPLE: Two of the numbers are missing from this sorting diagram.

	Multiple of 3	Not a multiple of 3
Factor of 66	3 6 ?	2 11 22
Not a factor of 66	?	7

Which of the following could be the missing numbers?

A 36 and 12   B 3 and 25
C 66 and 33   D 33 and 12
E 81 and 19

1) Both of the missing numbers are multiples of 3, one is a factor of 66 and one isn't. Start off by finding which of the answer options have two multiples of 3.

   3, 12, 33, 36, 66 and 81 are all multiples of 3. 19 and 25 are not.
   Options A, C and D all have two multiples of 3.

2) Now work out which one of these options has only one factor of 66.

   A 36 and 12 are not factors of 66.
   C 66 and 33 are both factors of 66.
   D 33 is a factor of 66, but 12 is not — D is the answer.

Section Two — Number Knowledge

Factors, Multiples and Primes

 **Indira bought some sweets and gave them all away to her friends. Each friend got an equal number of sweets and they were all given more than one sweet. How many sweets could she have bought?**

The question doesn't say how many friends Indira has — but she has more than one because it says she has "friends" and not "a friend".

    A 19   B 23   C 24   D 29   E 31

1) You might recognise that <u>all</u> of the amounts, <u>except 24</u>, are <u>prime numbers</u> (prime numbers have no factors other than 1 and the number itself).

   If the number of sweets is a prime number, e.g. 23, then they can only be equally distributed between one friend or a group of 23 friends. The question shows that there is more than one friend and they all get more than one sweet. So none of these are right.

2) The <u>answer</u> to the question is 24 (option C) because that is the <u>only number</u> that has any <u>factors</u> other than <u>1</u> and <u>itself</u>. For example, if Indira had 24 sweets she could give <u>8</u> friends <u>3</u> sweets each, or <u>4</u> friends could have <u>6</u> sweets each, etc.

3) If you're <u>not sure</u> if a number is <u>prime</u> then you can try to find the number's <u>factors</u>.

   For example, you could work out if 19 has any factors other than 1 or 19. Divide 19 by possible factors to see if you get a whole number. This will take time so it'd be useful to memorise some prime numbers.

 **Find the three prime numbers that multiply together to give 52.**

1) You need to find the set of <u>prime numbers</u> that <u>multiplies together</u> to make 52.
2) First find any <u>factor pair</u> of 52.

   52 = 2 × 26   *2 is a prime number, but 26 isn't.*

3) <u>Split</u> any factors that aren't prime into more factor pairs until you're <u>only left with prime numbers</u>.

   52 = 2 × 2 × 13   *26 splits into 2 × 13, which are both prime numbers.*

4) You've now got three primes that multiply to give 52, so you can stop. <u>2 × 2 × 13</u> is called the <u>prime factorisation</u> of 52.

Practice Questions

1) Which of these statements is true?
   - **A** All factors of 24 are multiples of 2.
   - **B** All numbers ending in a 3 are multiples of 3.
   - **C** 13 and 52 have no common factors.
   - **D** The highest common factor of 36 and 18 is 9.
   - **E** A prime number can be a multiple of 3.

2) Which of these numbers is not a factor of 72?   A 4   B 6   C 7   D 8   E 9

Make sure you don't get factors and multiples mixed up...

Remember that you need to *multi*ply a number to find its *multi*ples, while its factors divide into it.

Section Two — Number Knowledge

Fractions

Fractions are a bit tricky at first, but you'll be fine with a bit of practice.

Fractions are Parts of a Whole Number

1) A fraction looks like this:

   The bottom number of a fraction is the denominator. It tells you how many equal parts something is split into. $\frac{4}{9}$ The top number of a fraction is the numerator. It tells you how many equal parts you've got.

2) Fractions can be shown using shapes.

   This triangle is split into 9 equal parts. 4 out of the 9 parts are shaded. So the fraction of the triangle that's shaded is $\frac{4}{9}$.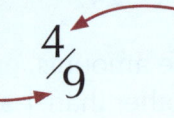

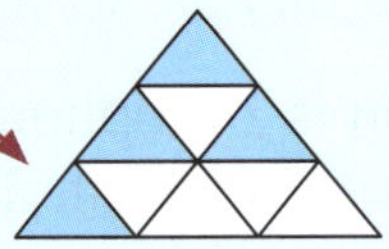

3) To find a fraction of a number (e.g. four-fifths of 15), divide the number by the fraction's denominator. Then multiply the result by the fraction's numerator.

   Divide by the denominator.
   $\frac{4}{5}$ of 15. 15 ÷ 5 = 3. Then, 4 × 3 = 12
   Multiply by the numerator.   So $\frac{4}{5}$ of 15 is 12.

   Alternatively, you can multiply by the numerator then divide by the denominator.

4) You can see this more clearly with a diagram:

   To find $\frac{4}{5}$ of 15 apples, start by dividing 15 by 5. That gives you 5 groups of 3 apples. So $\frac{4}{5}$ = 4 groups of 3 apples, or 12 apples.

Equivalent Fractions are Fractions that are Equal

1) For example, $\frac{1}{4}$ and $\frac{2}{8}$ are equivalent fractions because they're equal. You can show this using shapes:

2) To find an equivalent fraction, multiply the numerator and the denominator by the same number. So $\frac{2}{5}$ is equivalent to $\frac{4}{10}$, $\frac{6}{15}$ and $\frac{8}{20}$.

   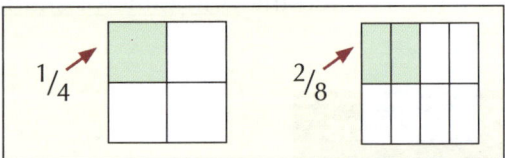

3) You can also find equivalent fractions by dividing both the numerator and the denominator by the same number. This is called simplifying a fraction. For example, $\frac{55}{100}$ is equivalent to $\frac{11}{20}$.

   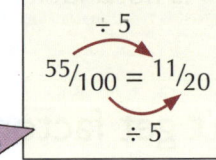

   A fraction is in its 'simplest form' if you can't divide the numerator and the denominator by the same amount any more.

Section Two — Number Knowledge

Fractions

Some **Fractions** are **Bigger Than 1**

1) You can write fractions that are bigger than 1 as improper fractions or mixed numbers.

2) Improper fractions have a numerator that's bigger than the denominator. For example:  1 whole is the same as 8 eighths (or $^8/_8$) so this fraction is greater than 1. 13 eighths is the same as 1 whole plus another $^5/_8$.

3) Mixed numbers have both a whole number and a fraction. For example: $1\,^5/_8$ This fraction is greater than 1 — there is 1 whole plus another $^5/_8$.

You can **Add, Subtract, Order, Multiply** and **Divide Fractions**

1) Adding and subtracting fractions is easy if they both have the same denominator. All you need to do is add or subtract the numerators and keep the denominator the same.

$$^2/_5 + ^2/_5 = ^4/_5 \qquad ^4/_5 - ^1/_5 = ^3/_5$$

2) To add or subtract fractions which have different denominators, change them so they have the same denominator. You can do this by making them into equivalent fractions.

$^2/_5 + ^3/_{10}$ — to add these fractions you need to change them so they have the same denominator. One way to do this is to make $^2/_5$ a fraction with 10 as its denominator.

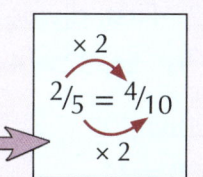

Both fractions now have the same denominator, so you can add them together.

$$^4/_{10} + ^3/_{10} = ^7/_{10}$$

3) You can also use equivalent fractions to order fractions with different denominators.

To compare the fractions $^3/_5$ and $^7/_{10}$, you need to make their denominators the same. Make $^3/_5$ a fraction with 10 as its denominator.

×2
$^3/_5 = ^6/_{10}$
×2

Now compare numerators: 7 is bigger than 6, so $^7/_{10}$ is bigger than $^3/_5$.

4) To multiply fractions, just multiply the numerators together and the denominators together.

$$^2/_5 \times ^3/_7 = ^6/_{35} \qquad ^2/_3 \times ^2/_7 = ^4/_{21}$$

5) To multiply a fraction by a whole number, multiply the numerator by the whole number. To divide a fraction by a whole number, multiply the denominator by the whole number.

You might be able to simplify your answer. Always check to see whether you can divide the numerator and denominator by the same amount.

$$^5/_6 \times 2 = ^{10}/_6 = ^5/_3 \qquad ^2/_5 \div 3 = ^2/_{15}$$

Section Two — Number Knowledge

Fractions

11+ Example Questions

**EXAMPLE:** Ginny has made 108 cupcakes. She sells 72 of them at the school fair. What fraction of her cupcakes did she sell?
Give your answer as a fraction in its simplest form.

1) Ginny sold <u>72 out of 108</u> or $^{72}/_{108}$ cupcakes.

2) <u>Simplify</u> the fraction by finding <u>common factors</u>.

   9 is a common factor of both 72 and 108, so divide the numerator and the denominator by 9. $\quad\xrightarrow{\div 9}\quad ^{72}/_{108} = {}^{8}/_{12}$

   4 is a common factor of both 8 and 12, so divide the numerator and the denominator by 4. $\quad\xrightarrow{\div 4}\quad ^{8}/_{12} = {}^{2}/_{3}$

3) 2 and 3 don't have any common factors — the fraction is in its <u>simplest form</u>.

**EXAMPLE:** A coat is originally priced at £32.
Its price is reduced to $^{3}/_{4}$ of the original price.
What is the price of the coat now?

1) You need to find $^{3}/_{4}$ of <u>£32</u>. First, <u>divide 32</u> by the <u>denominator</u> of the <u>fraction</u>.
   4 is the denominator in $^{3}/_{4}$. So, 32 ÷ 4 = 8. This means that $^{1}/_{4}$ of £32 = £8.

2) Now <u>multiply 8</u> by the <u>numerator</u>.
   If $^{1}/_{4}$ = 8, then $^{3}/_{4}$ is 3 × 8 = 24.

3) The coat costs £24.

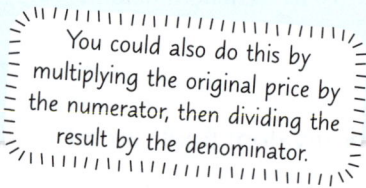
You could also do this by multiplying the original price by the numerator, then dividing the result by the denominator.

Practice Questions

1) Lydia and Rose each have a pie. Their pies are exactly the same size. Lydia gave two-fifths of her pie to Gemma. Rose gave Gemma one-fifth of her pie. Which statement is correct?

   A Gemma has more pie than Lydia.   **B** Gemma has the same amount of pie as Rose.
   C Gemma has more pie than Rose.   **D** Gemma has the same amount of pie as Lydia.
   E Rose and Lydia together have exactly twice as much pie as Gemma.

2) Tia had a sack of apples. She gave Alex $^{2}/_{3}$ of the apples and kept the rest. Alex split his apples into 3 equal piles. What fraction of the sack of apples are in each of Alex's piles?

   A $^{1}/_{3}$ **B** $^{1}/_{6}$ **C** $^{2}/_{9}$ **D** $^{2}/_{6}$ **E** $^{6}/_{9}$

 **Don't get confused by equivalent fractions...**
You might need to simplify your answer to a question so it matches one of the multiple choice options — just divide the top and bottom of the fraction by the same number.

Section Two — Number Knowledge

Ratio and Proportion

The difference between ratio and proportion can be tricky, so read this page carefully.

Ratios Compare One Part to Another Part

1) Ratios look like this: **1 : 3** — You read this as '1 to 3'. It means there's one of the first type of thing for every three of the second type.

2) They are most clearly shown using shapes or objects:

   The diagram shows that for every two limes there are six lemons.

   So for every lime there are three lemons. The ratio is 1 lime to 3 lemons or 1 : 3.

3) Finding equivalent ratios is a lot like finding equivalent fractions (see page 32). You have to multiply or divide all the parts of the ratio by the same number.

   If there were 12 lemons, how many limes would there be?

   × 4 ⟮ 3 lemons for every 1 lime ⟯ × 4
         12 lemons for every ? limes

   Like with fractions, both parts of the ratio have been multiplied by the same number — so there would be 1 × 4 = 4 limes.

Proportions Compare a Part to the Whole Thing

1) Proportions are written like this: **1 in every 4** — The 4 represents the whole thing and the 1 represents a part of the whole thing.

2) In the example above, 2 in every 8 fruits are limes, which is the same as 1 in every 4.

3) Proportions are another way of writing fractions. The proportion '1 in every 4' is the same as the fraction $1/4$. So you can answer proportion questions as you would fractions questions.

   If there were 24 fruits, how many limes would there be?
   The proportion of fruits that are limes is 1 in every 4, or $1/4$.
   To find $1/4$ of 24, divide 24 by the denominator. ⟶ 24 ÷ 4 = 6.
   You don't need to multiply by the numerator here, because it's 1.
   There would be 6 limes if there were 24 fruits.

Similar Shapes have Side Lengths in the Same Ratio

You can change the size of a shape by multiplying each side by the same number — called a scale factor. The two shapes are called similar, and have pairs of sides in the same ratio.

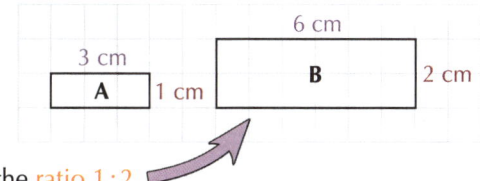

E.g. Shape A has been enlarged by a scale factor of 2 to give Shape B. Shape B's sides are twice as long as Shape A's — the pairs of sides are in the ratio 1 : 2.

Section Two — Number Knowledge

Ratio and Proportion

11+ Example Questions

EXAMPLE: Divide £490 in the ratio 4 : 3.

1) First add together the numbers in the ratio to find out how many parts £490 needs to be divided into.

   4 + 3 = 7

2) Next divide the total amount by 7 to find out how much one part is.

   £490 ÷ 7 = £70

3) Then multiply £70 by 4 to find out how much four parts are, and by 3 to find out how much three parts are.

   £70 × 4 = £280
   £70 × 3 = £210

4) The answer is £280 : £210.

EXAMPLE: 8 copies of the same magazine cost £16.40. How much will 3 copies cost?

1) Divide the total cost by 8 to work out how much one magazine costs.

   £16.40 ÷ 8 = £2.05

2) Then multiply by three to find the cost of 3 magazines.

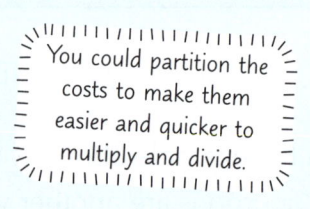

   £2.05 × 3 = £6.15

You could partition the costs to make them easier and quicker to multiply and divide.

Practice Questions

1) A farmer has 48 orange Highland cows and 96 black and white cows. What is the ratio of orange cows to black and white cows? Write your answer in its simplest form.

2) Maya has a box of coloured building blocks. 5 in every 7 of them are green. If there are 84 blocks in total, how many green blocks are there?

Ratios are all about sharing things out...

If ratio questions are getting you in a muddle, just remember to work out how much one part of the ratio is worth. First add to find the total number of parts, then divide by the total to find the value of one part. Then, you can multiply this by the number of parts you need to get the answer.

Section Two — Number Knowledge

Percentages, Fractions and Decimals

You can write a proportion of something as a decimal, a fraction or a percentage. This page will show you how percentages, fractions and decimals are related, and how to convert between them.

You can Convert between Percentages, Fractions and Decimals

Decimals can be Converted into Percentages

1) To turn a decimal into a percentage, multiply the decimal by 100, e.g. 0.53 × 100 = 53%.

2) Divide the percentage by 100 to get back to the decimal, e.g. 72% = 72 ÷ 100 = 0.72.

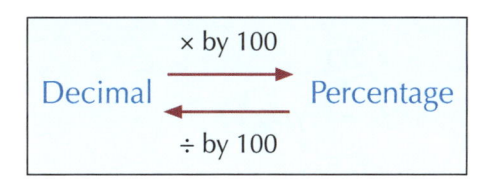

Decimal ⇄ Percentage
× by 100
÷ by 100

Fractions can be Converted into Percentages

1) Converting fractions with 100 as the denominator into percentages is easy. The numerator is the percentage, e.g. $^{23}/_{100}$ = 23%.

2) For other fractions, just make an equivalent fraction (see p.32) with 100 as the denominator.

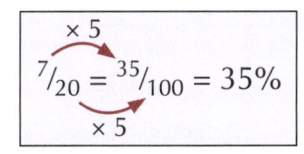

$^7/_{20}$ = $^{35}/_{100}$ = 35% (× 5)

Find an equivalent fraction over 100
Fraction ⇄ Percentage
Put the percentage over 100

3) You can write any percentage as a fraction. Put the percentage on the top (the numerator) and 100 on the bottom (the denominator), e.g. 17% = $^{17}/_{100}$.

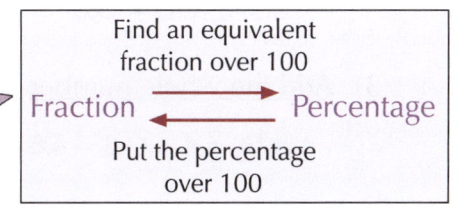

"Per cent" just means "out of 100" — it's usually written as %. So 17 per cent is 17 out of 100, which can also be written as 17%.

Fractions can also be Converted into Decimals

1) To convert a fraction into a decimal, you can often just find an equivalent fraction with 100 as its denominator.

2) Then divide the numerator by 100 to get the decimal.

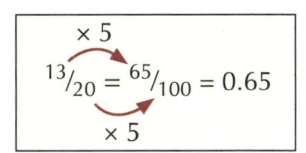

$^{13}/_{20}$ = $^{65}/_{100}$ = 0.65 (× 5)

Find the equivalent fraction over 100 and divide its numerator by 100
Fraction ⇄ Decimal
× by 100 and put this number over 100

3) To convert a decimal into a fraction you just multiply the decimal by 100, then put this as the numerator above a denominator of 100. E.g. 0.29 = $^{29}/_{100}$.

(If the decimal has more than 2 decimal places, multiply by a bigger number and put that as the denominator — e.g. 0.625 × 1000 = 625, so 0.625 = $^{625}/_{1000}$)

These are very common fractions as percentages and decimals — make sure you know them:
$^1/_4$ = 25% or 0.25 $^3/_4$ = 75% or 0.75 $^1/_2$ = 50% or 0.5 $^1/_{10}$ = 10% or 0.1 $^1/_5$ = 20% or 0.2

Section Two — Number Knowledge

Percentages, Fractions and Decimals

11+ Example Questions

EXAMPLE: What is $4\frac{4}{5}$ as a decimal?

1) Change the fraction part to a decimal.
   Find an equivalent fraction with 100 as the denominator.

   $$\frac{4}{5} = \frac{80}{100} \quad (\times 20)$$

2) Next divide the numerator of the equivalent fraction by 100.

   $80 \div 100 = 0.8$

3) Add the whole number part.

   $4\frac{4}{5} = 4 + 0.8 = 4.8$

EXAMPLE: Which one of these is the greatest?

A $\frac{1}{5}$ of 45   B 25% of 40   C $\frac{1}{3}$ of 30   D 80% of 20   E $\frac{3}{4}$ of 20

1) Work out the value of each option which involves a fraction. To work out the fraction of a number, divide the number by the denominator and multiply it by the numerator.

   A: $\frac{1}{5}$ of 45. $45 \div 5 = 9$. $9 \times 1 = 9$.

   C: $\frac{1}{3}$ of 30. $30 \div 3 = 10$. $10 \times 1 = 10$.

   E: $\frac{3}{4}$ of 20. $20 \div 4 = 5$. $5 \times 3 = 15$.

2) Work out the value of each option which involves a percentage. To work out the percentage of a number you could convert the percentage to a fraction. Then follow the method for working out the fraction of a number.

   B: 25% of 40 is the same as $\frac{1}{4}$ of 40. $40 \div 4 = 10$. $10 \times 1 = 10$.

   D: 80% of 20 is the same as $\frac{8}{10}$ of 20. $20 \div 10 = 2$. $2 \times 8 = 16$.

3) The answer is D because 80% of 20 is the greatest number.

Alternatively, to find a percentage of a number you can divide the number by 100 and multiply the result by the percentage you want to find.

Section Two — Number Knowledge

Percentages, Fractions and Decimals

EXAMPLE: **Find the correct statement.**

  A $7\frac{1}{4} < 7.2$ B $7\frac{1}{5} > 7.2$ C $7\frac{1}{10} > 7.2$

  D $7\frac{1}{5} = 7.2$ E $7\frac{1}{2} < 7.2$

1) Convert each of the fractions into a decimal so you can compare the numbers.

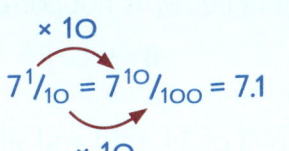

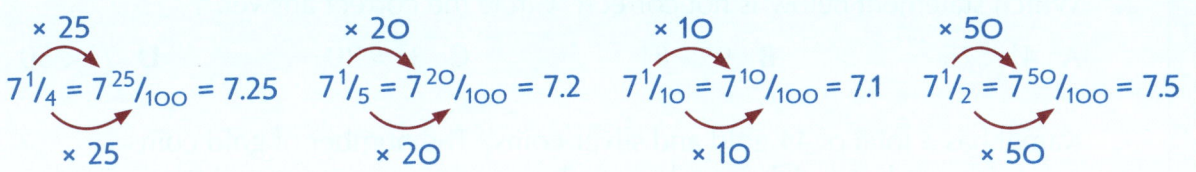

$7\frac{1}{4} = 7\frac{25}{100} = 7.25$ (× 25) $7\frac{1}{5} = 7\frac{20}{100} = 7.2$ (× 20) $7\frac{1}{10} = 7\frac{10}{100} = 7.1$ (× 10) $7\frac{1}{2} = 7\frac{50}{100} = 7.5$ (× 50)

2) Now you can check each statement.
   Remember, '<' means less than and '>' means greater than.

   A 7.25 < 7.2. Incorrect.
   B 7.2 > 7.2. Incorrect.
   C 7.1 > 7.2. Incorrect.
   D 7.2 = 7.2. Correct. So D is the answer.
   E 7.5 < 7.2. Incorrect.

Practice Questions

1) What percentage of the triangle on the right is shaded?

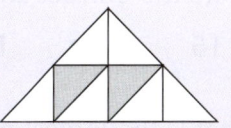

   A 10%   B 20%   C 25%   D 30%   E 40%

2) Marek asked all the children in Year 5 what their favourite colour was. He made a chart to show his results.

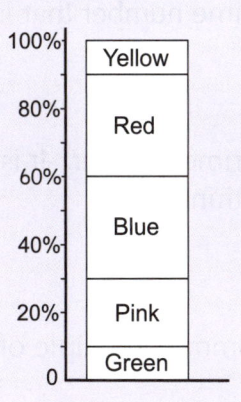

   There are 90 children in Year 5.

   How many children chose pink as their favourite colour?

   A 12   B 18   C 27   D 30   E 33

3) Which one of these is the smallest?

   A 25% of 4   B $\frac{3}{4}$ of 8   C $\frac{2}{5}$ of 10   D 10% of 25   E $\frac{2}{6}$ of 18

REVISION TIP

Practise switching between the different forms...

Memorising some common fractions as decimals and percentages will make answering these questions easier. Make sure you know the ones on page 37 really well.

Section Two — Number Knowledge

Practice Questions

Once you're done with the Number Knowledge section, find out how much you've learned by having a go at these Practice Questions.

1. Which of the following temperatures is the lowest? Circle the correct answer.
   A −4 °C   B 0 °C   C −12 °C   D −14 °C   E −9 °C

2. Which statement below is not correct? Circle the correct answer.
   A $4^3 < 75$ B $9^2 > 81$ C $3^3 > 20$ D $7^2 < 50$

3. Kamal has a total of 44 gold and silver coins. The number of gold coins is a cube number and the number of silver coins is a square number. How many gold coins does he have?

4. Which Roman numeral has the highest value? Circle the correct answer.
   A MXVI   B MCIX   C CMXC   D DCCX   E MLXI

5. What is the highest common factor of 40 and 72?

6. Verity shares a box of doughnuts equally between herself and five friends. Which of the following could be the number of doughnuts in the box? Circle the correct answer.
   A 15   B 20   C 8   D 25   E 18

7. What is the largest prime number that is smaller than 40?

8. Zoe is thinking of a prime number. It is a common factor of 35 and 84. What number is Zoe thinking of?

9. What is the lowest common multiple of 9 and 15?

10. Which fraction below is not equivalent to $^{10}/_{25}$? Circle the correct answer.
    A $^{12}/_{30}$ B $^{2}/_{5}$ C $^{4}/_{10}$ D $^{6}/_{15}$ E $^{30}/_{50}$

11. What is $2^3/_7$ as an improper fraction? Circle the correct answer.
    A $^{6}/_{7}$ B $^{10}/_{7}$ C $^{23}/_{7}$ D $^{3}/_{14}$ E $^{17}/_{7}$

Section Two — Number Knowledge

Practice Questions

12. What is $5/6 \div 3$? Circle the correct answer.

    A $5/18$ B $1/3$ C $6/15$ D $15/6$ E $15/18$

13. The table shows the fractions of a crossword puzzle that four children have completed.

Aidan	Beth	Cindy	Dev
$2/5$	$5/6$	$1/3$	$4/9$

    a) Who has completed the most? Circle the correct answer.

       A Aidan   B Beth   C Cindy   D Dev

    b) Cindy and Dev didn't get any of the same answers. How much of the puzzle did they complete in total? Circle the correct answer.

       A $1/9$ B $4/27$ C $5/9$ D $7/9$ E $5/3$

    c) How much more of the puzzle did Beth complete than Aidan? Circle the correct answer.

       A $3/11$ B $1/3$ C $13/30$ D $3/5$ E $13/15$

14. Izumi has read $7/9$ of a book. She has 12 pages left. How many pages does the book have?

15. There are 24 pens and 6 pencils in a box.

    a) What is the ratio of pens to pencils? Give your answer in its simplest form.

    b) 1 in every 8 pens is a ballpoint pen. How many ballpoint pens are there?

16. Divide 360 in the ratio 1 : 5.

17. In a swimming pool, there are 4 people for every 3 inflatables.

    a) How many people are there if there are 12 inflatables? Circle the correct answer.

       A 16   B 12   C 24   D 7   E 4

    b) How many inflatables are there if there are 80 people?

Section Two — Number Knowledge

Practice Questions

18. Look at the rectangle below. What is the ratio of a : b?

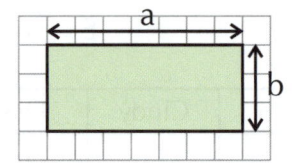

    ☐☐ : ☐☐

19. Richard has 20 identical screws in his pocket. They have a total mass of 180 g. He uses 4 of the screws. What is the mass of the screws he has left?

    ☐☐☐☐ g

20. What is $^{17}/_{20}$ as a decimal?

    ☐.☐☐

21. What percentage of the rectangle below is shaded?

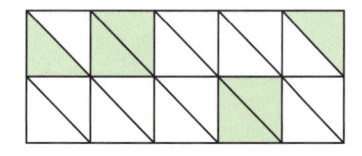

    ☐☐ %

22. What is $^{3}/_{50}$ as a percentage?

    ☐☐ %

23. A supermarket had 400 tins of tomatoes. They sold 45% of them. How many tins of tomatoes do they have left?

    ☐☐☐

24. What is 35% as a fraction? Circle the correct answer.

    A $^{7}/_{10}$ **B** $^{3}/_{10}$ **C** $^{3}/_{7}$ **D** $^{7}/_{20}$ **E** $^{13}/_{20}$

25. Sam used $^{7}/_{25}$ of a bag of flour to make some pasta and 24% to make a cake. What percentage of the flour is left?

    ☐☐ %

26. Which of the following statements is not true? Circle the correct answer.

    A 0.25 < 30%   **B** $^{1}/_{5}$ > 15%   **C** 0.9 = 90%
    D $^{4}/_{5}$ < 0.8   **E** $^{3}/_{10}$ > 0.25

27. What is 5% of 2100?

    ☐☐☐

Section Two — Number Knowledge

Section Three — Number Problems

Algebra

Algebra isn't as scary as it sounds. Make sure you're happy with the basics of how it works and then practise, practise, practise...

Algebra is using Letters or Symbols to Represent Numbers

1) Algebra uses letters or symbols to represent numbers that you don't know.

2) An algebraic expression contains both numbers and letters or symbols. For example, if z is an unknown number you want to add 3 to, an expression could be: ➡ $z + 3$

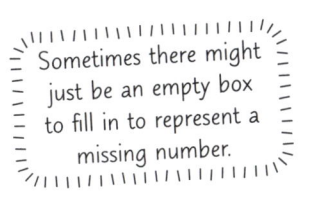

   Sometimes there might just be an empty box to fill in to represent a missing number.

3) Algebra doesn't always use multiplication signs before letters or symbols. You just write the number next to the letter or symbol. For example:

   | 3△ means 3 × △ | 2ab means 2 × a × b | $\frac{1}{2} x$ means $\frac{1}{2} \times x$ |

4) A letter or symbol written over a number means that you have to divide by that number. For example: ➡ $x/8$ means $x \div 8$

5) Algebraic expressions also use square numbers. These show that a letter or symbol is multiplied by itself. ➡ $\bigcirc^2$ means $\bigcirc \times \bigcirc$

6) Brackets are used to keep parts of an expression together. You should always work out the part in brackets first. For example:

   $3(a + b)$ means $(a + b) + (a + b) + (a + b)$

   Work out the part in brackets first, $(a + b)$, and then find 3 lots of the answer.

Use Algebra to turn Wordy Problems into Maths

You can write expressions to show what's happening in a word problem. For example:

> I think of a number, add 2, divide by 3 then subtract 10. Write an expression to show this word problem.
>
> Use a letter to represent the missing number, e.g. z. Build up the expression bit-by-bit.
>
> $z + 2$ — First, 2 is added to the number.
>
> Then the result is divided by 3. — $\dfrac{z + 2}{3}$
>
> $\dfrac{z + 2}{3} - 10$ — Then 10 is subtracted.

Section Three — Number Problems

Algebra

Do the Opposite Operation to solve an Equation

1) Equations have an equals sign in them to show that the values on the left-hand side are equal to the values on the right-hand side.

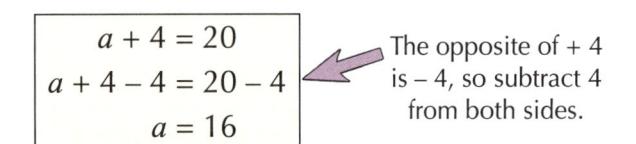

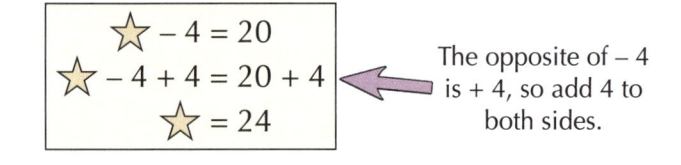

$4 + x = 9$

x represents a number that you don't know. When you add 4 to x you get 9.

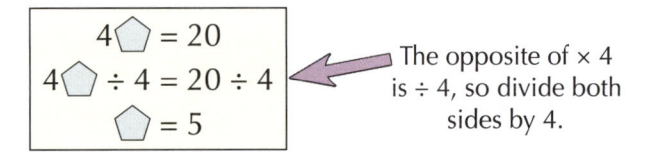

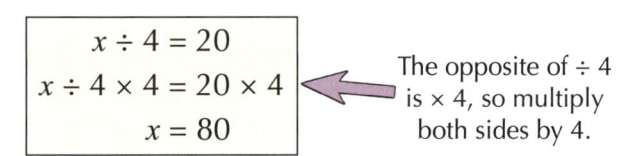

2) You can solve algebraic equations by finding the value of the letter.
3) You need to remove parts of the equation until the letter is left on its own on one side of the equals sign.
4) To remove part of an equation, do the opposite operation to both sides of the equation. For example:

$+$ and $-$ are opposites, and $\times$ and $\div$ are opposites.

$a + 4 = 20$
$a + 4 - 4 = 20 - 4$
$a = 16$

The opposite of $+ 4$ is $- 4$, so subtract 4 from both sides.

$\star - 4 = 20$
$\star - 4 + 4 = 20 + 4$
$\star = 24$

The opposite of $- 4$ is $+ 4$, so add 4 to both sides.

$4\pentagon = 20$
$4\pentagon \div 4 = 20 \div 4$
$\pentagon = 5$

The opposite of $\times 4$ is $\div 4$, so divide both sides by 4.

$x \div 4 = 20$
$x \div 4 \times 4 = 20 \times 4$
$x = 80$

The opposite of $\div 4$ is $\times 4$, so multiply both sides by 4.

A Formula is Used to Work Out an Amount

1) A formula tells you how to work out one quantity when you know a different quantity. For example, the formula below is for working out how many wheels a group of cars has in total.

w = total number of wheels $w = 4c$ c = number of cars

2) You can substitute different known values into a formula to work out the unknown value. For example:

How many wheels do 8 cars have?

$w = 4c$ There are 8 cars, so $c = 8$.
$= 4 \times 8$ Substitute 8 for c in the formula.
$w = 32$ wheels in total

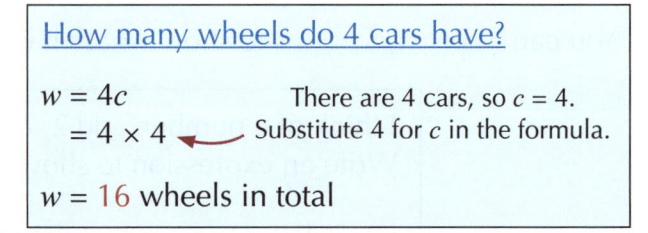

How many wheels do 4 cars have?

$w = 4c$ There are 4 cars, so $c = 4$.
$= 4 \times 4$ Substitute 4 for c in the formula.
$w = 16$ wheels in total

3) You can write formulas to help you solve word problems. For example:

Spiders have 8 legs.
Write a formula for the total number of legs, l, of t spiders.

Total number of legs = number of spiders $\times$ 8   This is the formula in words.

$l = t \times 8$ ...or... $l = 8t$ Substitute the letters in to create the formula.

Section Three — Number Problems

Algebra

11+ Example Questions

EXAMPLE: At a restaurant, a hamburger costs £3 and a hotdog costs £2. Which expression gives the total cost, in pounds, of buying x hamburgers and y hotdogs?

    A $2x + y$ B $5y - x$ C $3xy$ D $3x + 2y$ E $x \times y$

1) Make the expression one part at a time.

2) Start by finding the cost (in pounds) of <u>x hamburgers</u>:

    Cost of hamburgers = $3x$ The cost of the hamburgers is the number you're buying (x) multiplied by the price (£3). So this should be written as $3x$.

3) Next, add the cost (in pounds) of <u>y hotdogs</u> to <u>complete</u> the expression:

    $3x + 2y$ Each hotdog costs £2, so the price of y hotdogs is $2y$ pounds.
    To find the total cost, add the cost of the hotdogs to the cost of the hamburgers.

4) That gives you the <u>finished expression</u>. The correct answer is $3x + 2y$ — option D.

EXAMPLE: Solve the equation below to find the value of z.

$4 + 2z = 16$

Quick Method

The quickest way is just to use your <u>knowledge of maths</u> to <u>reason out</u> the answer.

1) Think "<u>what do you add to 4 to make 16?</u>" — it's 12, so $2z$ is the same as 12.
    $2z = 12$

2) Think "<u>2 times what is 12?</u>" — it's 6, so z is the same as 6.
    $z = 6$

Written Method

1) You need to <u>remove</u> parts of the equation so that the letter is left <u>on its own</u>.

2) The opposite of + 4 is – 4, so <u>subtract 4</u> from both sides
    $4 + 2z - 4 = 16 - 4 \longrightarrow 2z = 12$

3) The opposite of × 2 is ÷ 2, so <u>divide</u> both sides <u>by 2</u>.
    $2z \div 2 = 12 \div 2 \longrightarrow z = 6$

Section Three — Number Problems

Algebra

One More 11+ Example Question

EXAMPLE: A farm calculates the cost of eggs in pence (C) using this formula:

$C = 40 + 2x^2$

x is the number of eggs bought.

A man buys 9 eggs. What is the total cost in pounds?

1) The man buys 9 eggs, so change x in the formula to 9.
   $C = 40 + 2 \times 9^2$

2) Work out the calculation one part at a time.
   Remember to follow BODMAS (see page 21).

   First, work out 9^2...
   $C = 40 + 2 \times 81$ $9^2 = 9 \times 9 = 81$

   ...then do the multiplication...
   $C = 40 + 162$ $2 \times 81 = 162$

   ...then work out the addition to find the cost in pence...
   $C = 202$ $162 + 40 = 202$

   ...then divide by 100 to find the cost in pounds.
   $C = 202p = £2.02$

   Don't forget this last step. The question asked for the answer in pounds.

Practice Questions

1) The cost (in pounds) of calling out an electrician (C) is given by the formula:
   $C = 25 + 10h + p$, where h is the number of hours and p is the cost (in pounds) of any parts.
   What is the cost of the electrician when they work for 3 hours and need £20 worth of parts?

2) Solve the following equation to find the value of x.
   $x \div 8 - 6 = 2$

3) The width of a room is 3 m. The length of the room is four times the width of the room. The height of the room is y m. Which of these is the correct expression for finding the volume of the room in m³?

   A $12y \times 4$ B $3y \times 4y$ C $12y + 3y$ D $36y$ E $y + 36$

   Volume is calculated by length × width × height.

TEST TIP — **Make sure to check your answer...**
When you have to solve an equation, you can check that your answer is correct by substituting it back into the original equation. Even if you're short for time in the test, it's worth taking a few seconds to make sure you've come up with the correct answer.

Section Three — Number Problems

Number Sequences

You need to follow the rule of a sequence to get from one number to the next.

Some **Number Sequences** follow a **Pattern** you **Already Know**

1) You might spot a pattern in a number sequence because you recognise the numbers.

> 2, 3, 5, 7... — are all prime numbers going up in order.
> 25, 20, 15, 10... — are all multiples of 5 going down in order.
> 1, 4, 9, 16... — are all square numbers going up in order.

2) Once you know the pattern you can work out what the next number in the sequence will be.

> 1, 3, 5, 7... are all odd numbers going up in order.
> So the next number in the sequence will be 9.

3) You can also work out later numbers in the sequence. For example, to find the seventh number in this sequence of odd numbers, follow the same pattern until the seventh number.

> 1, 3, 5, 7, 9, 11, 13 — the seventh number in this sequence is 13.

You might need to **Find** the **Rule** for a **Number Sequence**

1) You might be given a more difficult number sequence, e.g. 4, 5, 7, 10, 14.

2) You'll need to work out the rule that the number sequence follows. One way to do this is to look at the difference between each number in the sequence.

> 4, 5, 7, 10, 14
> +1, +2, +3, +4
> The amount you need to add to get the next number in the sequence goes up by 1 each time. The next number in the sequence will be 14 + 5 = 19.

3) Make sure you look at all the values in the sequence when you're working out the rule. For example, the start of this sequence looks like it follows the same rule as the one above — but if you look at all the values, you can see the rule is actually to add together the previous two numbers in the sequence:

> 2, 3, 5, 8, 13 → 2 + 3 = 5, 3 + 5 = 8, 5 + 8 = 13.

The **Rule** for the nth Term helps you to find **Any Term**

1) You could be asked to find the 100th or even the 1000th term of a sequence. To find this you need to work out the rule for the nth term.

The numbers in a sequence are called the 'terms' of the sequence.

2) You use the nth term rule like a formula — substitute the term number for n to work out what the term is. For example, if the nth term rule was $8n + 1$, then the 100th term would be $8 \times 100 + 1 = 801$.

Section Three — Number Problems

Number Sequences

11+ Example Questions

EXAMPLE: Scott made a sequence by starting from the number 14 and counting back in steps of 6. Which of these numbers is in Scott's sequence?

A 4   B 1   C 0   D −2   E −4

1) Write out the number sequence for this question and see which number is included in it. Writing out the sequence will help you avoid any mistakes.

Make sure you apply the correct rule — subtract 6 each time.   14 → 8 → 2 → −4
                                                                 −6 −6 −6

2) Out of the options you're given, only −4 appears in the sequence. So the answer is E.

EXAMPLE: Look at the sequence 212, 205, 198, ☐, 184 ...
What is the missing number in this sequence?

1) First work out the rule for the sequence.

212 → 205 → 198
  −7   −7

2) The numbers in the sequence go down in steps of 7.
So the missing number is 198 − 7 = **191**

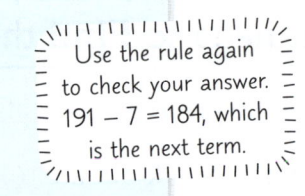

Use the rule again to check your answer. 191 − 7 = 184, which is the next term.

EXAMPLE: There are 9 small triangles in this shape. The shape is three triangles high. How many small triangles would there be in a shape that's five triangles high?

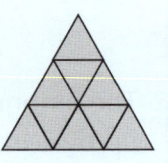

1) You need to find what the sequence is.

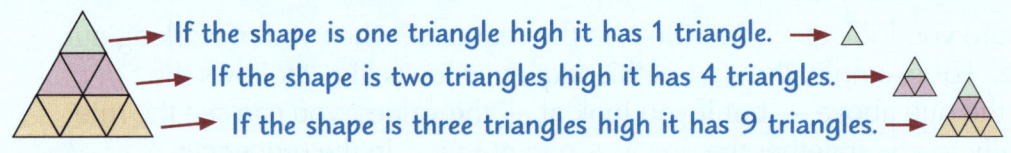

→ If the shape is one triangle high it has 1 triangle.
→ If the shape is two triangles high it has 4 triangles.
→ If the shape is three triangles high it has 9 triangles.

2) So the sequence for the number of triangles is 1, 4, 9. To find the 5th number in this sequence you need to work out if there's a pattern.

3) The difference between each number in the sequence increases by 2 each time — each row added has two more small triangles than the last one. Now work out what the 5th number in the sequence will be.

The difference increases by two each time, so apply this rule until you reach the 5th number.

1 → 4 → 9 → 16 → 25
 +3 +5 +7   +9

4) If the shape was five triangles high it would have **25** small triangles in it.

This is actually a sequence of the square numbers.

Section Three — Number Problems

Number Sequences

EXAMPLE: Gael uses squares to make the first three terms of a sequence.

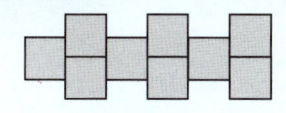

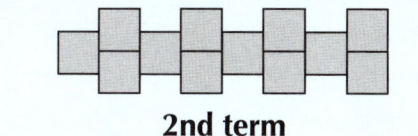

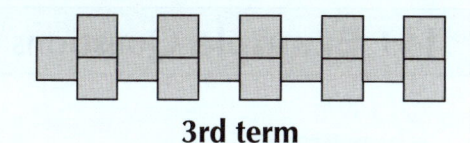

1st term   2nd term   3rd term

Write the expression for the number of squares in the nth term of the sequence.

1) Look for the relationship between the <u>number of squares</u> in each term.

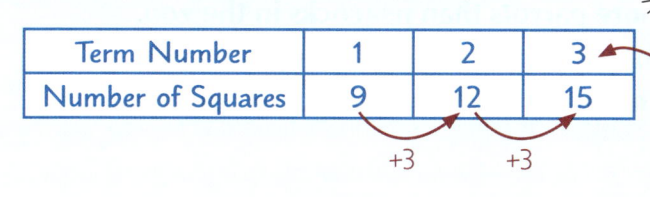

Term Number	1	2	3
Number of Squares	9	12	15

   +3   +3

   If you have multiple choice options for a question like this, you could just test each option to see which expression works for the sequence.

   The number of squares increases by 3 between each term. The sequence is following the three times table, so you need to multiply by three in the expression.

2) <u>Start</u> your expression with '<u>$3n$</u>'.

   For the 1st term, $n = 1$. So $3n = 3 × 1 = 3$. The table says term 1 has 9 squares. So if you add 6, you have made a rule that works for the 1st term of the sequence, $3n + 6$.

3) Check your expression is <u>correct</u> by testing the <u>other terms</u>.

   For the 2nd term, $3n + 6 = 3 × 2 + 6 = 12$.
   For the 3rd term, $3n + 6 = 3 × 3 + 6 = 15$.

4) The expression works for <u>all three terms</u>. So the correct answer is $3n + 6$.

Practice Questions

1) Jake is building a wall. He lays 4 bricks in the first hour, 5 in the second and 6 in the third. Each hour he continues to add one more brick than he laid in the previous hour. How many bricks will he have laid after 6 hours?

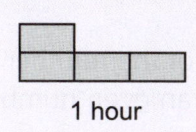

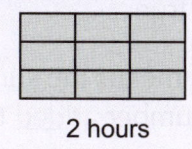

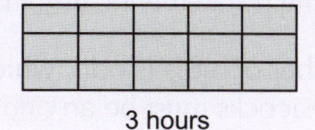

   1 hour   2 hours   3 hours

2) Here is a sequence of numbers:

   7   12   17   22   27

   Find the expression for the nth term of this sequence.

Think about using the expression for the nth term...

A question might not tell you that you should find the expression for the nth term — you'll have to decide yourself whether it's worth coming up with it. It's often a good idea to start by finding the expression when you need to find a term that's far along in the sequence (e.g. the 50th term).

Section Three — Number Problems

Word Problems

Word problems can be tricky — you need to read them very carefully to work out what they're asking. Then you can work out the best way to answer them quickly and correctly.

11+ Example Questions

EXAMPLE: A zoo has a total of 39 parrots and peacocks.
Which of these statements cannot be true?

A There are more parrots than peacocks in the zoo.
B There are more peacocks than parrots in the zoo.
C There are three more parrots than peacocks in the zoo.
D There are seven more peacocks than parrots in the zoo.
E There are twelve more parrots than peacocks in the zoo.

Method 1

1) Try to find a pair of numbers that works for each statement.

   A For example, there could be 20 parrots and 19 peacocks — so this could be true.

   B For example, there could be 20 peacocks and 19 parrots — so this could be true.

   C For example, there could be 21 parrots and 18 peacocks — so this could be true.

   D For example, there could be 23 peacocks and 16 parrots — so this could be true.

   E There isn't a pair of whole numbers that differ by twelve and add up to 39 — so this cannot be true.

2) The correct answer is option E.

Method 2

1) Use your knowledge of odd and even numbers to work out which statement cannot be true.

2) The total number of birds is odd, which means the sum of the number of parrots and peacocks must be an odd number added to an even number.

3) The difference between an odd and an even number is always odd — so option E cannot be true as the difference between the number of birds is even.

4) The total number of birds is odd, so there must be more of one type of bird than the other. So either statement A or statement B could be true — but there isn't enough information in the question to work out which.

5) The correct answer is option E.

Section Three — Number Problems

Word Problems

EXAMPLE: Beanthwaite School ordered 6 boxes of rulers in March and 4 boxes in April. Each box contained 130 rulers.

How many rulers did the school order in total?

1) Work out the total number of boxes ordered.

   6 boxes were ordered in March and
   4 were ordered in April, so 6 + 4 = 10.

2) Multiply the total number of boxes by the number of rulers in each box.

   10 × 130 = 1300 rulers in total.

EXAMPLE: Raisa went to a restaurant with two friends. They ordered from the menu:
3 plates of lasagne, 2 soups and 4 lemonades.

Raisa pays with a £50 note.

How much change should she receive?

Luigi's Restaurant
Lemonade................ 90p
Soup.......................£2.50
Carbonara..............£7.50
Pizza......................£6.00
Lasagne.................£8.50

1) Work out how much each item will cost. Make sure that all the amounts are in pounds.

   3 plates of lasagne is 3 × £8.50.
   Split £8.50 into £8 and £0.50:
   3 × £8 = £24 and 3 × £0.50 = £1.50.
   So 3 × £8.50 = £24 + £1.50 = £25.50

   2 soups is 2 × £2.50.
   2 × £2.5 = £5.00

   4 lemonades is 4 × 90p.
   4 × 90p = 360p
   360p = £3.60

2) Now find the total cost of all of the items.

   You could use partitioning to find the total amount.
   Add up all the pounds. 25 + 5 + 3 = £33.
   Add up all the pence. 50 + 60 = 110p = £1.10
   Now add them together. £33 + £1.10 = £34.10

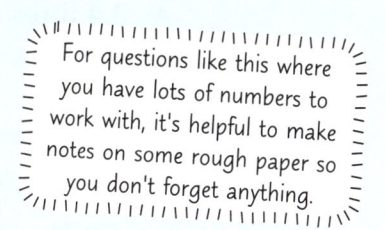

   For questions like this where you have lots of numbers to work with, it's helpful to make notes on some rough paper so you don't forget anything.

3) Now find the difference between the total cost of the items and £50.

   You can count on from £34.10 to £50.
   Count on to £35. £34.10 + 90p = £35
   Then count on to £50. £35 + £15 = £50
   Add the two numbers to find the difference. £15 + 90p = £15.90.

4) So the answer is £15.90.

Section Three — Number Problems

Word Problems

More **11+ Example** Questions

EXAMPLE: I am thinking of a positive number.
If I multiply it by 3, then square it, I get 36.

What number am I thinking of?

A 2   B 4   C 6
D 8   E 10

You know the final answer — to find the number at the start you need to work backwards through the calculation given in the question. You can do this in two steps.

1) The number at the end is 36. To get 36 a number was squared. The only positive number that could be squared to give 36 is 6.

2) To get 6 a number was multiplied by 3.
To find this number you just divide 6 by 3. 6 ÷ 3 = **2**.

EXAMPLE: A drinks company makes 250 litres of tropical punch each week.

Look at the ingredients used to make the punch.

The company sells the tropical punch in 50-litre barrels.

Tropical Punch
Mango Juice..........95.4 litres
Orange Juice.........45.5 litres
Pineapple Juice.....62.1 litres
Apple Juice.............47 litres

How many litres of orange juice are in one barrel of tropical punch?

A 3.4 litres   B 8.5 litres   C 18.0 litres
D 9.1 litres   E 11.6 litres

1) First you need to work out what fraction of 250 litres makes up 1 barrel of tropical punch.

   1 barrel = 50 litres. 250 ÷ 50 = 5, so 1 barrel is $\frac{1}{5}$ of 250 litres.

2) There are 45.5 litres of orange juice in 250 litres of tropical punch, so you need to find $\frac{1}{5}$ of 45.5 litres.

   To find $\frac{1}{5}$ of 45.5 you need to divide 45.5 by 5.

   There are options to choose from, so you could make an estimate.
   45 ÷ 5 = 9, so the answer to 45.5 ÷ 5 will be a little greater than 9.

   Option D is **9.1 litres** — so this is the correct answer.

Section Three — Number Problems

Word Problems

EXAMPLE: A counter is worth 5 points and has a diameter of 3.5 cm. A row of counters was lined up along a wall, with each counter touching the next. The values on the line of counters added up to 1500 points.

Find the length of the row of counters, in metres.

1) Work out how many counters there are in total.

   There are 1500 points worth of 5 point counters.
   So the total number of counters is 1500 ÷ 5.
   1500 is 100 times larger than 15, so 1500 ÷ 5 must be 100 times larger than 15 ÷ 5.
   15 ÷ 5 = 3. So 1500 ÷ 5 = 100 × 3 = 300

2) Now find the length of the line of counters.

   Each counter is 3.5 cm in diameter, and there are 300 in total — so work out 300 × 3.5.
   Partition 3.5 into 3 and 0.5:
   300 × 3 = 900
   300 × 0.5 = 150 (it's the same as half of 300).
   Then add up the result:
   900 + 150 = 1050 cm.

3) Don't forget to convert your answer into metres: 1050 cm ÷ 100 = 10.5 m.

Practice Questions

1) A bunch of seven tulips costs £4.50. A bunch of six roses costs £3.50.
   Lena wants 42 tulips and 42 roses. How much does she need to pay?
   - A £24.50
   - B £147.00
   - C £189.00
   - D £27.00
   - E £51.50

2) Benni buys 5 sandwiches that all cost the same amount.
   He pays with a £10 note and gets £1.50 change.
   How much is one sandwich?

3) Simone made bracelets to sell. Each bracelet cost her 20p to make and she sold them for 50p each. She sold 57 bracelets in total.
   How much money did she make, after she subtracted the cost of making the bracelets?

TEST TIP

Word questions are often about familiar situations...

Think about what a sensible answer could be and keep it in mind when working through a problem — you'll be able to catch yourself if you stray too far off course.

Section Three — Number Problems

Practice Questions

You've seen a wide range of Number Problems in this section.
Now it's time to put your skills to the test and have a go at these Practice Questions.

1. If $n = 12$, work out the value of $6n + 5$.

2. Which of these expressions is the same as $3(t + 4)$?
   Circle the correct answer.

   A $3t + 3$ B $3t + 4$ C $3t + 12$ D $4t + 3$ E $4t + 12$

3. A mug can hold x ml of water and a glass can hold y ml. Which of these is the correct expression for the amount of water in ml that 7 mugs and 3 glasses can hold?
   Circle the correct answer.

   A $3x + 7y$ B $7x + 3$ C $10(x + y)$ D $7x + 3y$ E $7x + y$

4. What is the value of x when $5x - 6 = 24$?

5. The amount you pay at a bowling alley (£B) is given by the formula: $B = 5g + p + 2$ where g is the number of games and p is the number of players.

   a) How much would it cost for 3 players to play 4 games?

   £

   b) If 5 players have to pay £17 in total, how many games did they play?

6. Sharla thinks of a number, n. She subtracts five, divides by two, then adds seven.
   Which expression shows this? Circle your answer.

   A $(n - 7) \div 2 + 5$ B $n - (5 \div 2) + 7$ C $n - 5 \div (2 + 7)$
   D $n - 5 \div 2 + 7$ E $(n - 5) \div 2 + 7$

7. The first five terms of a sequence are 4, 9, 14, 19, 24...
   Which of these is the correct expression for the nth term in this sequence?
   Circle the correct answer.

   A $4n + 5$ B $5n - 1$ C $9n - 4$ D $4n + 1$ E $5n + 4$

Section Three — Number Problems

Practice Questions

8. The rule $n/2 + 4$ is used to generate a sequence.
   What is the 100th term in the sequence?

9. What is the missing number in the sequence 7, ___, 23, 31, 39?

10. The first four terms of a sequence are 3, 7, 11, 15...
    What is the 50th term in the sequence?

11. How many dots will be in the next shape in this sequence?

12. Nazeem has 79 grapes and eats 7 every hour.

    a) How many hours will it be before he has fewer than 50 grapes?

    ____ hours

    b) How many grapes will Nazeem have left after eight hours?

13. Chris has £10 of credit on a pay-as-you-go mobile phone. Calls cost 5p per minute.
    After how many minutes of call time would his credit be reduced by half?

    ____ minutes

14. Louise thinks of a number. She squares it and then adds six.
    The result is 70. What number did she start with?

15. Alfie has swimming sessions on Tuesdays and Thursdays. He swims 3.5 km every session.
    How many weeks will it take him to swim a total distance of 140 km?

    ____ weeks

Section Three — Number Problems

Practice Questions

16. Mac has £5 to spend on fruit. He buys 1 pineapple, 1 watermelon, and as many kiwi fruit as he can afford. How much money does he have left?
    Circle the correct answer.

    Fruit Prices
    Pineapple............£0.95
    Watermelon.......£2.75
    Kiwi fruit.......15p each

    A 5p   B 10p   C 15p   D 20p   E 25p

17. Daniel hires a costume for a party. He pays £5 per hour, plus a fixed fee of £10. He hires the costume for 3 hours. Which calculation gives him the total cost?
    Circle the correct answer.

    A £5 × £10 + 3   B £5 + £10 × 3   C £5 × 3 + £10
    D 3 × (£5 + £10)   E £5 × 3 × £10

18. Tiana donated some jumpers and T-shirts to charity. She gave a total of 27 items of clothing. Circle the statement that cannot be true.

    A Tiana donated twice as many jumpers as T-shirts.
    B Tiana donated seven fewer T-shirts than jumpers.
    C Tiana donated more jumpers than T-shirts.
    D Tiana donated five more T-shirts than jumpers.
    E Tiana donated eight fewer T-shirts than jumpers.

19. A plumber charges a £30 call-out fee and £20 per hour, plus the cost of the parts they use. If they work for 3 hours and charge £195, what is the cost of the parts?

    £ ☐☐☐

20. A quiz show awards 7 points for answering a hard question and 3 points for answering an easy question. Sanjay earned 149 points in total. He answered 17 easy questions. How many hard questions did Sanjay answer?

    ☐☐☐

21. A set of five spoons costs £2.25. A set of four mugs costs eight times as much as the set of five spoons. How much does each mug cost? Circle the correct answer.

    A £2.25   B £3.60   C £3.75   D £4.00   E £4.50

22. Aaron shares out carrots equally between his horses. Each horse ends up with 7 carrots and Aaron has 4 left over.
    Circle the number of carrots that Aaron could have started with.

    A 21   B 22   C 24   D 25   E 26

Section Three — Number Problems

Section Four — Data Handling

Data Tables

Data is just any set of facts or information. It's often easier to understand and use if you organise it into a table, particularly if there's a lot of it.

11+ Example Questions

EXAMPLE: The table below shows the activities chosen by a group of people at a watersports centre. Which activity was the most popular?

Activity	Kayaking	Canoeing	Sailing	Windsurfing
Number of children	12	18	8	4
Number of adults	15	7	22	18

Add up the numbers in the column for each activity:

Kayaking: 12 + 15 = 27   Canoeing: 18 + 7 = 25
Sailing: 8 + 22 = 30   Windsurfing: 4 + 18 = 22

Sailing was the most popular activity, as the largest number of people chose it.

EXAMPLE: Ryan does a survey to find out how much the shops in his town charge for a can of cola. He groups his results into price bands and puts them in this table.
Which of these statements is definitely true?

Frequency just means how many times something happens.

Price	Frequency
50p – 59p	4
60p – 69p	10
70p – 79p	12
80p – 89p	8
90p – £1.00	6

A The most expensive can of cola Ryan found costs £1.00.

B Ryan recorded the prices of 42 cans of cola.

C More than half of the cans of cola cost between 70p and 79p each.

D Three-quarters of the cans of cola cost less than 80p each.

E More than half of the cans of cola cost 70p or more each.

Look at each option and work out whether it's definitely true.

A The table only tells you that the most expensive can of cola is between 90p and £1.00. It might not be exactly £1.00 though — so you don't know if the statement is definitely true.

B To find the total number of cans of cola, add up all the frequencies in the table. 4 + 10 + 12 + 8 + 6 = 40 — so the statement isn't true.

C Half of the total number of cans is 40 ÷ 2 = 20. There are only 12 cola cans in the 70p – 79p price band — so the statement isn't true.

D One quarter of the total number of cans is 40 ÷ 4 = 10, so three quarters is 30. Add together the first three rows to find the number of cans that cost less than 80p: 4 + 10 + 12 = 26. 26 isn't three-quarters of the total number of cans — so the statement isn't true.

E Add together the last three rows of the table to find the total number of cans that cost 70p or more = 12 + 8 + 6 = 26. This is more than half of the total number of cans (20) — so this statement is true. E is the correct answer.

Data Tables

EXAMPLE: Years 5 and 6 are having a party. They all choose between meat pie and cheese pie. This table shows some of their choices. How many children are there in Year 5?

	Year 5	Year 6	Total
Meat pie		12	
Cheese pie	21		39
Total			64

1) This is a <u>two-way table</u>. There's a total for each row and column.

	Year 5	Year 6	Total
Meat pie		12	
Cheese pie	21		39
Total			64

- Total number of cheese pies eaten.
- Total number of pies eaten and the total number of children in Year 5 and Year 6.
- This is the space for the number of children in Year 5.
- Number of meat pies eaten by Year 6.

2) You don't have enough <u>information</u> to work out how many children there are in Year 5 straight away — you need to <u>fill in</u> some of the other <u>empty</u> boxes first.

	Year 5	Year 6	Total
Meat pie	13	12	25
Cheese pie	21		39
Total			64

First find out how many meat pies were eaten in total.
Total number − total cheese pie eaters = 64 − 39 = 25
Now you can find out how many meat pies Year 5 ate.
Total meat pie eaters − Year 6 meat pie eaters
= 25 − 12 = 13

3) <u>Add</u> the numbers in the <u>Year 5 column</u> of the table to find the number of children in Year 5.

Year 5 children = Year 5 meat + Year 5 cheese
                  pie eaters   pie eaters
= 13 + 21 = **34**

	Year 5	Year 6	Total
Meat pie	13	12	25
Cheese pie	21		39
Total	**34**		64

Practice Questions

1) The table on the right shows the numbers of DVDs owned by some children. How many children own more than 15 DVDs?

   A 9   B 19   C 28   D 27   E 13

DVDs	Frequency
0 – 5	14
6 – 10	13
11 – 15	9
16 – 20	13
21 – 25	6

Ticket	Price	Number needed	Total cost
Child	£5	32	£160
Adult	£8	4	£32
Senior Citizen		3	
		Booking Fee	£2.50
		Amount to pay	£212.50

2) The table on the left shows an order form for some pantomime tickets. Some boxes have been left empty. Calculate the cost of a senior citizen ticket.

TEST TIP

Don't let unfamiliar tables put you off...
You might come across a table that looks a bit different to the ones you've seen before. Don't panic — just look at the row and column labels to work out what the table shows.

Displaying Data

Charts and graphs aren't just an excuse for a bit of colouring. They're a really important way of showing data — they can help you understand information at a glance.

Bar Charts Make it Easy to Compare things

Bar charts have two axes. The horizontal axis is called the x-axis.
The vertical axis is called the y-axis — it usually shows the frequency.

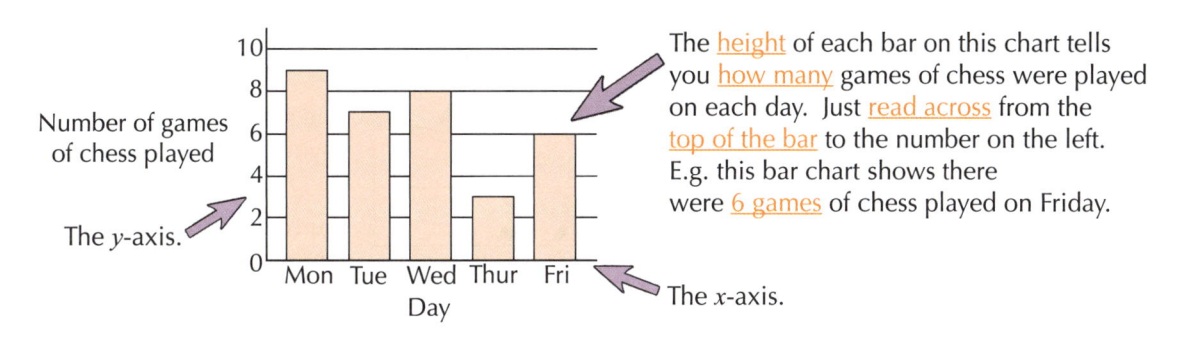

The height of each bar on this chart tells you how many games of chess were played on each day. Just read across from the top of the bar to the number on the left. E.g. this bar chart shows there were 6 games of chess played on Friday.

The y-axis.

The x-axis.

Line Graphs Often Show things that Change over Time

1) Line graphs show you how one thing (shown on the y-axis) changes as another thing changes (shown on the x-axis).

2) Time is often on the x-axis. For example, this graph shows how the temperature in an oven changes over time.

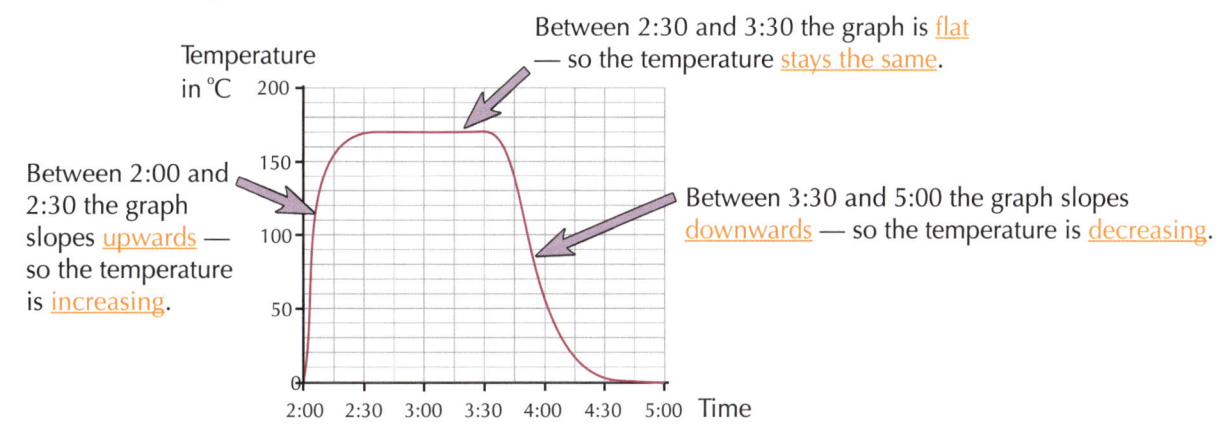

Between 2:00 and 2:30 the graph slopes upwards — so the temperature is increasing.

Between 2:30 and 3:30 the graph is flat — so the temperature stays the same.

Between 3:30 and 5:00 the graph slopes downwards — so the temperature is decreasing.

3) Here's how to read off a value from a line graph, e.g. the temperature at 3:45 from this line graph.

Step 1 — Find 3:45 on the x-axis. Follow a line straight up to the graph line.

Step 2 — Now follow a line straight across to the y-axis.

Step 3 — Read the temperature value from the y-axis — 140 °C.

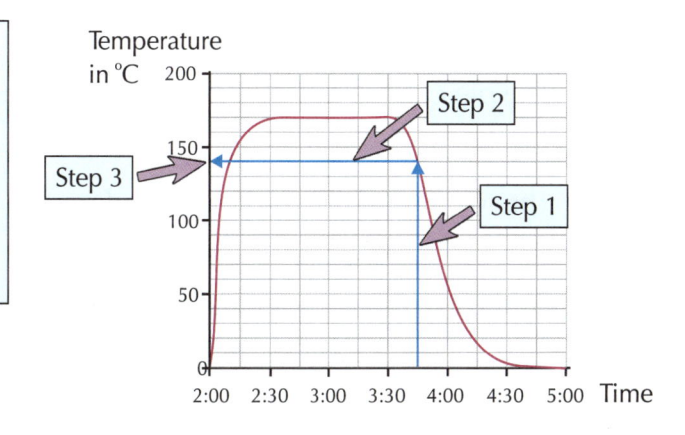

Section Four — Data Handling

Displaying Data

Pictograms use Symbols to Show Frequency

1) In pictograms, simple pictures show numbers of things or how often something happens.
2) The key is really important — it tells you how many things each picture stands for.

This pictogram shows how many chess games were played each day.

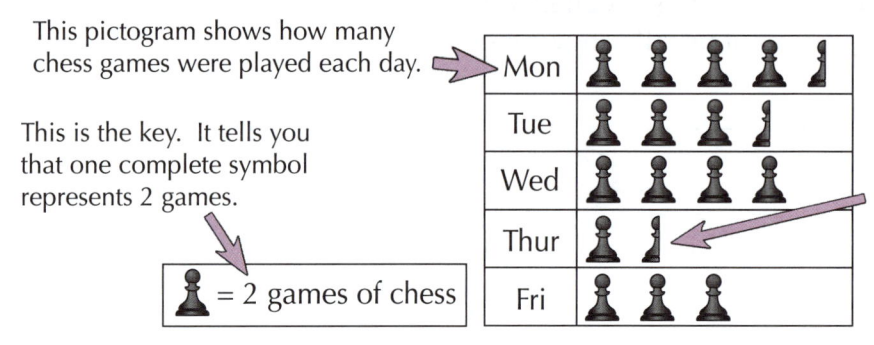

This is the key. It tells you that one complete symbol represents 2 games.

♟ = 2 games of chess

Mon	♟ ♟ ♟ ♟ ♟
Tue	♟ ♟ ♟ ♟
Wed	♟ ♟ ♟ ♟
Thur	♟ ♟
Fri	♟ ♟ ♟

One symbol = 2 games, so half a symbol = 2 ÷ 2 = 1 game.
There are 1½ symbols for Thursday, so there were 2 + 1 = 3 games played on Thursday.

Pie Charts Show Things as Proportions

Proportion just means the fraction of the total amount.

1) Each 'slice' of a pie chart is called a sector. You can work out the number of things shown by each sector on a pie chart.
2) For example, the pie chart below shows what 60 four-year-old boys said they wanted to be when they grow up. You can find how many boys said each thing by working out what fraction a sector is of the whole pie.

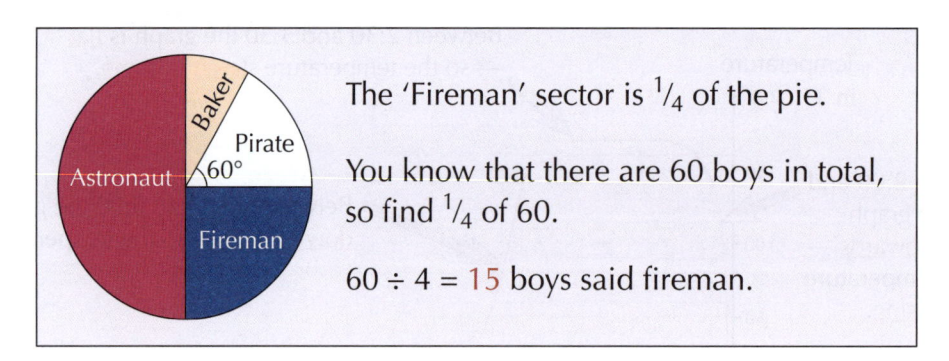

The 'Fireman' sector is ¼ of the pie.

You know that there are 60 boys in total, so find ¼ of 60.

60 ÷ 4 = 15 boys said fireman.

You can also use the number of degrees (see p.71) that make up a sector to work out how many boys said each thing.

The 'Pirate' sector has an angle of 60°.

The pie chart is a circle, so the total angle of all the sectors is 360°.

The fraction of the whole pie made up by the pirate sector is $\frac{60°}{360°} = \frac{1}{6}$ (÷ 60)

So the number of boys that want to be a pirate is ⅙ of 60 = 60 ÷ 6 = 10.

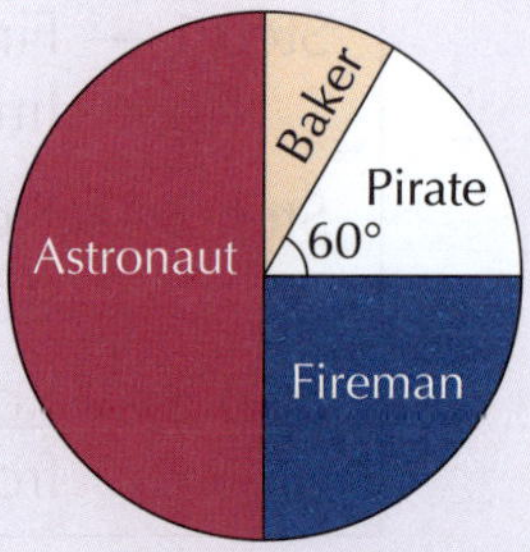

Section Four — Data Handling

Displaying Data

11+ Example Questions

EXAMPLE: The bar chart shows the scores a year group of students got in a maths test. How many more students got 41-60 marks than 21-40 marks?

A 30   B 35   C 40
D 45   E 50

1) Work out how many students got 41-60 marks, and how many students got 21-40 marks.

   41-50 bar = 45 students
   51-60 bar = 30 students
   45 + 30 = 75 students got 41-60 marks.

   21-30 bar = 10 students
   31-40 bar = 25 students
   10 + 25 = 35 students got 21-40 marks.

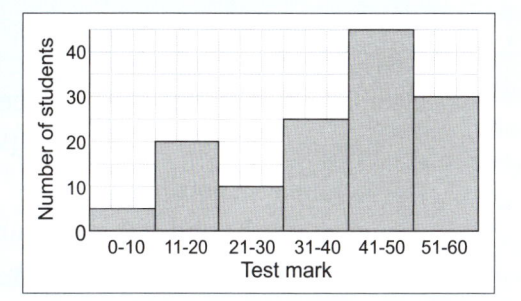

2) Subtract the number of students who got 21-40 marks from the number who got 41-60 marks.

   75 − 35 = 40 students

3) The answer is option C — 40 students.

EXAMPLE: A chef uses 35 oz of pastry to make some apple pies. She needs to use 4 apples for every 400 g of pastry.

Use the graph to work out how many apples she needs if she uses all the pastry to make apple pies.

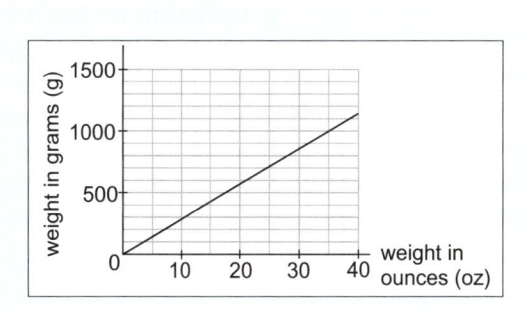

1) Read off how much 35 oz of pastry is in grams from the graph.
   35 oz = 1000 g.

2) Find the amount of pastry used for 1 apple.
   For 400 g of pastry you need 4 apples.
   So she uses 400 ÷ 4 = 100 g of pastry for 1 apple.

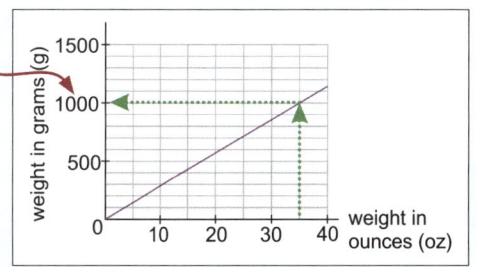

3) She needs 1 apple for every 100 g of pastry and she's using 1000 g of pastry.
   1000 ÷ 100 = 10 — she needs 10 apples.

Section Four — Data Handling

Displaying Data

EXAMPLE: The pictogram shows the number of differently shaped sweets in a bag.
How many more animal shaped sweets than fruit shaped sweets are there in the bag?

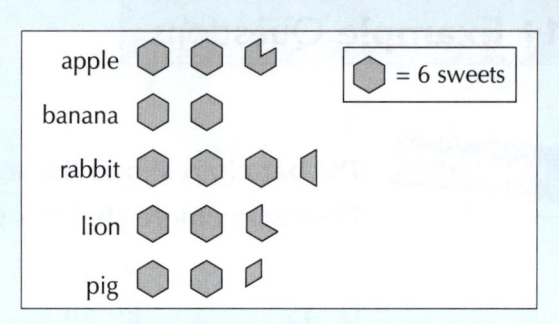

apple	⬡ ⬡ ⬔
banana	⬡ ⬡
rabbit	⬡ ⬡ ⬡ ◁
lion	⬡ ⬡ ⌐
pig	⬡ ⬡ ◿

⬡ = 6 sweets

1) First work out <u>how many</u> sweets are <u>animal shaped</u> (i.e. either a rabbit, a lion or a pig).
   There are 7 whole symbols for the animal sweets. 7 × 6 = 42 sweets.
   The rabbit shape also has $^3/_6$ of a symbol on the end = 3 sweets, the lion shape has $^4/_6$ of a symbol on the end = 4 sweets and the pig shape has $^2/_6$ of a symbol on the end = 2 sweets.
   Add these together to get the total number of animal shaped sweets.
   42 + 3 + 4 + 2 = 51 sweets.

2) Now use the same method to work out <u>how many fruit shaped sweets</u> there are.
   There are 4 whole symbols for fruit shaped sweets. 4 × 6 = 24 sweets.
   The apple shape also has $^5/_6$ of a symbol on the end = 5 sweets.
   Total number of fruit shaped sweets = 24 + 5 = 29 sweets.

3) Then <u>subtract</u> to find the <u>difference</u> between the two.
   There are 51 − 29 = 22 more animal shaped sweets than fruit shaped sweets.

EXAMPLE: The table shows the ingredients in 300 ml of a salad dressing. Ben wants to draw a pie chart to show the proportion of each ingredient in the dressing. What angle would the vinegar sector of the pie chart have?

Ingredient	Amount
Vinegar	50 ml
Olive oil	200 ml
Lemon juice	50 ml

1) First find what <u>fraction</u> of the dressing is made up of vinegar.
   50 ml out of 300 ml is vinegar.
   The fraction of the total dressing that's vinegar is $^{50}/_{300} = ^1/_6$ (÷ 50)

   Divide the numerator and the denominator by 50 to simplify.

2) The <u>total angles</u> in a pie chart are <u>360°</u>, so find $^1/_6$ of 360°.
   $^1/_6$ of 360° = 360° ÷ 6 = 60°.

Practice Question

1) A class of children were asked what their favourite colour is. Two children chose brown. This was represented on a pie chart by a 20° sector. How many children are in the class?

There are lots of different ways of displaying data...
Make sure you can interpret all these graphs and charts — any type could come up in your test.

Section Four — Data Handling

Analysing Data

One way to analyse a data set is to calculate the mean, a type of average.
An average is one number which summarises a whole set of numbers.

Practise Finding the Mean

The Mean Involves Adding and Dividing

1) To work out the mean:
   - Add up all the numbers in the data set.
   - Divide the total by how many numbers there are.

2) So to work out the mean of the data set on the right, first add up all the numbers: 13 + 8 + 7 + 4 + 11 + 2 = 45.

   | 13, 8, 7, 4, 11, 2 |

3) There are six numbers, so divide the total by six: 45 ÷ 6 = 7.5.

11+ Example Questions

EXAMPLE: Safiya records how long she exercises each day for 5 days:

| 24 mins | 25 mins | 35 mins | 39 mins | 32 mins |

What is the mean time she spends exercising?

1) Add together all the times.
   24 + 25 + 35 + 39 + 32 = 155 mins

2) She records her times on five different days, so divide the total by five.
   The mean time she spends exercising is 155 ÷ 5 = 31 mins

EXAMPLE: Marcus works on a stall that sells fruit smoothies.
The table below shows the price of each type of smoothie.

Banana	£2.70
Mango	£3.10
Strawberry	£2.50
Raspberry	£2.70

What is the mean price of a smoothie from Marcus's stall?

1) Add together the prices of all the smoothies.
   £2.70 + £3.10 + £2.50 + £2.70 = £11

2) There are four different types of smoothie, so divide the total by four.
   The mean price of a smoothie is £11 ÷ 4 = £2.75

Section Four — Data Handling

Analysing Data

EXAMPLE: The bar chart shows five children's marks in three tests.

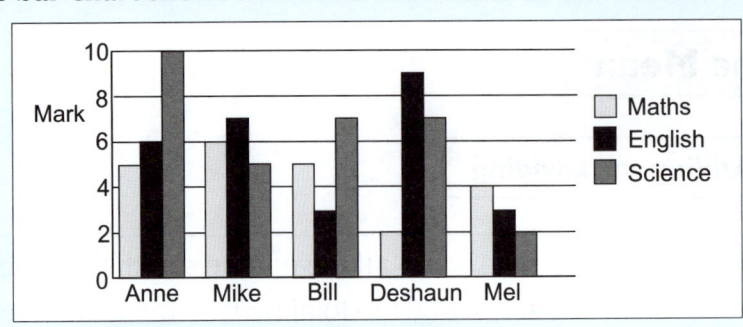

[Bar chart showing marks for Anne, Mike, Bill, Deshaun, Mel in Maths, English, Science]

Which child had the highest mean mark across all the tests?

1) <u>Add</u> together each child's marks and <u>divide</u> them by <u>three</u> to find each mean mark.
   Anne: (5 + 6 + 10) ÷ 3 = 7   Mike: (6 + 7 + 5) ÷ 3 = 6   Bill: (5 + 3 + 7) ÷ 3 = 5
   Deshaun: (2 + 9 + 7) ÷ 3 = 6   Mel: (4 + 3 + 2) ÷ 3 = 3

2) <u>Compare</u> the means — the highest is 7, so the answer is Anne.

EXAMPLE: Derek has a set of five numbers. He calculates that the mean of his numbers is 11.5.

| 8 | 13 | 18 | 7.5 | 11 |

He forgets one of his numbers. The mean of the four numbers he can remember is 12.5. Which number has he forgotten?

1) First work out the <u>total</u> of the numbers <u>he can remember</u>.
   If the mean of the four numbers he can remember is 12.5, he must have divided a number by 4 to get 12.5. So multiply 12.5 by 4 to find the total. 12.5 × 4 = 50.

2) Then work out the <u>total</u> of the <u>original five numbers</u>.
   8 + 13 + 18 + 7.5 + 11 = 57.5

3) <u>Subtract</u> the total of the four numbers he can <u>remember</u> from the <u>original total</u>.
   57.5 − 50 = 7.5 — the number he forgot was 7.5.

Practice Question

1) The data set on the right shows how many tea bags were used in the Smith household each day. What was the mean number of tea bags used per day?

Mon	Tue	Wed	Thur	Fri
22	23	17	17	26

REVISION TIP: Remember to divide by how many numbers there are...
It's really important that you learn the 2-step method to find the mean.
Once you know it, you can use it as normal or reverse it to find a missing number.

Section Four — Data Handling

Misleading Data

People often use data to try to prove a point they're making. However, you have to think really hard about data to make sure it's not being twisted to make you believe something that's not true.

11+ Example Question

EXAMPLE:

> **CHILDREN PREFER PLAYING COMPUTER GAMES TO PLAYING SPORT**
> A group of school children were asked, 'What is your favourite weekend activity?'. 20% of them said 'playing computer games', while only 1 in 4 children said their favourite activity was 'playing sport'.

Why is this newspaper article misleading?

A The article doesn't say what other activities the children picked.

B According to the numbers given in the article, more children said they liked playing sport than playing computer games.

C The article doesn't tell you how many boys and girls were in the group asked.

D The figures in the article show that fewer children chose sport than computer games.

E The article doesn't tell you what sports or computer games the children like to play.

1) Read the article and work out what the article is claiming to be true.

   The headline says that children prefer playing computer games to playing sport.

2) Look carefully at any figures you're given, to see if they back up what the article is claiming. Put the figures into the same form (e.g. fractions, decimals or percentages) to compare them.

   20% of children said their favourite activity was playing computer games.
   1 in 4 children said playing sport — which is the same as 25%.
   25% is greater than 20%, so more children said playing sport than playing computer games.

3) Look at the options to see which one is correct.

   Options A, C, and E are all true, but they don't mean that the article is misleading.
   Option D is incorrect — the figures show that more children chose sport than computer games.
   Option B is correct. The article is misleading because it says that fewer people picked sport than computer games, when the figures show that more people picked sport than computer games.

Section Four — Data Handling

Misleading Data

Another 11+ Example Question

EXAMPLE: This graph is used to show the increase in the number of chickens eaten by the population of a country between 2018 and 2019.
Why is the graph misleading?

A Only two years are shown on the graph.
B The scale on the vertical axis is uneven.
C The graph doesn't show how many turkeys were eaten.
D We are not told which country the data is about.
E The chicken picture for 2019 is more than double the area of the 2018 picture.

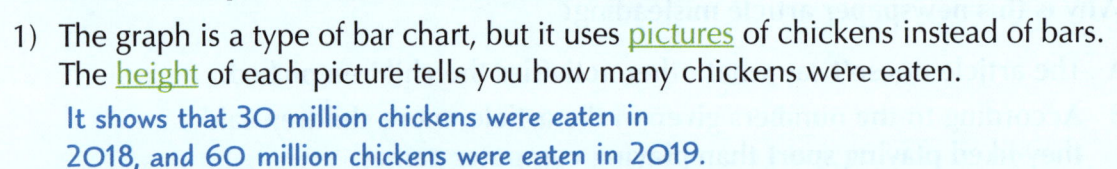

1) The graph is a type of bar chart, but it uses <u>pictures</u> of chickens instead of bars. The <u>height</u> of each picture tells you how many chickens were eaten.
   It shows that 30 million chickens were eaten in 2018, and 60 million chickens were eaten in 2019.

2) Look at each answer and decide if it's a <u>good reason</u> why the graph is misleading.
   A: The graph is only about 2018 and 2019, so it's not misleading that only two years are shown.
   B: This isn't true. The values are evenly spaced.
   C: It doesn't matter how many turkeys are eaten — the graph is about chickens.
   D: You haven't been led to believe that the data is about anywhere in particular, so this isn't the answer.
   E: From reading the graph you know that about twice as many chickens were eaten in 2019 than 2018. The trouble is, the area of the chicken for 2019 is about 4 times as big as the area of the chicken for 2018. This means that at a glance, the graph makes it look like the difference between the years was far greater than it actually was. **E is the correct answer.**

Practice Question

1) A newspaper report with a graph has the headline:
Sales of pencils plummet. Why is the report misleading?

A There are no crosses on the graph to mark the plotted points.
B The graph does not show how many pens were sold.
C The y-axis doesn't start on zero so it makes the drop in sales look worse than it is.
D The graph doesn't show what happened before 2012.
E The pencil manufacturers want you to go and buy more pencils.

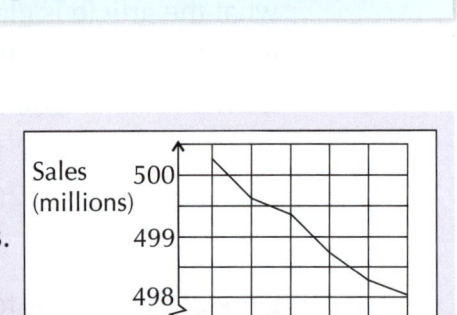

Misleading graphs try to make you think the wrong thing...

Watch out for graphs that have part of the y-axis missing (shown by a zigzag line). E.g. These bar charts show the same data, but the second one makes the difference in the heights of the bars look much bigger than the first.

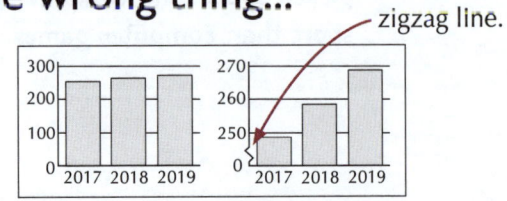

Here's the zigzag line.

Section Four — Data Handling

Practice Questions

Try out your Data Handling skills on these Practice Questions.

1. The pupils in Year 6 are split into two classes, A and B. They were asked to choose between swimming, cricket and gymnastics. The results are shown in the table below.

	Class A	Class B	Total
Swimming	12		21
Cricket	6		10
Gymnastics		12	
Total	28		

   a) How many pupils in Class B chose swimming?

   b) Which activity was the most popular? Circle the correct answer.

      A Swimming   **B** Cricket   **C** Gymnastics

   c) How many pupils are there in Year 6 in total?

2. The pictogram below shows the number of different types of butterfly in a butterfly house.

Red Admiral	🦋 🦋 🦋
Tortoiseshell	🦋 🦋 🦋 🦋 🦋
Monarch	🦋 🦋
Purple Emperor	🦋 🦋

   Key: 🦋 = 4 butterflies

   a) What is the least common type of butterfly? Circle the correct answer.

      A Red Admiral   **B** Tortoiseshell   **C** Monarch   **D** Purple Emperor

   b) How many more Tortoiseshell butterflies than Red Admiral butterflies are there?

   c) How many butterflies are there in total?

Section Four — Data Handling

Practice Questions

3. The bar chart on the right shows the number of books borrowed from a library each day for five days.

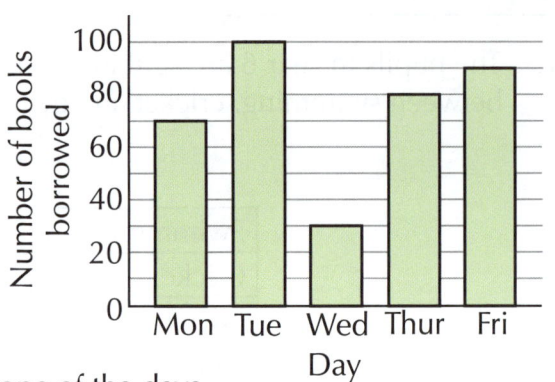

   a) How many more books were borrowed on Tuesday than on Monday?

   b) The library was only open for half a day on one of the days. Which day was this most likely to be? Circle the correct answer.

   A Monday   **B** Tuesday   **C** Wednesday   **D** Thursday   **E** Friday

   c) What was the mean number of books borrowed in a day?

4. Violet is going on holiday to America. The graph on the right shows the conversion between pounds (£) and American dollars ($).

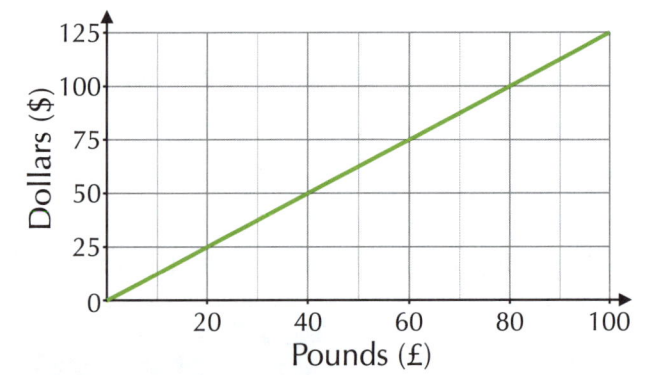

   a) How many dollars is £60 worth?

   $ ☐☐☐

   b) In total, she took $400 with her. How much is this in pounds?

   £ ☐☐☐

   c) At the end of the holiday, Violet had $27 left. Which is the most expensive souvenir she could afford? Circle the correct answer.

   A A hoodie costing £30   **B** A vase costing £27   **C** A scarf costing £19

5. Some children were asked what they had eaten for breakfast that morning. The results are shown in the pie chart on the right.

   a) What is the angle for the 'Fruit' sector? Circle the correct answer.

   A 45°   **B** 60°   **C** 360°   **D** 120°   **E** 90°

   b) 20 children had cereal for breakfast. How many children were asked in total?

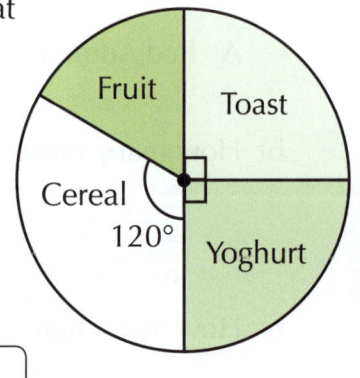

Section Four — Data Handling

Practice Questions

6. On a summer's day, Mrs Singh starts filling a paddling pool with water. The graph on the right shows the depth of water in the paddling pool over time.

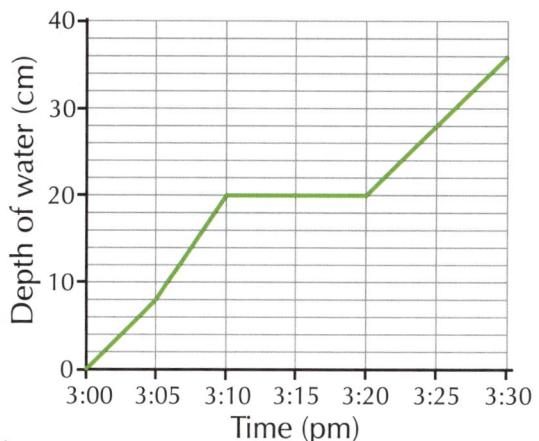

   a) At what time was the water 28 cm deep?

   ☐ : ☐☐ pm

   b) Mrs Singh turned the water off while she answered the phone. Between which two times was the water turned off? Circle the correct answer.

   A 3:00 pm and 3:30 pm   **B** 3:10 pm and 3:15 pm
   C 3:05 pm and 3:10 pm   **D** 3:10 pm and 3:20 pm

   c) How deep was the water at 3:30 pm?

   ☐☐ cm

7. 72 children were asked to name their favourite type of flower. The results are shown in the pie chart on the right.

   Which of the statements below is true?
   Circle the letter next to the correct answer.

   A Irises were the least popular type of flower.
   B More children chose lilies than tulips.
   C 18 children chose roses.
   D The same number of children chose daisies and bluebells.
   E 9 children chose daisies.

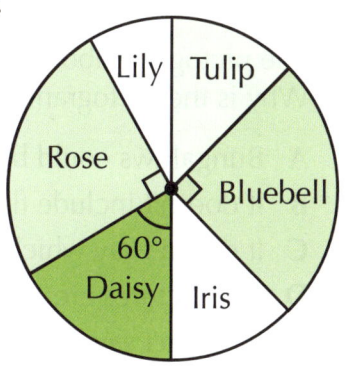

8. Dina records the amount of money she spends on comics each month. The amounts for five of the last six months are shown below:

   £4.80   £5.40   £3.90   £6.20   £4.30

   Dina has forgotten how much she spent in the other month, but she knows that the mean amount spent over the six months was £4.50. How much did she spend in the missing month?

   £ ☐ . ☐☐

Section Four — Data Handling

Practice Questions

9. Gleb measured the temperature and wind speed at 12 noon every day for a week. His results are shown in the table below.

	Mon	Tues	Wed	Thurs	Fri	Sat	Sun
Temperature (°C)	11	9	8	10	12	13	14
Wind speed (mph)	9	11	7	14	8		

a) What was the mean temperature that week?

☐☐.☐ °C

b) The mean wind speed for the whole week was 9 mph. The wind speed on Sunday was 6 mph more than the wind speed on Saturday. What were the wind speeds on Saturday and Sunday?

Saturday: ☐☐ mph, Sunday: ☐☐ mph

10. The pictogram above shows the different types of houses in a village. Why is the pictogram misleading? Circle the letter next to the correct answer.

A Bungalows could be detached, semi-detached or terraced.
B It doesn't include flats.
C It doesn't say which village it is.
D The pictures are arranged differently, and are different sizes and shapes.
E It doesn't say how many people live in each house.

11. The misleading bar chart below shows the results of a school council election.

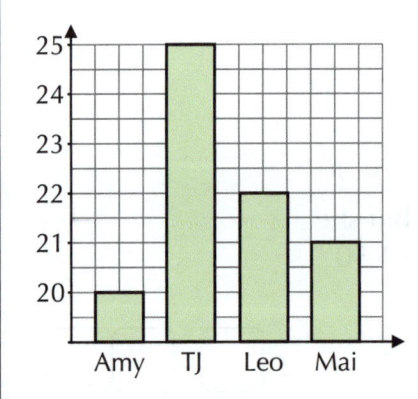

Which of the following statements is true? Circle the letter next to the correct answer.

A TJ received twice as many votes as Leo.
B Mai received $2/3$ of the number of votes that Leo received.
C Amy received half as many votes as Mai.
D Amy received $4/5$ of the number of votes that TJ received.
E Leo received 3 times as many votes as Amy.

Section Four — Data Handling

Section Five — Shape and Space

Angles

The three main types of angle you need to know are right angles, acute angles and obtuse angles.

Angles are Measured using Degrees (°)

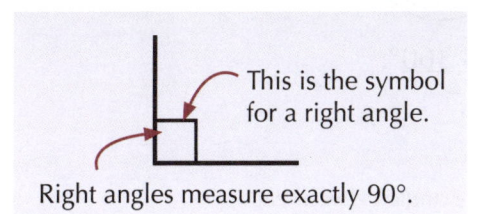

This is the symbol for a right angle.

Right angles measure exactly 90°.

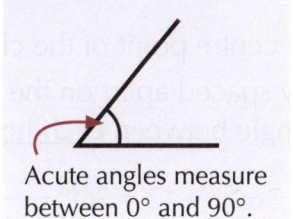

Acute angles measure between 0° and 90°.

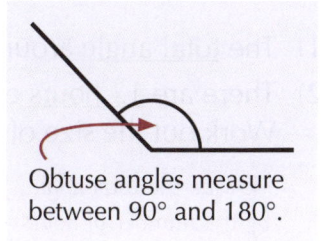

Obtuse angles measure between 90° and 180°.

You need to know these Rules about Angles

Angles around a Point Add Up to 360°

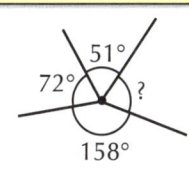

The four angles total 360°. So the missing angle is 360° − 51° − 72° − 158° = 79°.

Angles on a Straight Line Add Up to 180°

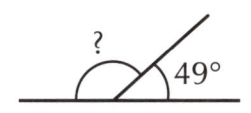

The two angles total 180°. So the missing angle is 180° − 49° = 131°.

Angles in a Triangle Add Up to 180°

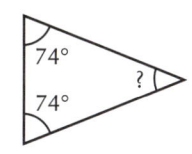

The three angles total 180°. So the missing angle is 180° − 74° − 74° = 32°.

Angles in a Quadrilateral Add Up to 360°

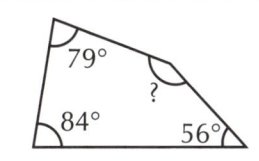

The four angles total 360°. So the missing angle is 360° − 84° − 79° − 56° = 141°.

11+ Example Questions

EXAMPLE: Estimate the size of angle x.
A 90°   B 30°   C 105°   D 75°   E 120°

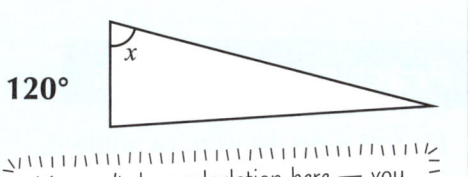

1) It's smaller than 90°, so it must be an acute angle. That means option A is incorrect — it's a right angle. Options C and E are also incorrect — they're obtuse angles.

   You can't do a calculation here — you don't know the sizes of the other angles.

2) That leaves options B and D. You need to decide which option is more realistic.

   If the angle was 30°, it would be three times smaller than a right angle.
   When you compare angle x to a right angle, it's only a little bit smaller.
   So, the angle must be 75° — it's the most realistic option.

   You can compare an unknown angle with a right angle using the corner of a sheet of paper.

3) The correct answer is option D — 75°.

Angles

EXAMPLE: What is the size of the angle marked *a* between the two hands on this clock?

1) The total angle around the centre point of the clock is 360°.

2) There are 12 hours equally spaced apart on the clock. Work out the size of the angle between each hour.

   Divide the total angle by the number of hours. → 360° ÷ 12 = 30° → The angle between each hour on the clock is 30°.

3) Work out how many hours apart the two hands are.

   The minute hand is at 12 and the hour hand is at 5. They are 5 hours apart.

4) Multiply the number of hours by 30° to find the value of the missing angle.

   5 × 30° = 150°. Angle *a* is 150°.

EXAMPLE: Ted made the following pattern using a rectangle and a triangle. What is the size of angle *x*?

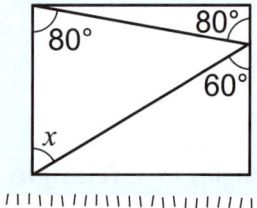

1) Work out the size of the other angle in the triangle.

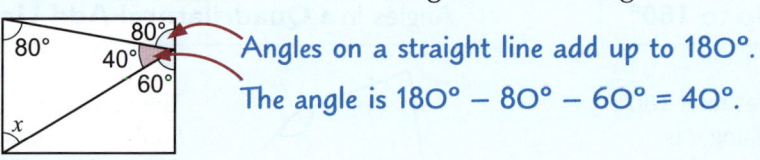

   Angles on a straight line add up to 180°.
   The angle is 180° − 80° − 60° = 40°.

   This is one of several different ways you could work out the answer to this question.

2) The three angles in a triangle add up to 180°. Use this rule to work out the size of *x*:

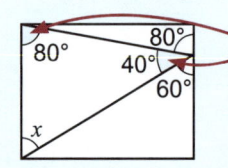

   You have two angles of the triangle. Their total is 80° + 40° = 120°.

   Angle *x* is the third angle in the triangle. It is 180° − 120° = 60°.

Practice Questions

1) Estimate the size of angle *c*.

   A 100°   B 125°   C 10°
   D 45°   E 90°

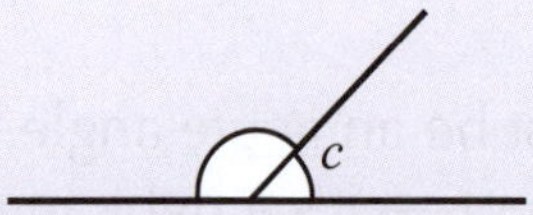

2) What is the size of the angle between the north-east and south points on this compass?

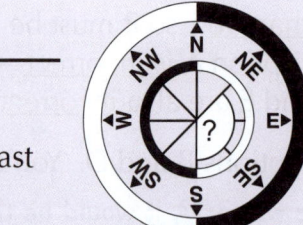

   Think about the total number of points on the compass.

Look out for triangles and quadrilaterals in a busy diagram...

It can be hard to know where to start when you have to find a missing angle. Spotting triangles and quadrilaterals in the diagram is a good first step, since you know what their angles add up to.

Section Five — Shape and Space

2D Shapes

2D shapes are flat — they have length and width but no depth.

Quadrilaterals are shapes with Four Sides

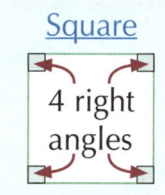

Parallel lines have exactly the same slope.

Square
4 right angles
4 equal sides and 2 pairs of parallel sides

Trapezium
1 pair of parallel sides

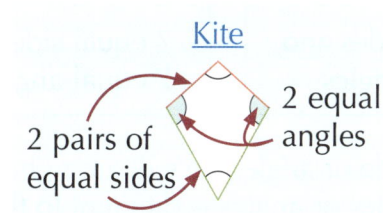

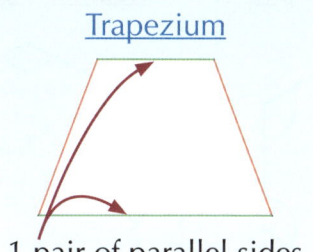

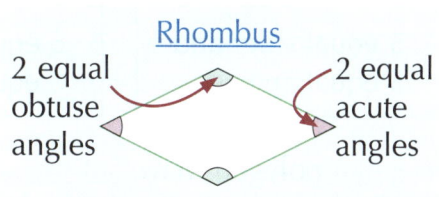

Parallelogram
2 equal obtuse angles
2 equal acute angles
2 pairs of equal sides and 2 pairs of parallel sides

Rectangle
4 right angles
2 pairs of equal sides and 2 pairs of parallel sides

Kite
2 pairs of equal sides
2 equal angles

Rhombus
2 equal obtuse angles
2 equal acute angles
4 equal sides and 2 pairs of parallel sides

There are Different Types of Triangle

The angles in a triangle add up to 180° (see page 71).

1) Equilateral Triangle
3 equal angles — each angle measures 60°.
3 equal sides

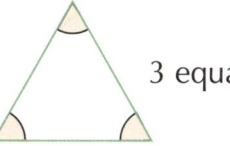

2) Isosceles Triangle
2 equal angles
2 equal sides

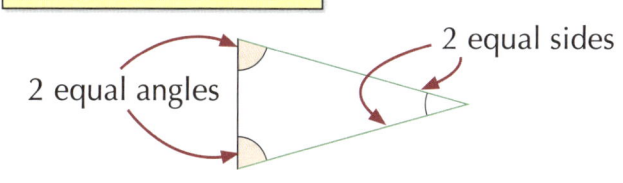

3) Right-angled Triangle
1 right angle

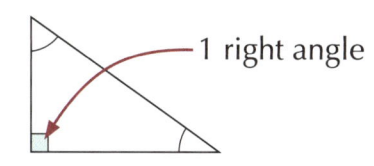

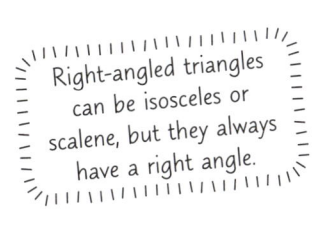

Right-angled triangles can be isosceles or scalene, but they always have a right angle.

4) Scalene Triangle
No equal sides or angles

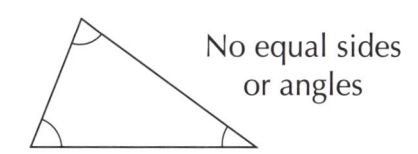

Know the Parts of a Circle

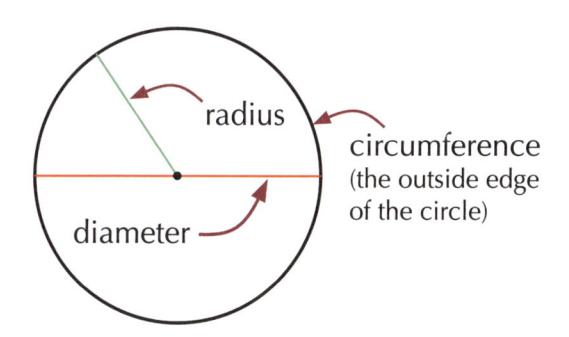

radius
circumference (the outside edge of the circle)
diameter

The Diameter is Twice the Radius

You can use this rule to work out the diameter or the radius.

The radius of this circle is 6 cm.
So the diameter = 2 × 6 = 12 cm

diameter 6 cm

Section Five — Shape and Space

2D Shapes

Regular Polygons have Equal Sides and Angles

A polygon is a 2D shape with straight lines.

Regular Pentagon	Regular Hexagon	Regular Heptagon	Regular Octagon
5 equal sides and 5 equal angles	6 equal sides and 6 equal angles	7 equal sides and 7 equal angles	8 equal sides and 8 equal angles

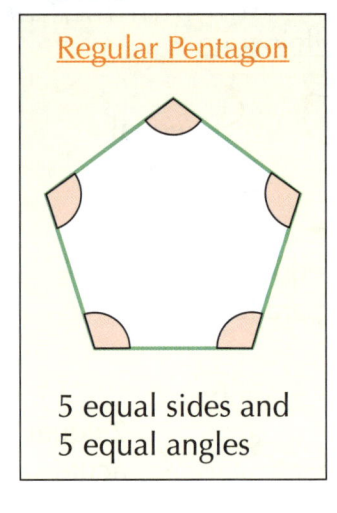

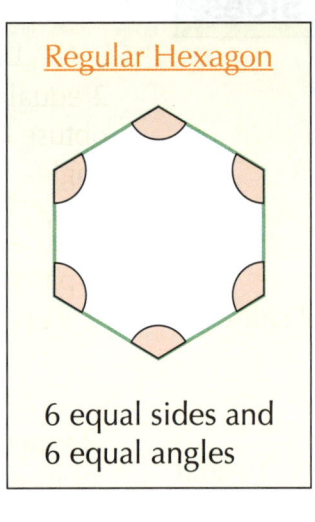

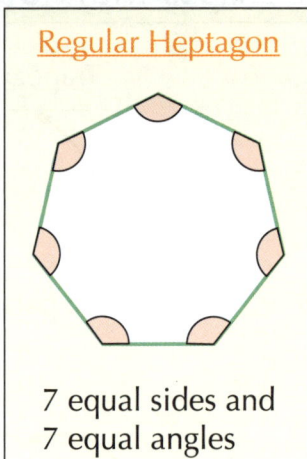

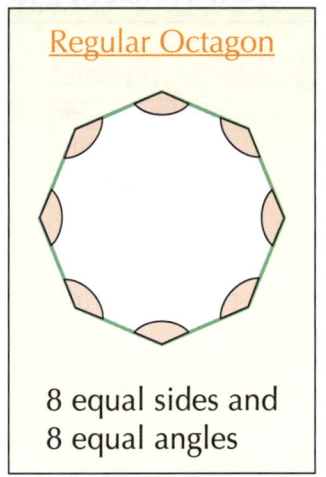

Irregular polygons have at least one side or angle that's different in size. E.g. an irregular pentagon has five sides but at least one of the sides or angles is different to the others.

11+ Example Questions

EXAMPLE: Which of the following shapes should be placed in area Z of the Venn diagram?

A Square
B Rectangle
C Rhombus
D Isosceles Triangle
E Trapezium

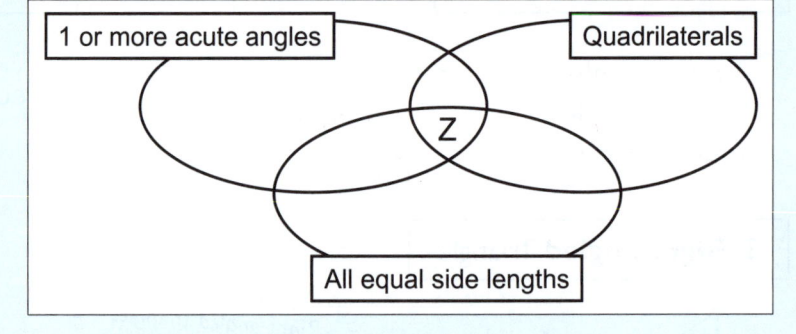

(Venn diagram with three overlapping ovals labelled "1 or more acute angles", "Quadrilaterals", and "All equal side lengths", with Z at the centre intersection.)

1) Area Z is in the centre of the Venn diagram. You need to find the option that's a quadrilateral with 1 or more acute angles and all equal side lengths.

2) First, eliminate any options that aren't quadrilaterals.
   An isosceles triangle has 3 sides so it's not a quadrilateral. The answer isn't option D.

3) Next, eliminate the options that don't have all equal side lengths.
   Rectangles and trapeziums don't have all equal side lengths.
   The answer isn't option B or E.

4) That leaves A and C. Eliminate the option that doesn't have 1 or more acute angles.
   A square has 4 right angles. The answer isn't option A.

5) The correct answer must be a rhombus — option C.
   It's a quadrilateral with 2 acute angles and 4 equal sides.

Section Five — Shape and Space

2D Shapes

EXAMPLE: Tariq put five shapes into a bag. He pulled one out at random. The shape had exactly one pair of equal sides, no parallel sides and no obtuse angles. Which of the following shapes did Tariq pull out of the bag?

A (trapezium)   B (pentagon)   C (kite)   D (triangle)   E (rhombus)

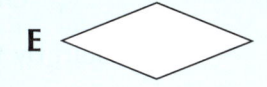

1) Work through each option until you find the one that matches the description of the shape.

   Option A has one pair of parallel sides so it's incorrect.

   Option B has five equal sides and five obtuse angles so it's incorrect.

   Option C has two pairs of equal sides and two obtuse angles so it's incorrect.

   Option D has one pair of equal sides, no parallel sides and no obtuse angles.

2) Option D matches the description of the shape that Tariq chose — this is the correct answer.

3) You can check option E to make sure you haven't made a mistake.

   Option E has four equal sides, two pairs of parallel sides and two obtuse angles so it's incorrect.

EXAMPLE: Which shape should go in the grey box of the sorting table?

A Regular hexagon
B Equilateral triangle
C Regular pentagon
D Parallelogram
E Rectangle

	At least one obtuse angle	No obtuse angles
All sides equal lengths		
Exactly two pairs of equal length sides	(grey box)	

1) First rule out the shapes that don't fit in the 'at least one obtuse angle' column.

   Equilateral triangles and rectangles don't have any obtuse angles so you can rule out B and E.

2) Then rule out the shapes that don't fit in the 'two pairs of equal length sides' row.

   Regular hexagons and regular pentagons both have all equal length sides — you can rule out A and C.

3) So, the only shape that fits in the 'at least one obtuse angle' column and the 'two pairs of equal length sides' row is a parallelogram. The correct answer is option D.

Section Five — Shape and Space

2D Shapes

One More 11+ Example Question

EXAMPLE: Fran has a box containing identical rhombus tiles. One of the tiles is shown. What is the size of angle c?

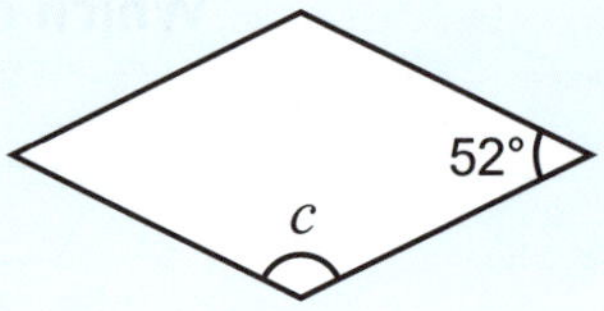

1) Start by working out the size of the other acute angle.

   A rhombus has two equal acute angles. So, this angle is also 52°.

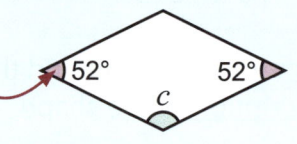

   There's more about acute angles and obtuse angles on page 71.

2) Work out the total size of the two obtuse angles.

   A rhombus is a quadrilateral, so the total size of the angles is 360°. This means that the total size of the two remaining angles is 360° − 52° − 52° = 256°.

3) You can now calculate the size of angle c.

   A rhombus has two equal obtuse angles, so the size of angle c is 256° ÷ 2 = **128°**.

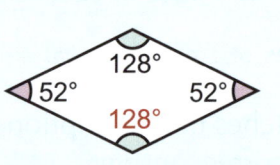

Practice Questions

1) Rhona is describing a triangular tile to her friends. She says that it has no right angles, no equal sides and no equal angles. What is the shape of the tile that Rhona is describing?

   A Equilateral triangle
   B Isosceles triangle
   C Scalene triangle
   D Right-angled triangle

2) Which shape should go in the grey box of the sorting table?

   A Trapezium
   B Square
   C Rectangle
   D Equilateral triangle
   E Rhombus

	All equal angles	Angles aren't all equal
All equal side lengths		
Side lengths aren't all equal		

3) Naomi is thinking of a shape. She gives David some clues about it:
   - The shape has no obtuse angles.
   - The shape has no right angles.
   - Two of its sides are equal in length.

   What shape is Naomi thinking of?

4) Lucas draws the biggest circle possible on a square piece of paper, as shown on the right. What is the radius of the circle he has drawn? (18 cm)

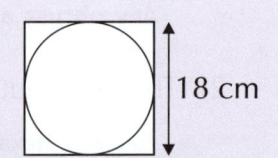

REVISION TIP

Don't just memorise the properties of 2D shapes...

It's tempting to think you're all set once you've learnt the properties on pages 73 and 74. You'll need to know how to apply these properties in the test though, so make sure you're comfortable with questions like the examples above before you move on.

Section Five — Shape and Space

2D Shapes — Area and Perimeter

The length around the edge of a shape is its perimeter. The space covered by a shape is its area.

Perimeter is the Length Around a Shape

1) To calculate the perimeter of a shape, add up the length of every side of the shape.

The shapes on this page aren't drawn to scale.

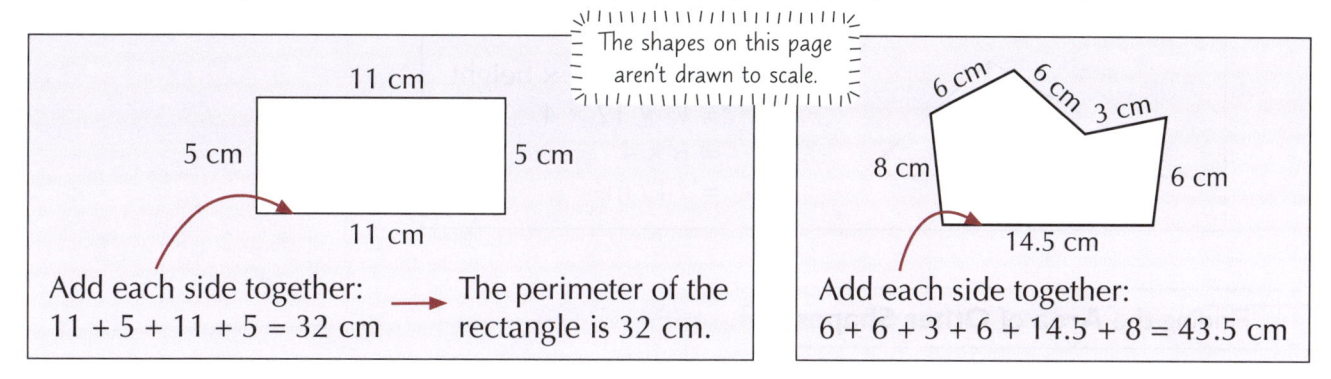

Add each side together:
11 + 5 + 11 + 5 = 32 cm → The perimeter of the rectangle is 32 cm.

Add each side together:
6 + 6 + 3 + 6 + 14.5 + 8 = 43.5 cm

2) Sometimes you don't know the length of every side. You need to work out the missing lengths.

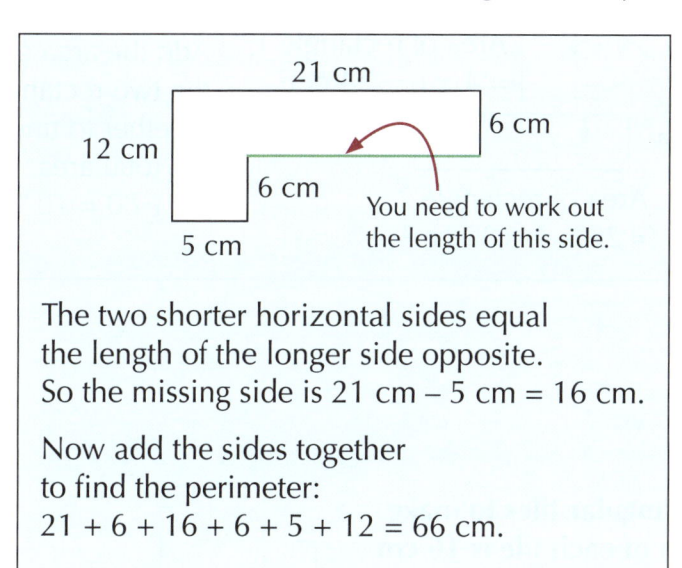

You need to work out the length of this side.

The two shorter horizontal sides equal the length of the longer side opposite. So the missing side is 21 cm − 5 cm = 16 cm.

Now add the sides together to find the perimeter:
21 + 6 + 16 + 6 + 5 + 12 = 66 cm.

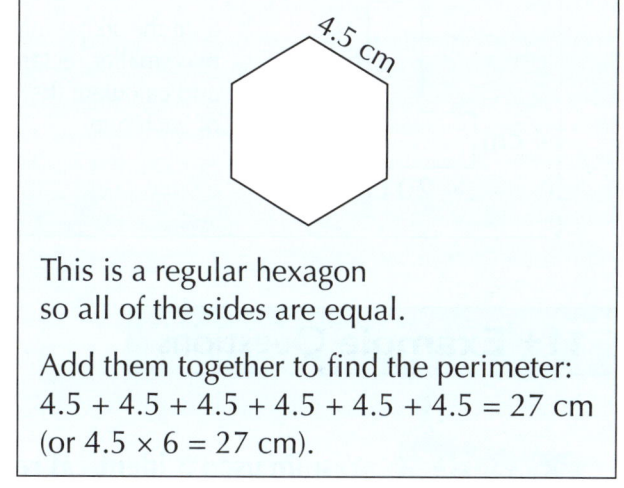

This is a regular hexagon so all of the sides are equal.

Add them together to find the perimeter:
4.5 + 4.5 + 4.5 + 4.5 + 4.5 + 4.5 = 27 cm
(or 4.5 × 6 = 27 cm).

Area is the Space Inside a Shape

Finding the Area of a Square or Rectangle

Multiply the length by the width to work out the area of a square or rectangle.

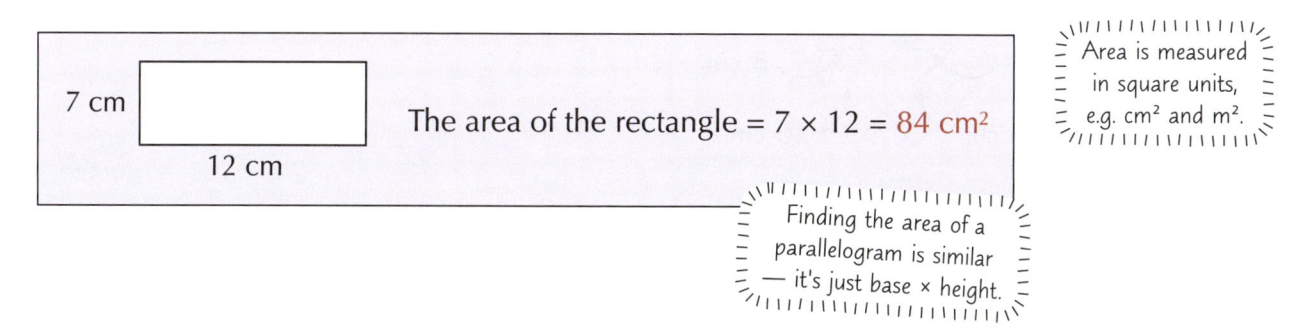

The area of the rectangle = 7 × 12 = 84 cm²

Area is measured in square units, e.g. cm² and m².

Finding the area of a parallelogram is similar — it's just base × height.

Section Five — Shape and Space

2D Shapes — Area and Perimeter

Finding the Area of a Triangle

Calculate the area of a triangle by multiplying half of the base length by the height.

You might see this as the formula: area = ½ × base × height

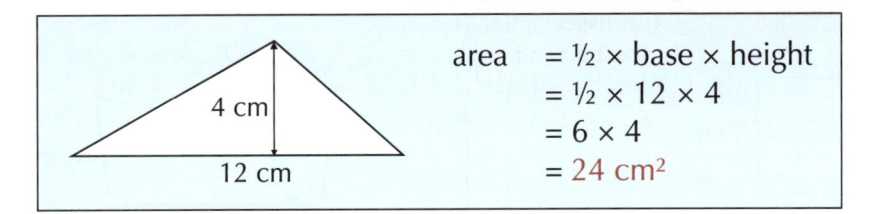

area = ½ × base × height
= ½ × 12 × 4
= 6 × 4
= 24 cm²

(triangle: 4 cm height, 12 cm base)

Finding the Area of Other Shapes

Sometimes you need to split a more complex shape into smaller shapes to calculate its area.

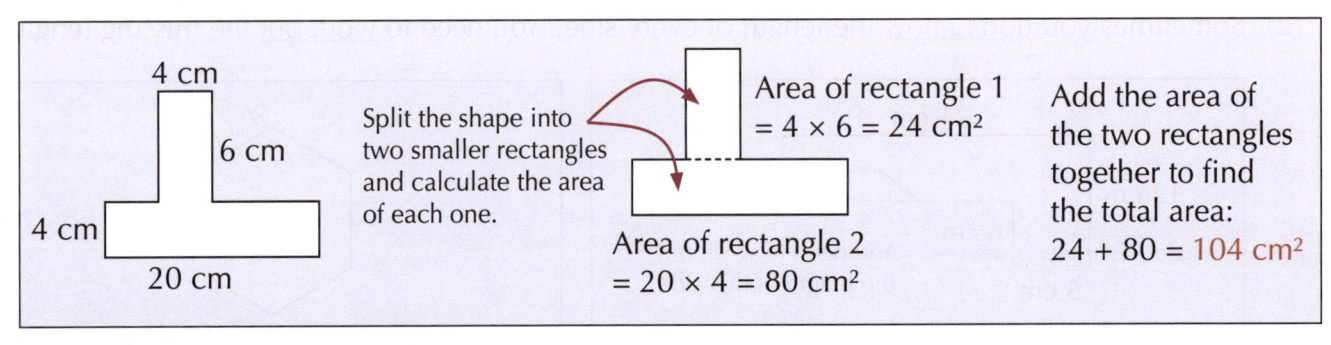

Split the shape into two smaller rectangles and calculate the area of each one.

Area of rectangle 1 = 4 × 6 = 24 cm²

Area of rectangle 2 = 20 × 4 = 80 cm²

Add the area of the two rectangles together to find the total area: 24 + 80 = 104 cm²

(T-shape: 4 cm, 6 cm, 4 cm, 20 cm)

11+ Example Questions

EXAMPLE: Yasmin used 5 identical rectangular tiles to make the shape shown. The length of each tile is 16 cm and the width of each tile is 8 cm.

What is the perimeter of the arrow shape that's been made inside the grey tiles?

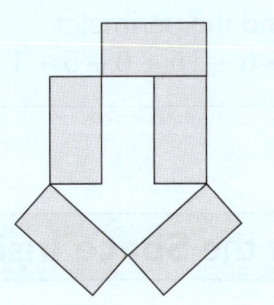

1) Work out the length of each part of the shape.

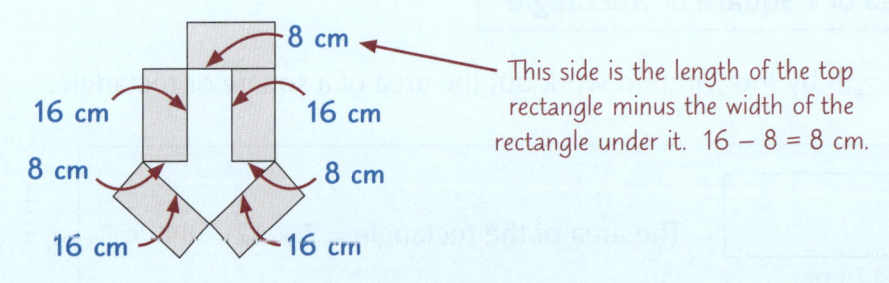

8 cm — This side is the length of the top rectangle minus the width of the rectangle under it. 16 − 8 = 8 cm.

16 cm, 16 cm, 8 cm, 8 cm, 16 cm, 16 cm

2) Add each side together to find the perimeter.

8 + 16 + 8 + 16 + 16 + 8 + 16 = **88 cm**

Section Five — Shape and Space

2D Shapes — Area and Perimeter

More 11+ Example Questions

EXAMPLE: Marcelo made this shape using one square and four identical isosceles triangles.

The total perimeter of the shape is 96 mm.

What is the length of line a?

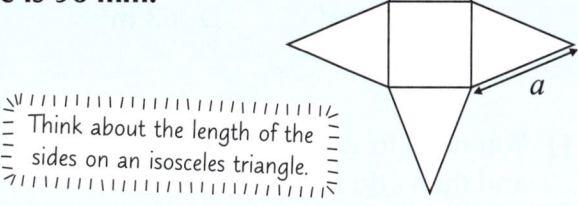

1) Look at the lines which make up the perimeter of Marcelo's shape.

   Think about the length of the sides on an isosceles triangle.

   The perimeter of the shape is made using the two equal sides of four isosceles triangles.
   There are eight lines that make up the perimeter of the shape.
   The isosceles triangles are identical, so all eight lines must be the same length.

2) You know that the perimeter of the shape is 96 mm. So, divide the total perimeter by the number of lines to work out the length of each line.

   96 ÷ 8 = 12 mm

3) That gives you the answer — the length of line a is 12 mm.

EXAMPLE: Mabel is building a new run for her rabbits. The run is made up of four rectangular fence panels which are each 200 cm in length and 40 cm in width. What is the total area of the fence panels that Mabel needs to make the run?

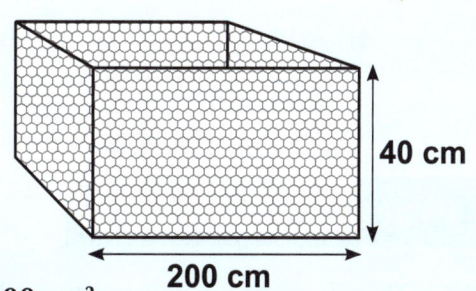

A 32 000 cm²   C 40 000 cm²   E 16 000 cm²
B 8000 cm²   D 24 000 cm²

1) Start by finding the area of each rectangular panel.

   The area of a rectangle = length × width
   So the area of each fence panel = 200 × 40 = 8000 cm²

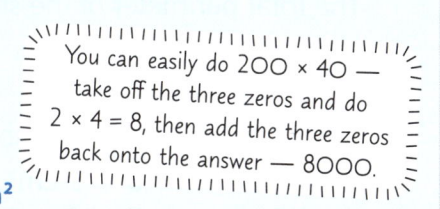

   You can easily do 200 × 40 — take off the three zeros and do 2 × 4 = 8, then add the three zeros back onto the answer — 8000.

2) Multiply this by the number of panels to find the total area of all of the fence panels.

   8000 × 4 = 32 000 cm²

3) The total area of the fence panels used by Mabel is 32 000 cm². So the correct answer is option A.

Section Five — Shape and Space

2D Shapes — Area and Perimeter

EXAMPLE: The diagram shows the downstairs of Stephen's house. Stephen wants to lay a new carpet in his living room and his dining room. What is the area of carpet that Stephen needs?

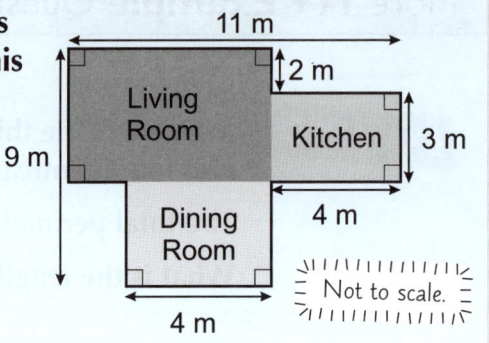

A 35 m²   C 99 m²   E 51 m²
B 16 m²   D 63 m²

1) You need to work out the areas of the living room and dining room separately, and then add them together.

2) Start by working out the unknown lengths.

The width of the living room is the width of the kitchen plus 2 metres.
3 + 2 = 5 m

The width of the dining room is the total width of the downstairs minus the width of the living room.
9 − 5 = 4 m

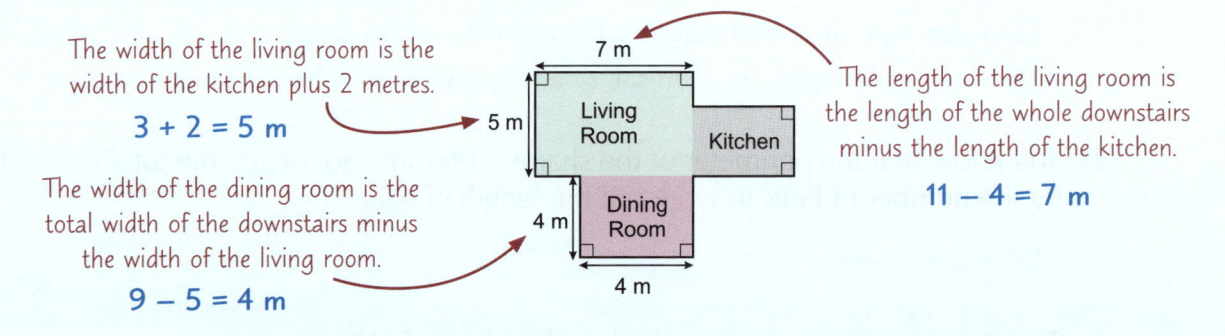

The length of the living room is the length of the whole downstairs minus the length of the kitchen.
11 − 4 = 7 m

3) Next, work out the area of the living room and the area of the dining room.

Area of the living room = 7 × 5 = 35 m²
Area of the dining room = 4 × 4 = 16 m²

4) Add the two areas together to find the total area of carpet that Stephen needs.

35 + 16 = 51 m² — option E is correct.

Practice Questions

1) This shape is made from two identical regular hexagons joined together. The total perimeter of the shape is 75 cm. How long is side Z?

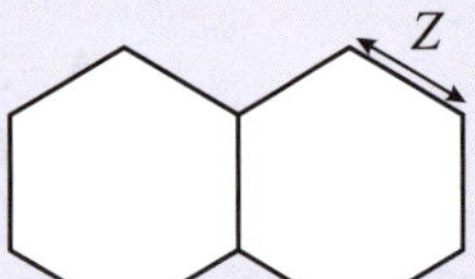

2) Calculate the area of this shape.
A 48 cm²   B 72 cm²   C 64 cm²
D 132 cm²   E 96 cm²

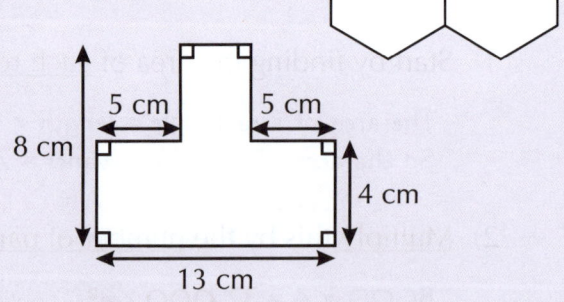

Only use the outside edges of the shape to work out the perimeter...

If the shape you need to find the perimeter of is made up of smaller shapes joined together (like the example on the previous page), you don't need to use the joined edges in your calculation.

Section Five — Shape and Space

Symmetry

Symmetrical shapes can be split into two identical halves. These halves are reflections of each other.

2D Shapes can be Symmetrical

1) If a shape has a line of symmetry, it means that both parts of the shape on each side of the line are reflections of each other.

line of symmetry

These two parts of the shape are reflections of each other.

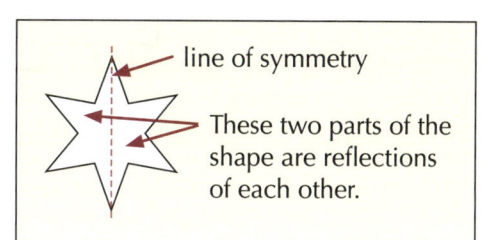

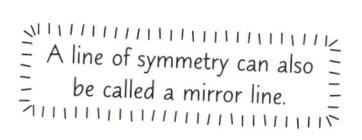

A line of symmetry can also be called a mirror line.

2) Shapes can have different numbers of lines of symmetry (or no lines of symmetry). For example:

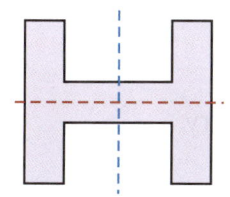

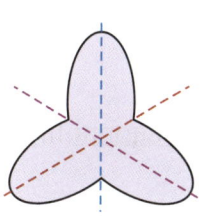

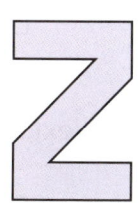

1 line of symmetry

2 lines of symmetry

3 lines of symmetry

No lines of symmetry

11+ Example Questions

EXAMPLE: Charlene has drawn half of a shape. She reflects it in the mirror line to make a whole shape. What is the name of the whole shape?

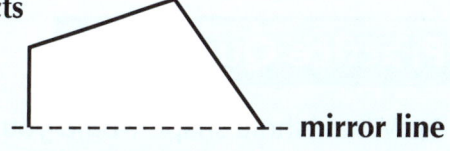

mirror line

A Rhombus   B Parallelogram   C Pentagon
D Hexagon   E Kite

1) You could sketch the shape and its reflection on some rough paper to show you what the whole shape will be.

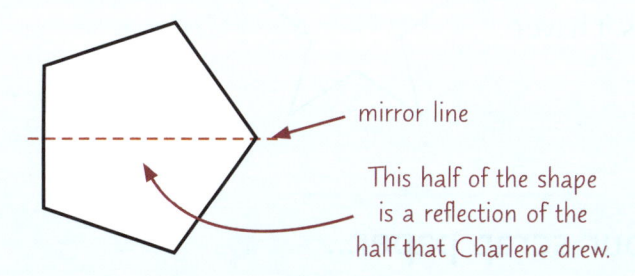

mirror line

This half of the shape is a reflection of the half that Charlene drew.

2) The whole shape has five sides. This means that it's a pentagon — option C.

Section Five — Shape and Space

Symmetry

> Another **11+ Example** Question

EXAMPLE: How many lines of symmetry does this shape have?

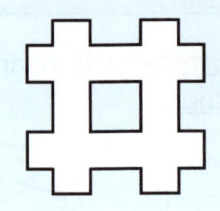

1) Start by looking for any <u>horizontal</u> or <u>vertical lines of symmetry</u>.

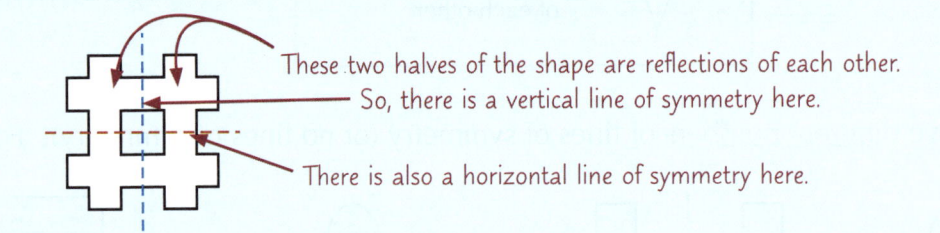

These two halves of the shape are reflections of each other.
So, there is a vertical line of symmetry here.

There is also a horizontal line of symmetry here.

2) Next, look for any <u>diagonal</u> lines of symmetry.

There are two diagonal lines of symmetry here.
The lines split the shape into two sets of identical halves.

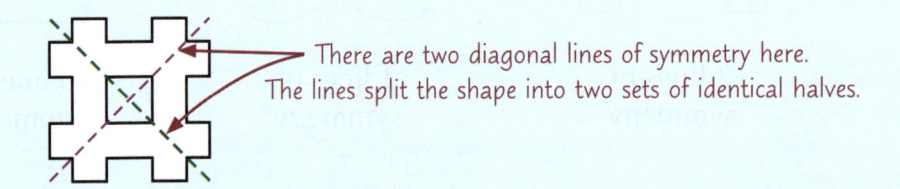

3) The shape has **four** lines of symmetry in total.

Practice Questions

1) What whole shape would you see when this half shape is reflected in the mirror line? 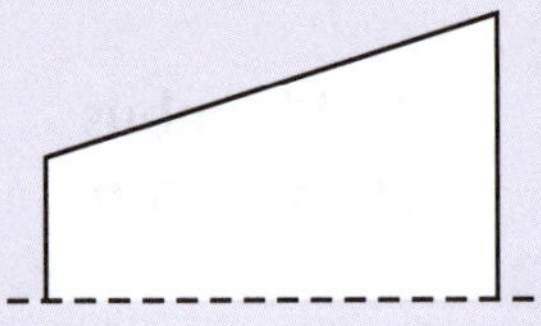
   - **A** Trapezium
   - **B** Parallelogram
   - **C** Rhombus
   - **D** Pentagon
   - **E** Hexagon

2) Elsa drew the following shape. How many lines of symmetry does it have?

> **TEST TIP** — **Make good use of your scrap paper...**
> If you're stuck in the exam, you can draw the shape on a scrap piece of paper and fold it in half. Unfold the paper and look to see whether the two halves of the shape on either side of the fold line are symmetrical. If they are, the fold line is a line of symmetry.

Section Five — Shape and Space

3D Shapes

3D shapes are different from 2D shapes — they have length and width, but they also have depth.

Know these common 3D Shapes

Cubes and Cuboids have Six Faces

Vertices are corners.

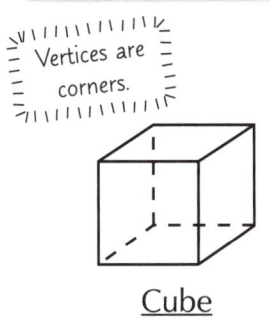

Cube
6 faces, 12 edges and 8 vertices

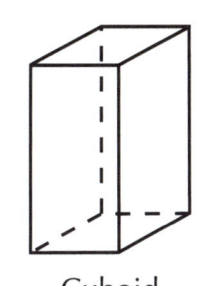

Cuboid
6 faces, 12 edges and 8 vertices

Pyramids have Triangular Faces that join at a Point

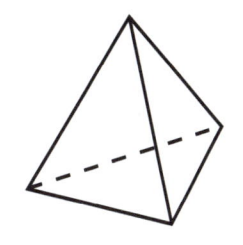

Triangle-based Pyramid
4 faces, 6 edges and 4 vertices

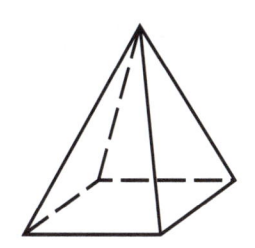

Square-based Pyramid
5 faces, 8 edges and 5 vertices

Prisms have the Same Face at Each End

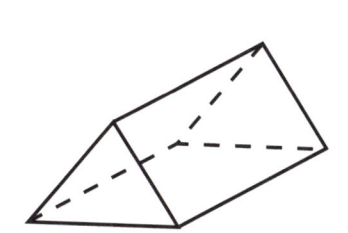

Triangular Prism
5 faces, 9 edges and 6 vertices

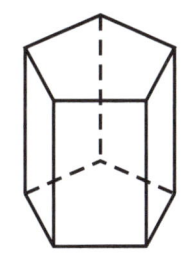

Pentagonal Prism
7 faces, 15 edges and 10 vertices

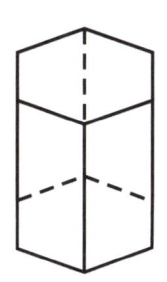

Hexagonal Prism
8 faces, 18 edges and 12 vertices

Nets Fold to make 3D Shapes

1) 3D shapes can be made using a net. A net is a 2D shape which can be folded to make a 3D shape.
2) The shapes that make up the net become the faces of the 3D shape.
3) There's often more than one net that you can use to make a 3D shape.

The net has six square faces... ...it folds to make a cube.

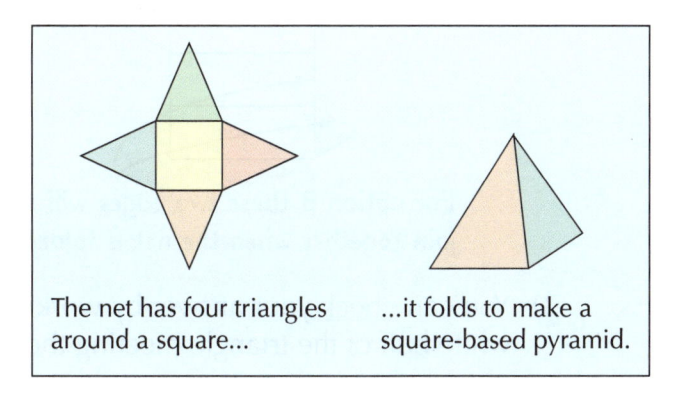

The net has four triangles around a square... ...it folds to make a square-based pyramid.

Section Five — Shape and Space

3D Shapes

Volume of Cubes and Cuboids = Length × Width × Height

1) <u>Volume</u> is the amount of space <u>inside</u> a shape.
2) You can work out the volume of a cube or a cuboid by <u>multiplying</u> the <u>length</u>, <u>width</u> and <u>height</u> together.

Volume is measured in cubed units — e.g. m³ or cm³.

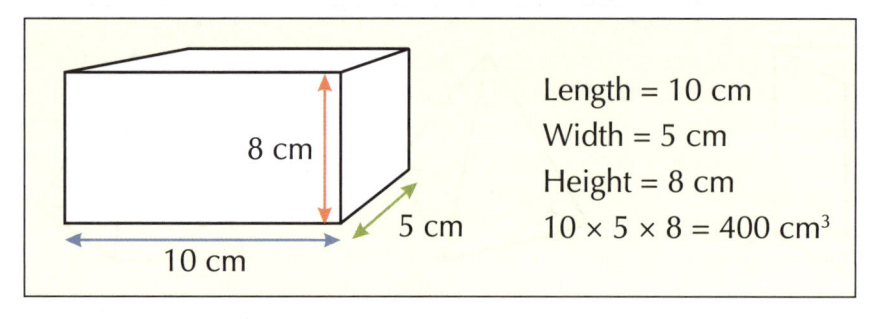

Length = 10 cm
Width = 5 cm
Height = 8 cm
10 × 5 × 8 = 400 cm³

11+ Example Questions

EXAMPLE: Sunita has made the 3D shape shown on the right, and shaded part of two faces.
Which of the nets below form Sunita's shape?

A   B   C   D   E

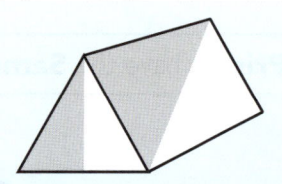

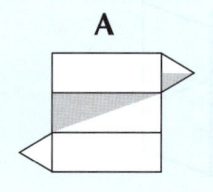

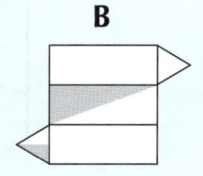

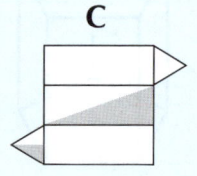

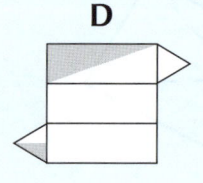

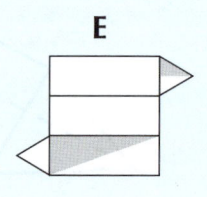

1) <u>Imagine</u> each net being folded up.
Work out which <u>edges of the shaded faces</u> will <u>join</u> together.
2) Work through the <u>options</u> until you find the <u>correct answer</u>:

The white half of the triangle must meet the grey half of the rectangle.

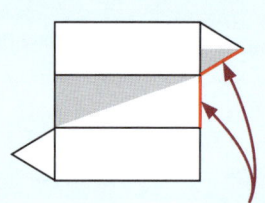

For option A these two edges will join together when the net is folded.

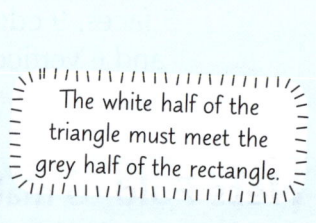

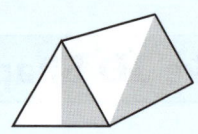

The patterned faces of the prism would look like this — it doesn't match the picture so it's incorrect.

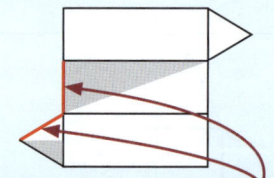

For option B these two edges will join together when the net is folded.

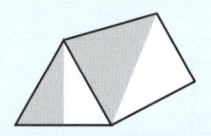

The patterned faces of the prism would look like this — it matches the picture so **option B** is the correct answer.

3) You can <u>check</u> your answer by working through <u>options C-E</u>. <u>None</u> of them have the white half of the triangle meeting the shaded half of the rectangle, so they're all <u>incorrect</u>.

Section Five — Shape and Space

3D Shapes

EXAMPLE: Chloe's swimming pool is shown. It can hold 48 m³ of water when full. What is the height of the swimming pool?

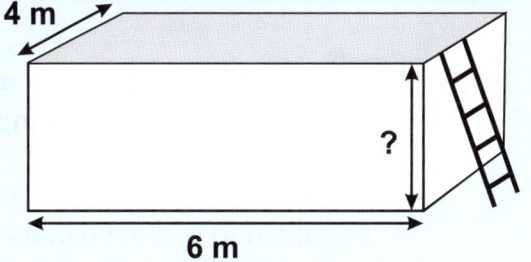

A 1.5 m B 4 m C 12 m
D 2 m   E 8 m

1) The formula to work out the volume of the pool is: length × width × height.
2) You know the volume, length and width, so you can use this to work out the height.

   length × width × height = 48 m³
   6 × 4 × height = 48 m³
   24 × height = 48 m³
   So height = 48 ÷ 24 = 2 m.

   You can check that your answer is correct by doing 6 × 4 × 2 = 48.

3) The height of the swimming pool is 2 m — option D.

EXAMPLE: Oscar has a bag of identical dice of side 2 cm. What is the maximum number of dice that he can fit in this box?

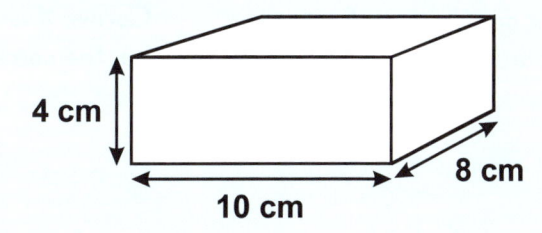

1) Start by working out how many dice fit along the length of the box.

   Each dice is 2 cm long and the box is 10 cm long.
   10 ÷ 2 = 5 dice.

2) Next, work out how many dice fit along the width of the box.

   Each dice is 2 cm wide and the box is 8 cm wide.
   8 ÷ 2 = 4 dice.

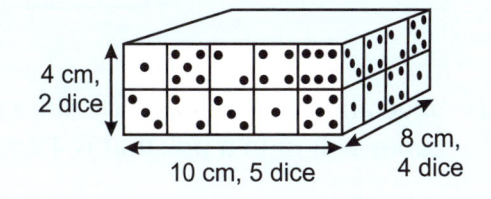

3) Then, work out how many dice fit up the height of the box.

   Each dice is 2 cm high and the box is 4 cm high.
   4 ÷ 2 = 2 dice.

4) To find the total number of dice that will fit in the box, multiply the number of dice that fit in the length by the number that fit in the width and the number that fit up the height.

   5 × 4 × 2 = 40. Oscar will be able to fit 40 dice in the box.

Section Five — Shape and Space

3D Shapes

One More 11+ Example Question

EXAMPLE: Joel folds this net to make a pentagonal prism. Which corner is going to join to corner X?

1) You need to imagine how the net will be folded to make the pentagonal prism.

2) Each corner of the two pentagons will join with a corner of a rectangle.

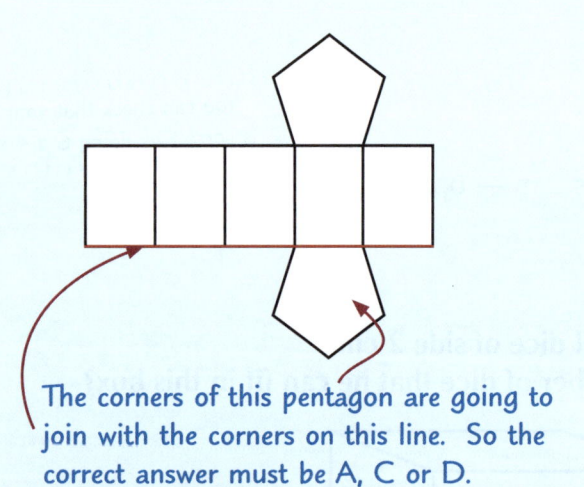

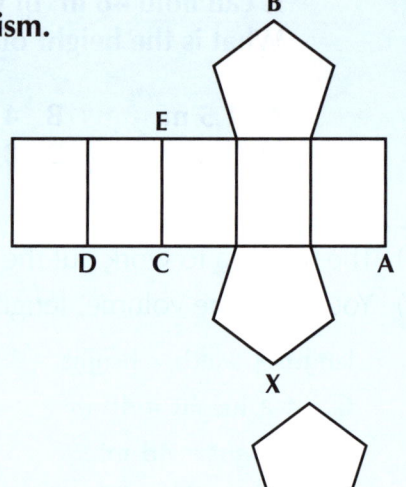

The corners of this pentagon are going to join with the corners on this line. So the correct answer must be A, C or D.

Corner X is going to join to corner D. So, the correct answer is option D.

Practice Questions

1) Which of these nets will not fold to make a cube?

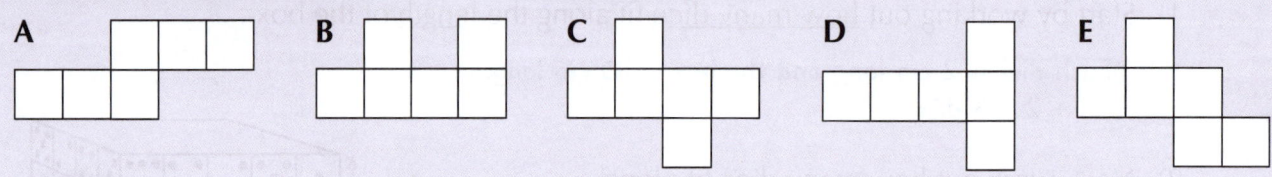

A   B   C   D   E

2) Vegetable stock cubes have sides that are 1 cm long. How many vegetable stock cubes will fit in a box that is 4 cm long, 8 cm wide and 2 cm high?

3) Frankie has made this net. What shape will be made when the net is folded?

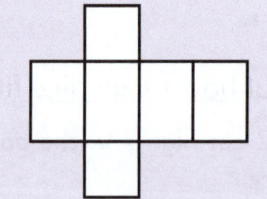

Make sure you're comfortable with sketching 3D shapes...

If you're asked about the properties of 3D shapes, it might help to draw them — it's easier to count the faces, edges or vertices that way. It's easy to miss one if you're just imagining the shape.

Section Five — Shape and Space

Shape Problems

Some questions will ask you to picture in your head what shapes will look like when they're flipped, rotated or moved around, or when you're looking at them from a different angle.

Plans and Elevations are 2D Drawings of 3D Shapes

1) A plan is the view from directly above a shape.
2) An elevation is the view from one side. Elevations can be different depending on which side you're looking at.

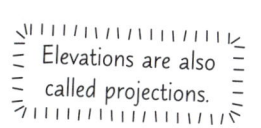

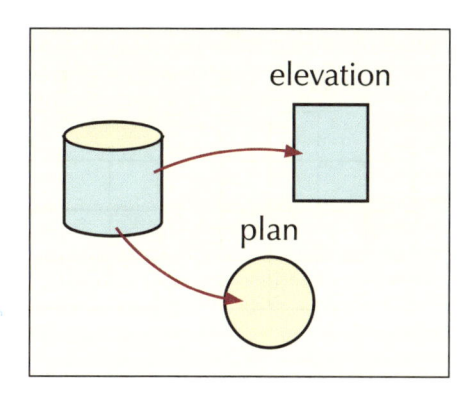

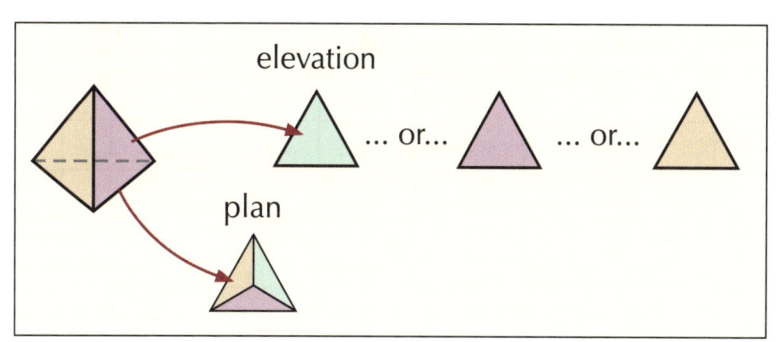

Elevations are also called projections.

11+ Example Questions

EXAMPLE: Some triangular tiles have been used to make a pattern. The tiles are reflected in a vertical mirror line to the right-hand side, then rotated 90° clockwise. Which of the options shows the shape now?

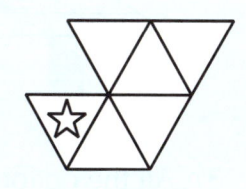

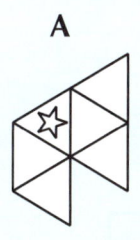

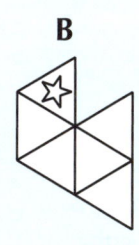

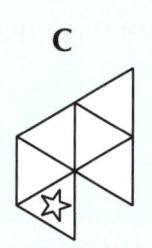

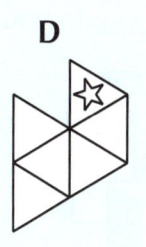

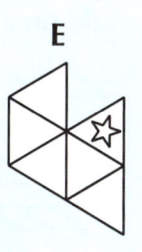

A   B   C   D   E

1) Imagine the tiles being reflected in a vertical mirror line, then rotated 90° clockwise.

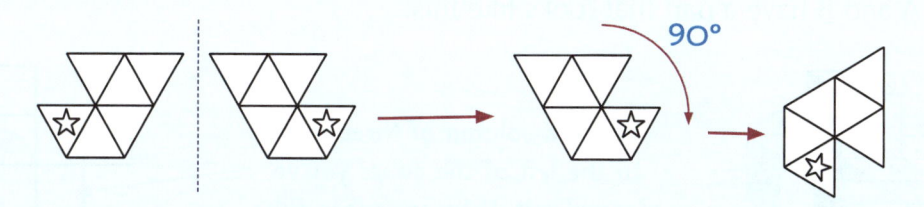

2) Option **C** is the correct answer.

Section Five — Shape and Space

88

Shape Problems

More 11+ Example Questions

EXAMPLE: Here is a 3D shape built out of cubes. Which of the following plans matches the shape?

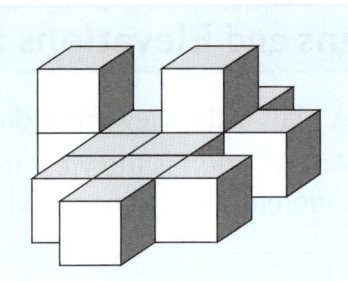

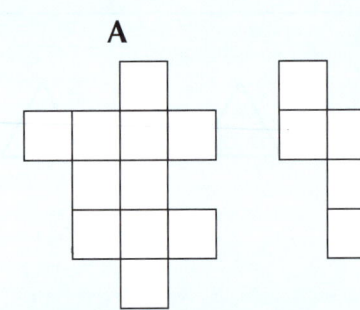

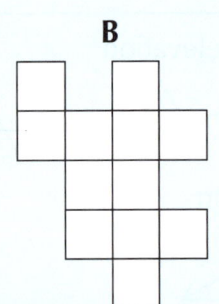

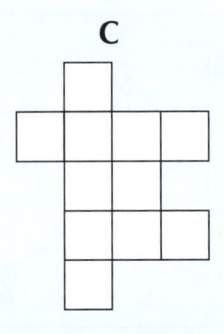

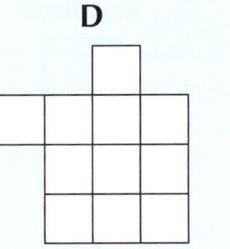

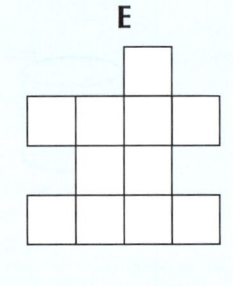

A   B   C   D   E

1) You can <u>ignore</u> the cubes on the bottom of other cubes — you <u>wouldn't see them</u> from above.
2) It can be helpful to choose a part of the shape and use it as a <u>point of reference</u>.

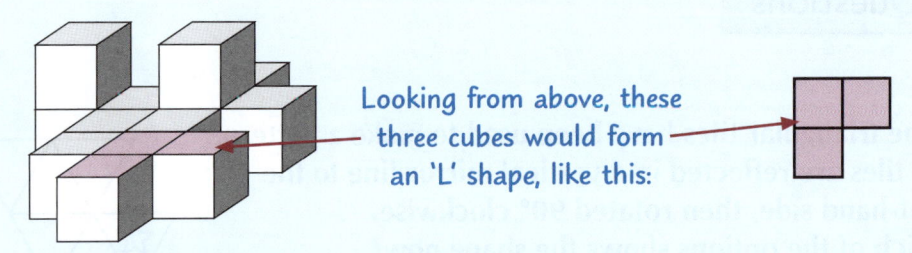

Looking from above, these three cubes would form an 'L' shape, like this:

3) <u>All</u> the options have a part that looks like this, so add on a <u>bit more</u> to your point of reference.

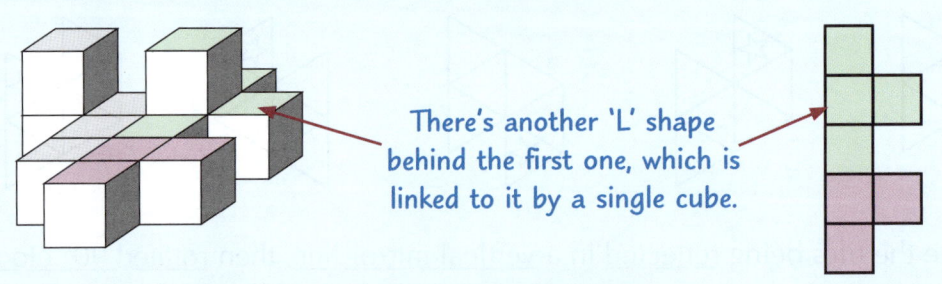

There's another 'L' shape behind the first one, which is linked to it by a single cube.

4) Options <u>A</u> and <u>B</u> have a part that looks like this.

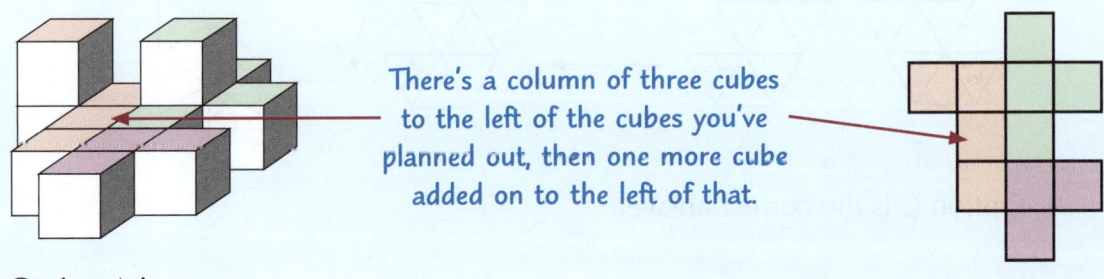

There's a column of three cubes to the left of the cubes you've planned out, then one more cube added on to the left of that.

5) Option A is correct.

Section Five — Shape and Space

Shape Problems

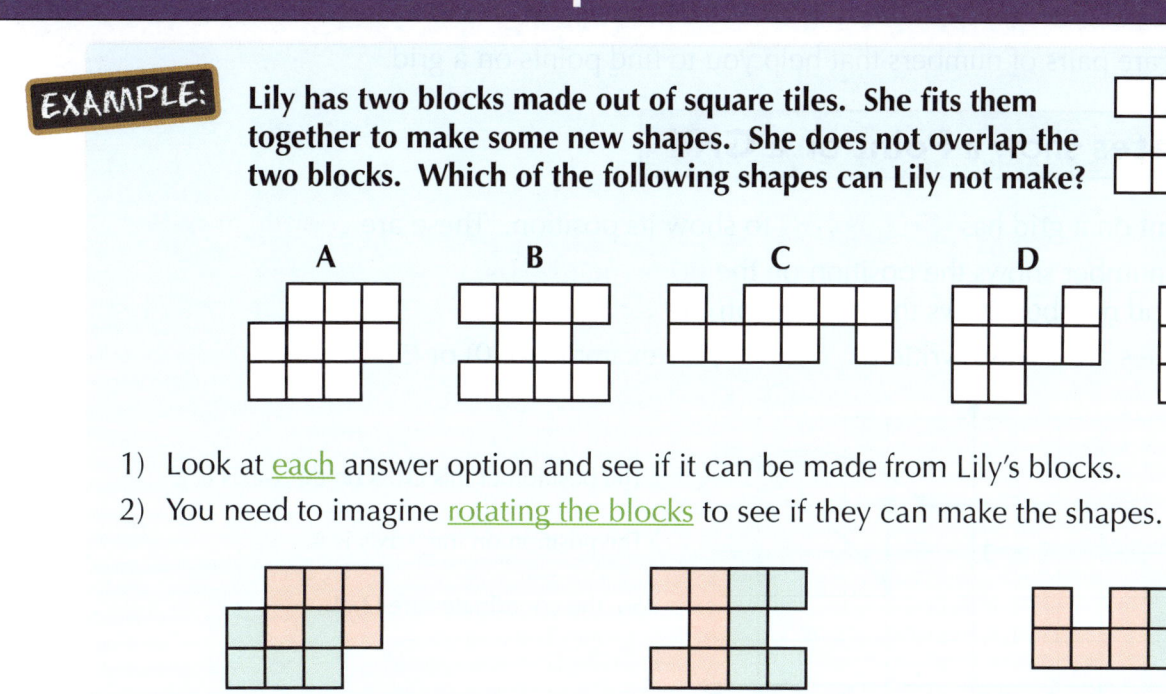

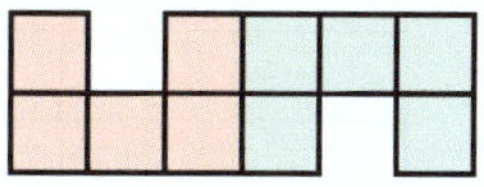

EXAMPLE: Lily has two blocks made out of square tiles. She fits them together to make some new shapes. She does not overlap the two blocks. Which of the following shapes can Lily not make?

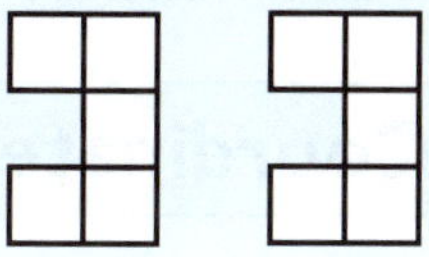

A   B   C   D   E

1) Look at <u>each</u> answer option and see if it can be made from Lily's blocks.
2) You need to imagine <u>rotating the blocks</u> to see if they can make the shapes.

Shape A can be made from Lily's blocks.

Shape B can be made from Lily's blocks.

Shape C can be made from Lily's blocks.

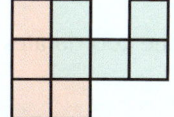

Shape D can't be made from Lily's blocks. The two blocks would have to overlap to make this shape.

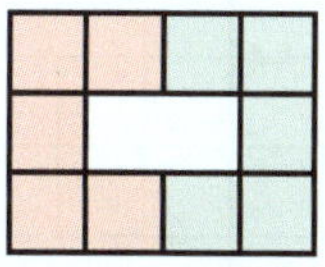

Shape E can be made from Lily's blocks.

3) Option D is the correct answer — it can't be made from the blocks used by Lily.

Practice Question

1) The diagram shows how a logo on a window appears when viewed from the front. Which of the following options shows the same logo when viewed from the back?

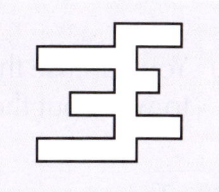

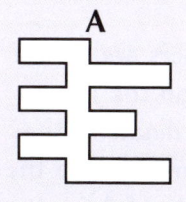

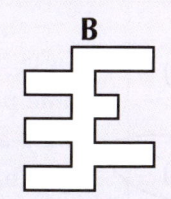

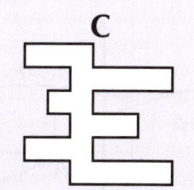

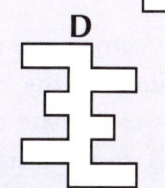

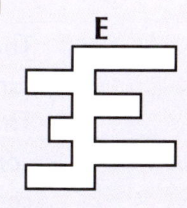

A   B   C   D   E

TEST TIP — You can draw it out if you get stuck...

For questions like the example above, you could sketch the options on a rough piece of paper. Then try to shade in the two blocks to see if both of them fit into the shape.

Section Five — Shape and Space

Coordinates

Coordinates are pairs of numbers that help you to find points on a grid.

Coordinates show a Point on a Grid

1) Each point on a grid has <u>two numbers</u> to show its position. These are <u>coordinates</u>.
2) The first number shows the position on the <u>horizontal x-axis</u>.
   The second number shows the position on the <u>vertical y-axis</u>.
3) Coordinates are always written <u>in brackets</u>, for example (0, 0) or (5, 4).

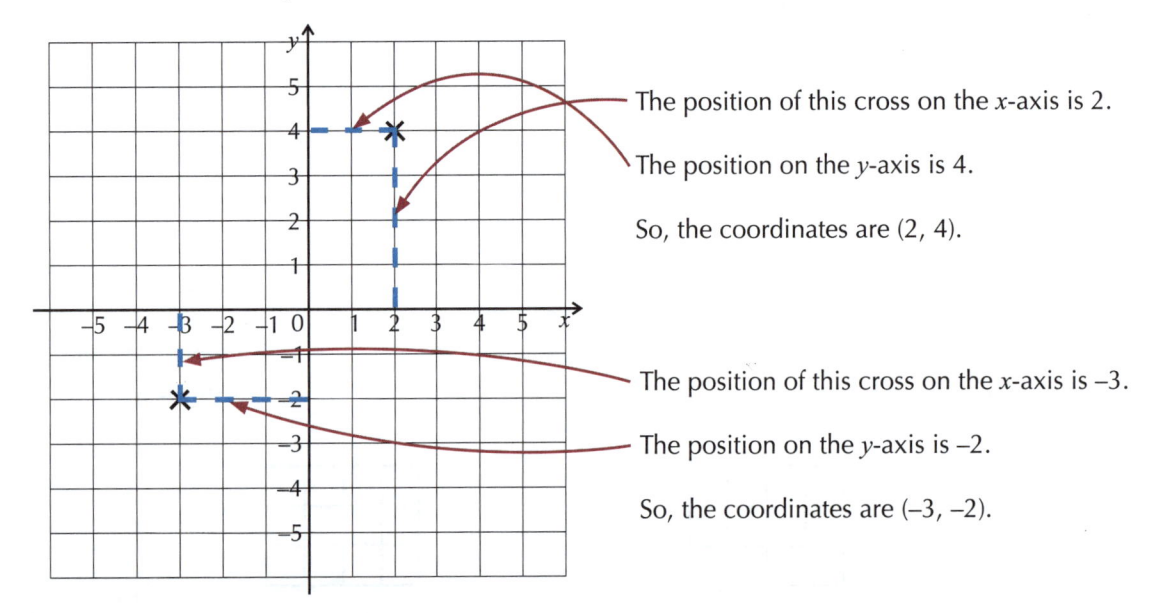

The position of this cross on the x-axis is 2.

The position on the y-axis is 4.

So, the coordinates are (2, 4).

The position of this cross on the x-axis is –3.

The position on the y-axis is –2.

So, the coordinates are (–3, –2).

11+ Example Questions

EXAMPLE: A rectangle was drawn on a coordinate grid. What are the coordinates of corner A?

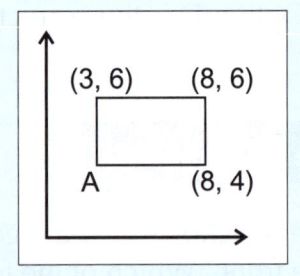

(3, 6)   (8, 6)

A   (8, 4)

1) You can use the coordinates you've been given to work out the coordinates of <u>corner A</u>.

   These two corners are on the same position on the x-axis. The x-axis coordinate of the top corner is 3, so the x-axis coordinate of A is also **3**.

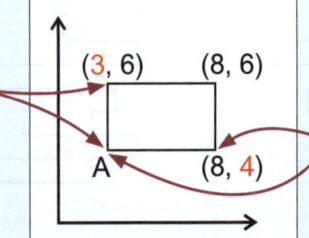

   (3, 6)   (8, 6)

   A   (8, 4)

   These two corners are on the same position on the y-axis. The y-axis coordinate of the right-hand corner is 4, so the y-axis coordinate of A is also **4**.

2) That gives you the <u>x-axis</u> and <u>y-axis</u> coordinates.
   So, the coordinates of corner A are **(3, 4)**.

Section Five — Shape and Space

Coordinates

EXAMPLE: Yohan draws a square on a grid. The coordinates of the four corners are (3, 5), (7, 5), (3, 9) and (7, 9). Which of the following points is inside Yohan's square?

A (7, 3)   B (6, 4)   C (9, 8)   D (6, 8)   E (5, 4)

1) You can use the coordinates that you've been given to work out which of the coordinates is within the square.

The x-coordinates of the corners of the square are 3, 7, 3 and 7.
So to be inside the square, the point must have an x-coordinate between 3 and 7.

The y-coordinates of the corners of the square are 5, 5, 9 and 9.
So to be inside the square, the point must have a y-coordinate between 5 and 9.

In option D, the x-coordinate (6) is between 3 and 7, and the y-coordinate (8) is between 5 and 9. So the point (6, 8) is inside Yohan's square.

2) That gives you the answer — option D is the only option that's inside the square.

Practice Questions

1) Nadine is plotting a parallelogram on this coordinate grid. She plots two of the corners at (1, 3) and (2, 6). Which of the following could be the coordinates of the other two corners?

A (4, 3) and (5, 4)   B (5, 5) and (7, 7)   C (6, 5) and (6, 4)
D (7, 6) and (6, 3)   E (3, 2) and (4, 7)

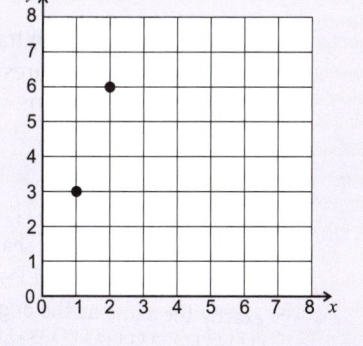

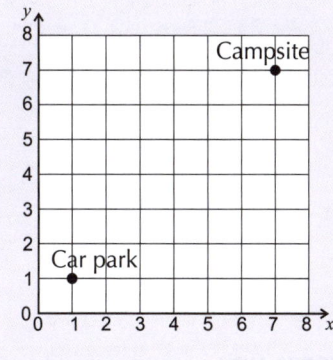

2) The farmhouse is exactly halfway between the campsite and car park. What are the coordinates of the farmhouse?

REVISION TIP — Remember — the x-axis goes across, and x is a cross...

Make sure you know the properties of quadrilaterals from page 73 — they'll come in really handy if you have to complete a shape on a coordinate grid. Squares and rectangles are pretty straightforward, but the others are a bit trickier so be careful.

Section Five — Shape and Space

Transformations

Transformations are where shapes are reflected or moved around a coordinate grid.

Shapes can be Transformed on a Coordinate Grid

Reflection in a Line

> The shape you get when a shape has been transformed is sometimes called its image.

1) Shapes can be reflected across a mirror line on a coordinate grid.
2) Each point and its reflection are exactly the same distance from the mirror line.

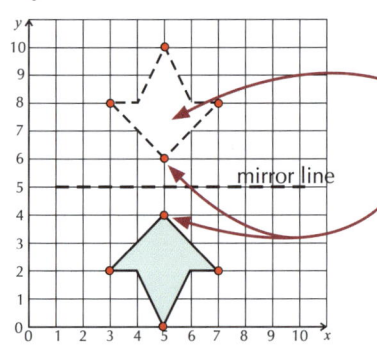

— This is the reflection of the shape.

— This point on the original shape is one square away from the mirror line. So, the same point on the reflected shape is also one square away from the mirror line.

Translation is Sliding a Shape

Translation is when a shape is moved from one place to another, without being flipped or rotated.

This shape has been translated by moving it 5 squares right and 4 squares down:

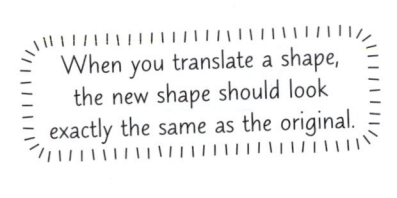

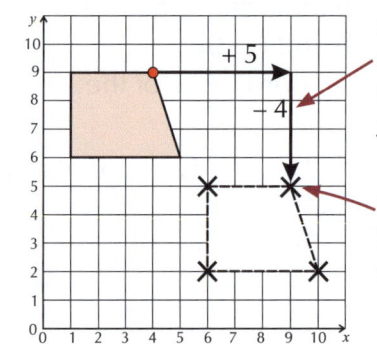

For the red point (4, 9), the x-coordinate on the translated shape will be 5 greater, and the y-coordinate will be 4 fewer.

The x-coordinate of this corner will be 4 + 5 = 9 and the y-coordinate will be 9 − 4 = 5 — (9, 5).

> When you translate a shape, the new shape should look exactly the same as the original.

11+ Example Questions

EXAMPLE: Point P (5, 2) is one vertex of a shape.
The shape is translated 4 squares to the left and 2 squares up.
What are the coordinates of the translated point P?

The x-coordinate of point P decreases by 4 and the y-coordinate increases by 2.

The coordinates of the translated point P are (5 − 4, 2 + 2) = **(1, 4)**

Section Five — Shape and Space

Transformations

EXAMPLE: Gurbaj drew this shape on a coordinate grid. She then reflected the shape in the mirror line. What are the coordinates of the image of point X?

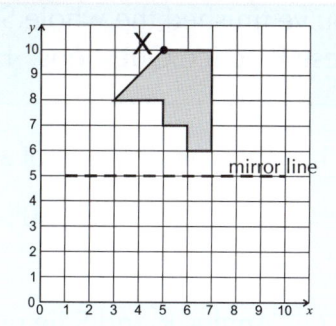

Point X on the image will be the same distance from the mirror line as point X is on the original shape.

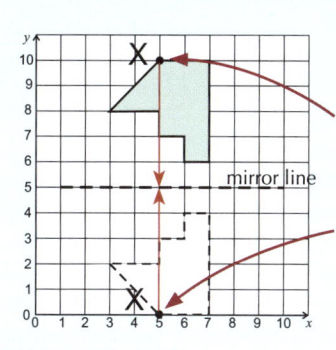

The shape has been reflected vertically, so the *x*-coordinate is still the same (5).

The *y*-coordinate of point X is 10, and the *y*-coordinate of the mirror line is 5. So, point X is 10 − 5 = 5 squares away from the mirror line.

The image of point X will also be 5 squares away from the mirror line. So, its *y*-coordinate will be 5 − 5 = 0.

The coordinates of the image of point X are (5, 0).

If you're allowed to write on the exam paper, you could draw the reflection of the shape.

Practice Questions

1) What will the coordinates of corner Y be after this triangle has been reflected in the mirror line?

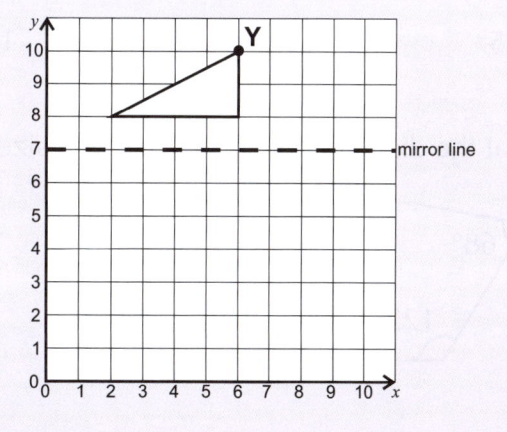

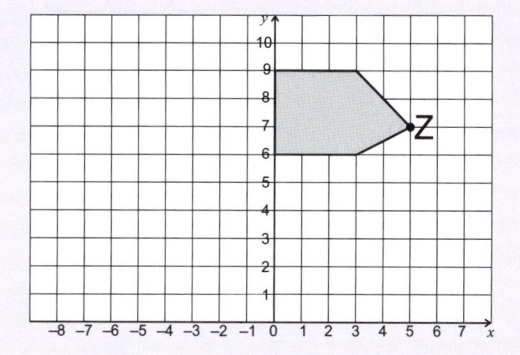

2) The shape on the coordinate grid is translated 6 squares to the left and 3 squares down. What are the new coordinates of point Z?

Translate shapes one corner at a time...

When you're translating a shape, start by translating each point. Then join up all of the points with straight lines. You can check your work by making sure that the two shapes are identical.

Section Five — Shape and Space

Practice Questions

You've finished the whole Shape and Space section, so now it's time to test your skills with these Practice Questions. Have another look at any of the topics you're struggling with.

1. Estimate the size of angle w. Circle the correct answer.

   A 35°   B 60°   C 20°   D 120°   E 90°

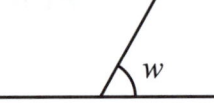

2. Angles R and S lie on a straight line.
   If angle R is 49°, what is angle S?

3. Look at the diagram below. What is the size of angle x?

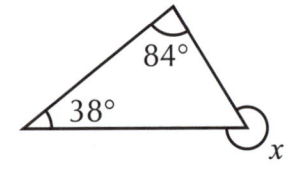

4. Angles g, h, j and k lie around a point. Angles g, h and j are obtuse.
   Which of the following could be the size of angle k? Circle the correct answer.

   A 215°   B 90°   C 150°   D 73°   E 98°

5. Look at the diagram below. What is the size of angle y?

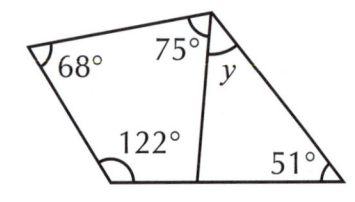

6. What is the name of the shape shown to the right?
   Circle the correct answer.

   A Rhombus   B Octagon

   C Hexagon   D Heptagon

   E Pentagon

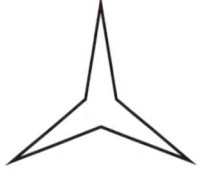

7. Niamh has five identical straight sticks. She uses all of the sticks to make different shapes by laying them end to end. Which of the following shapes could she not have made? Circle the correct answer.

   A Isosceles triangle   B Trapezium   C Regular pentagon   D Rectangle

Section Five — Shape and Space

Practice Questions

8. Robbie is making a circular watch face. He paints the outside edge of the watch face silver. What part of the circle does he paint silver? Circle the correct answer.

   A Radius   B Circumference   C Diagonal   D Vertex   E Diameter

9. How many pairs of equal angles does a kite have?

10. A circular dinner plate has a diameter of 240 mm. What is the radius of the plate?

    ___ mm

11. Jenny has drawn the isosceles triangle to the right. What is the size of angle m?

    ___ °

12. Bassam used four different equilateral triangles to make the pattern shown below. What is the size of angle b?

    ___ °

13. Linh has been asked to draw an irregular quadrilateral. Which of the following shapes should she not draw? Circle the correct answer.

    A Rhombus   B Kite   C Square   D Rectangle   E Parallelogram

14. A regular heptagon has a perimeter of 84 cm. What is the length of each side?

    ___ cm

15. George is painting the lines on the outside of the rugby pitch shown below. One can of paint covers 100 m. How many cans of paint will he need?

    70 m
    130 m

Section Five — Shape and Space

Practice Questions

16. Rhys uses three identical regular pentagons to make the pattern below.
    Each pentagon has a perimeter of 35 cm.
    What is the perimeter of the triangle in the centre of the pattern?

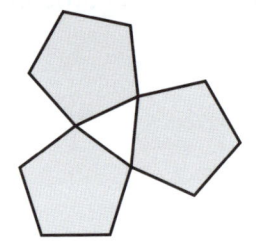

    ☐☐☐ cm

17. Irene owns field A, which has a fence all the way around the outside of it. She buys field B and wants to combine the two fields. She removes the section of fence between them and puts up new fencing around the rest of field B. How much longer is the new fence around the combined fields than the original fence around field A?

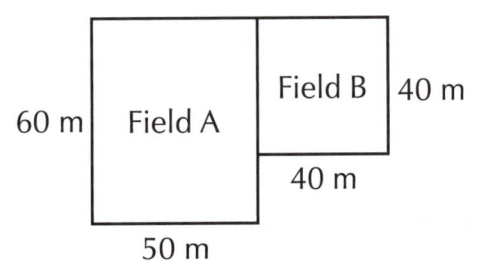

    ☐☐☐ m

18. A rectangle has an area of 56 cm². If the width of the rectangle is 7 cm, what is its length? Circle the correct answer.

    A 5 cm   B 6 cm   C 7 cm   D 8 cm   E 392 cm

19. A ship is flying the flag shown below. What is the area of the flag?

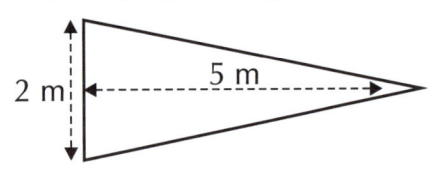

    ☐☐ m²

20. What is the area of the shape shown below?

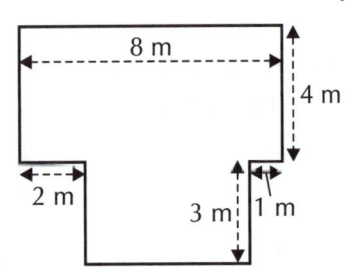

    ☐☐☐ m²

Section Five — Shape and Space

Practice Questions

21. Which of these shapes has the most lines of symmetry? Circle the correct answer.

    A Regular pentagon   B Equilateral triangle   C Square   D Rhombus

22. How many lines of symmetry does the shape below have?

23. What shape is made when this half shape is reflected in the mirror line? Circle the correct answer.

    A Octagon   B Hexagon   C Pentagon   D Heptagon   E Quadrilateral

24. Tessa has made a prism with 7 faces. What shape are the end faces? Circle the correct answer.

    A Square   B Triangle   C Hexagon   D Heptagon   E Pentagon

25. How many vertices does a triangle-based pyramid have?

26. Jay has made the net shown below. What shape will be made when the net is folded? Circle the correct answer.

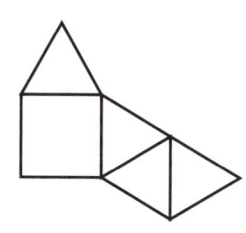

    A Triangle-based pyramid
    B Square-based pyramid
    C Triangular prism
    D Hexagonal prism
    E Cuboid

27. Marlon is putting sugar cubes into the container shown below. If the side length of each sugar cube is 2 cm, how many sugar cubes can he fit in the container?

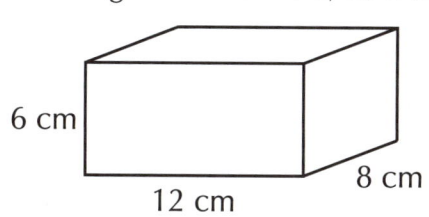

    6 cm   12 cm   8 cm

Section Five — Shape and Space

Practice Questions

28. Which of these nets will not fold to make a prism? Circle the correct answer.

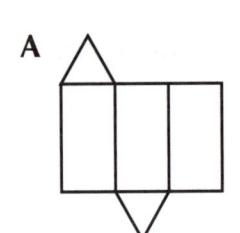

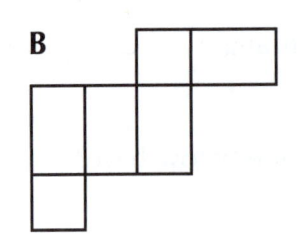

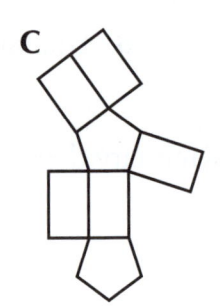

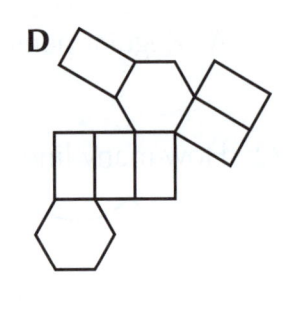

   A   B   C   D

29. Meera's planter is shown below. The planter can hold 5 m³ of soil. What is the length of the planter?

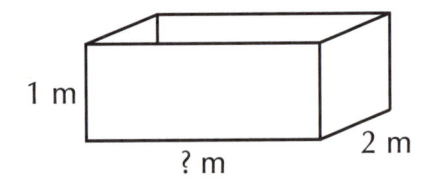

   1 m
   ? m
   2 m

   ☐.☐ m

30. Olly has 400 cm³ of water in a jug. He pours all of the water into the empty container shown below. How much more water does he need to add to fill the container?

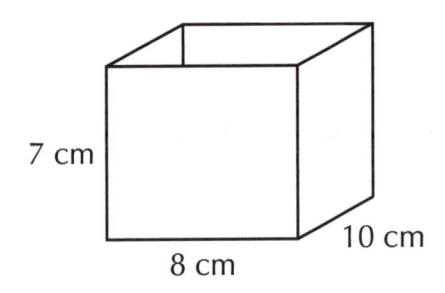

   7 cm
   8 cm
   10 cm

   ☐☐☐ cm³

31. Marianne used six wooden cubes to make the shape below. She then painted the outside of the shape. How many cube faces did she paint?

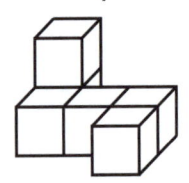

   ☐☐

32. Robert has cut these two shapes out of squared paper. He arranges them to make a new shape without overlapping the original shapes. Which of the following shapes could he have made? Circle the correct answer.

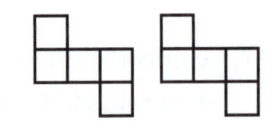

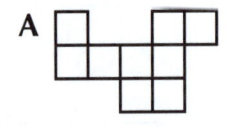

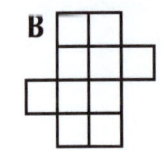

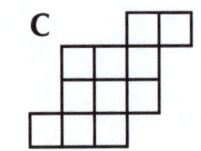

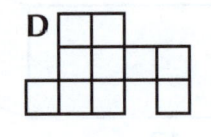

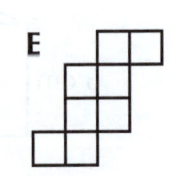

   A   B   C   D   E

Section Five — Shape and Space

Practice Questions

33. Nneka lives at point X. Point Y is exactly halfway between Nneka's house and her grandma's house. What are the coordinates of her grandma's house? Circle the correct answer.

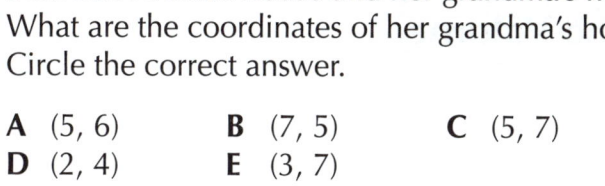

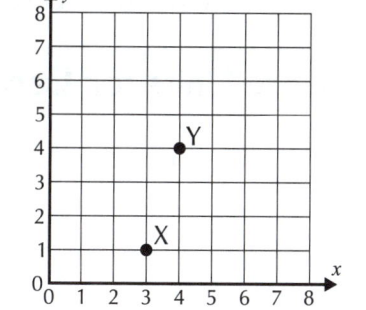

    A (5, 6)   B (7, 5)   C (5, 7)
    D (2, 4)   E (3, 7)

34. The shape shown below is a square. What are the coordinates of corner H?

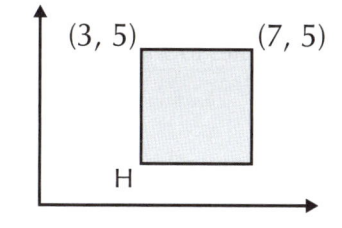

    (☐, ☐)

35. Alec has drawn the shape shown to the right.

    a) What are the coordinates of point A when he reflects the shape in the mirror line? Circle the correct answer.

        A (7, −2)   B (−6, 7)   C (6, −7)
        D (−2, 7)   E (0, 7)

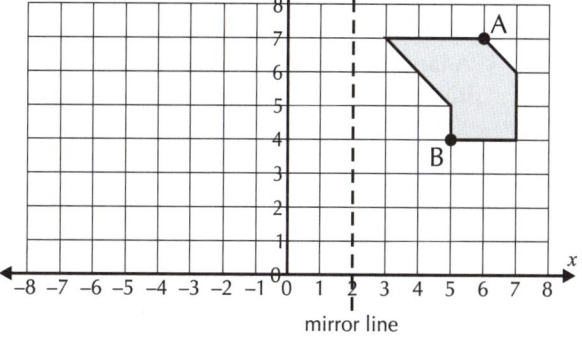

    b) Alec translates the original shape 2 squares down and 8 squares to the left. What are the coordinates of point B on the translated shape? Circle the correct answer.

        A (3, −4)   B (13, 6)   C (−3, 2)   D (13, 2)   E (−3, 6)

36. Ruby translates a shape as shown below. What are the coordinates of point T?

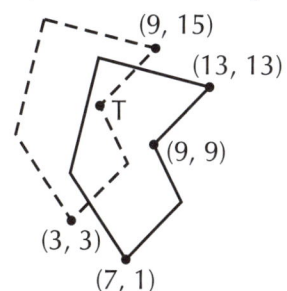

    (☐☐, ☐☐)

37. A map of a city square has been drawn on a coordinate grid. The four corners of the square are located at (4, 6), (8, 6), (8, 10) and (4, 10). Which of the following could be the coordinates of a statue located in the square? Circle the correct answer.

    A (3, 7)   B (5, 9)   C (12, 11)   D (9, 7)   E (7, 5)

Section Five — Shape and Space

Section Six — Units and Measures

Units

For the test, you'll need to be able to convert between different units for length, mass and volume, as well as know when it's best to use each one.

There are Units for **Length**, **Mass** and **Volume**

1) Here's a bit about the different units of length:

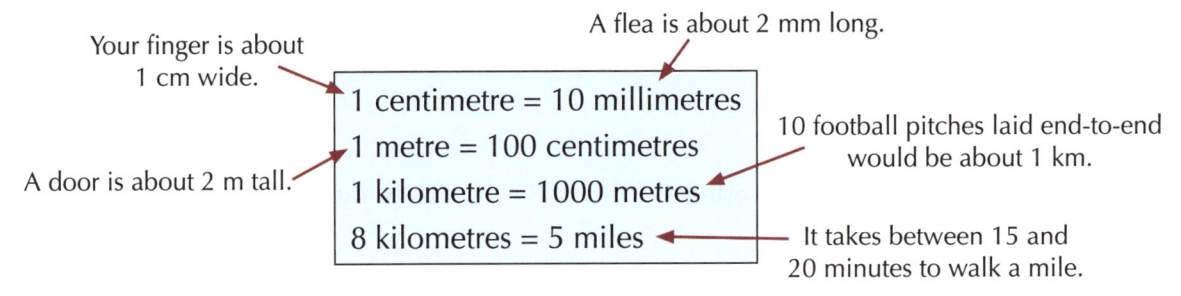

Your finger is about 1 cm wide.

A flea is about 2 mm long.

1 centimetre = 10 millimetres
1 metre = 100 centimetres
1 kilometre = 1000 metres
8 kilometres = 5 miles

A door is about 2 m tall.

10 football pitches laid end-to-end would be about 1 km.

It takes between 15 and 20 minutes to walk a mile.

2) Here's a bit about the different units of mass:

A medium-sized bag of sugar has a mass of 1 kg.

1 kilogram = 1000 grams

A paper clip has a mass of about 1 g.

3) Here's a bit about the different units of volume:

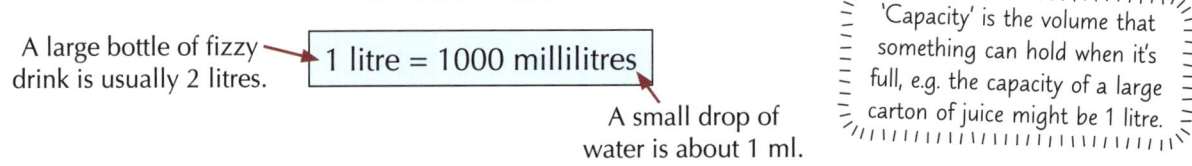

A large bottle of fizzy drink is usually 2 litres.

1 litre = 1000 millilitres

A small drop of water is about 1 ml.

'Capacity' is the volume that something can hold when it's full, e.g. the capacity of a large carton of juice might be 1 litre.

Some **Scales** are **Tricky** to **Read**

1) Units of measurement are often displayed using scales.

2) You need to be able to read values off scales, but not all divisions on scales are marked with a number. Here are some examples:

What value (in litres) is the arrow pointing to?
To work out what value the arrow is pointing to, you need to work out what each division is worth.
There are 5 divisions between the numbered marks.
The difference between the numbered marks is 0.1 litres.
So each division shows 0.1 litres ÷ 5 = 0.02 litres.
The arrow is pointing to 1.46 litres.

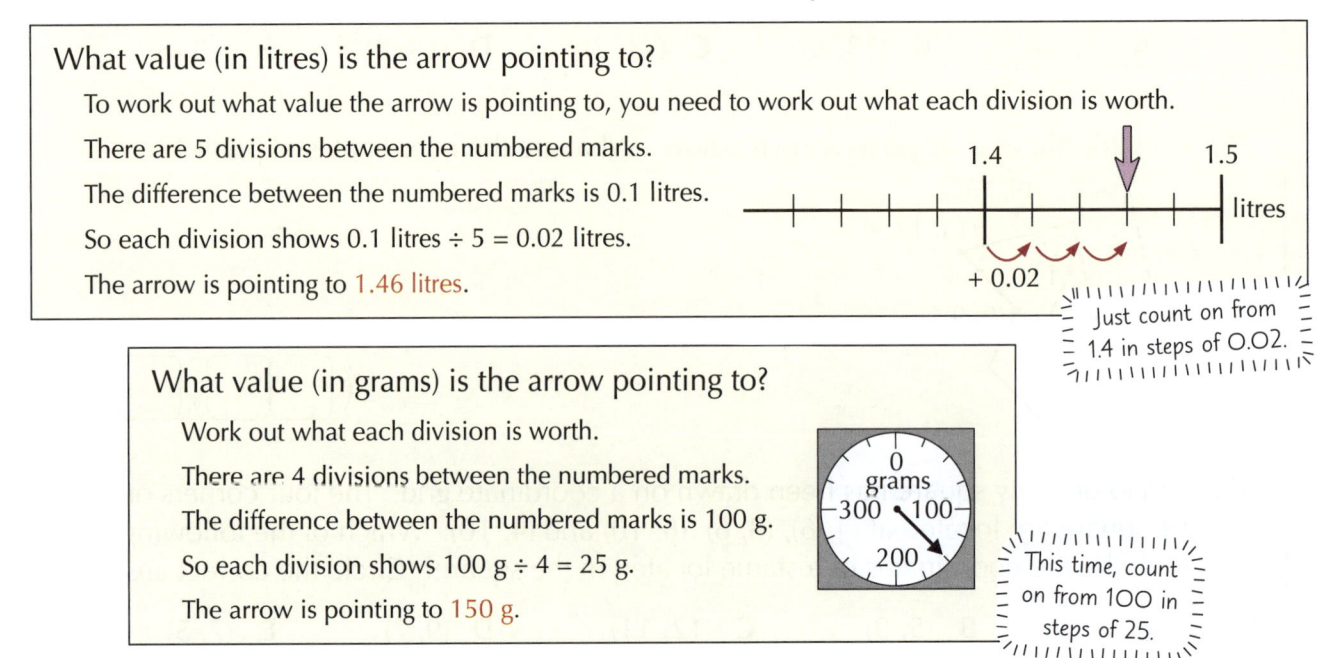

Just count on from 1.4 in steps of 0.02.

What value (in grams) is the arrow pointing to?
Work out what each division is worth.
There are 4 divisions between the numbered marks.
The difference between the numbered marks is 100 g.
So each division shows 100 g ÷ 4 = 25 g.
The arrow is pointing to 150 g.

This time, count on from 100 in steps of 25.

Units

Convert between Large and Small Units by Multiplying or Dividing

1) You might need to convert a smaller unit into a larger unit or a larger unit into a smaller one.
2) To convert a larger unit to a smaller unit you need to multiply. For example:

> To convert a mass that's in kg to a mass that's in g, multiply by 1000 (because there are 1000 g in a kg).
> 3.6 kg ⟶ 3.6 × 1000 = 3600 g

3) To convert a smaller unit to a larger unit you need to divide. For example:

> To convert a length that's in cm to a length that's in m, divide by 100 (because there are 100 cm in a m).
> 40 cm ⟶ 40 ÷ 100 = 0.4 m

Learn how to Convert between Miles and Kilometres

1) To convert km to miles, divide by 8 then times by 5. For example:

> 72 km ⟶ 72 ÷ 8 = 9, then 9 × 5 = 45 miles

2) To convert miles to km, divide by 5 then times by 8. For example:

> 55 miles ⟶ 55 ÷ 5 = 11, then 11 × 8 = 88 km

11+ Example Questions

EXAMPLE: How much water is there in this measuring jug?

A 0.95 litres B 0.8 litres
C 0.75 litres D 0.85 litres
E 0.9 litres

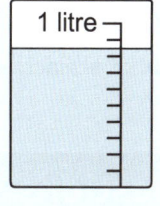

1) Work out how much each division on the scale is worth.
   There are 10 divisions in 1 litre.
   So each division shows 1 ÷ 10 = 0.1 litres.

2) The level of water in the jug is halfway between two marks on the scale. Work out the value of those two marks.
   Each division shows 0.1 litres. The water is between the eighth and ninth division, so there is between 0.8 and 0.9 litres.

3) Find the value halfway between the two marks.
   The difference between 0.8 and 0.9 is 0.1. Half of 0.1 is 0.05.
   So, halfway between 0.8 and 0.9 is 0.85, so the answer is D.

Section Six — Units and Measures

Units

EXAMPLE: Jo has 1.6 kg of hot chocolate powder. She puts 30 g of powder in each of 5 mugs of hot water. How much hot chocolate powder does Jo have left?

    A 1.57 kg   B 1.3 kg   C 1.45 kg   D 0.1 kg   E 1.585 kg

1) First work out how many grams of hot chocolate powder have been used.
   30 g in each of 5 mugs is a total of 30 × 5 = 150 g.

2) To find out how much hot chocolate powder is left you need to subtract 150 g from 1.6 kg, so make the units the same. The answers are in kg, so make the units both kg. ⟶ 150 g ÷ 1000 = 0.15 kg

3) Now subtract to find the mass of hot chocolate powder left.
   1.6 kg − 0.15 kg = 1.45 kg. So the answer is C.

EXAMPLE: A stalactite is hanging from a cave ceiling. It is currently 22 cm long. If it grows at a rate of 0.2 mm per year, how long, in centimetres, will it be in 200 years' time?

1) First, find out how much the stalactite will grow in 200 years by multiplying 0.2 mm by 200.
   The quick way to do 0.2 × 200 is to work out 0.2 × 100, and multiply the result by 2:
   0.2 × 100 = 20,   20 × 2 = 40 mm

2) You need to add the new growth to the stalactite's current length — but first make sure the units are the same.
   As you want the final answer in cm, convert the new growth to cm.
   1 cm = 10 mm, so divide 40 mm by 10 to get the number of cm: 40 ÷ 10 = 4 cm

3) Now add the current length and the new growth to find the length in 200 years' time.
   Length of stalactite = 22 cm + 4 cm = 26 cm

Practice Questions

1) Which of the following is most likely to be the mass of Tim's schoolbag with all of his books in?
     A 0.3 g   B 3 g   C 30 g   D 3 kg   E 30 kg

2) There are 28.75 litres of soup. 350 ml is spilt, and the rest is divided into 400 ml servings. How many servings are there?

3) Ashanti's stride is 50 cm. How many strides must she take to walk 10 km?
     A 20 000   B 2000   C 200 000   D 500   E 5000

TEST TIP — **Learn the conversions for length, mass and volume...**
The question might not specifically ask you to convert units, but if it uses a mixture, you'll need to convert at least one of the measurements so they all use the same unit.

Section Six — Units and Measures

Time

There's a lot to remember for this topic. Time to get prepared...

There are lots of **Different Units** for **Measuring Time**

1) Here's how some of the different units of time are related to each other.

   > 1 minute = 60 seconds
   > 1 hour = 60 minutes
   > 1 day = 24 hours
   > 1 year = 365 days (366 in a leap year)

   Leap years occur every 4 years. The extra day is added to February.

2) There are 7 days in a week and 52 weeks in a year.

3) Months are a bit more tricky — there are 12 months in a year, but the number of days in each month is different.

4) You can memorise the number of days in each month using this poem.

   > "30 days has September, April, June and November.
   > All the rest have 31, except February alone,
   > Which has 28 days clear, and 29 in each leap year."

Don't Get Confused between **Morning** and **Evening**

1) The hours on a 12-hour clock are shown by the numbers 1-12. The numbers then have either "am" or "pm" after them to show you whether it's morning or evening.
2) "am" runs from 12 midnight to 11:59 in the morning.
3) "pm" runs from 12 noon to 11:59 at night.
4) 24-hour time is the same as 12-hour time if it's morning, e.g. 9:00 am is the same as 09:00 on a 24-hour clock.
5) But you have to add on 12 hours if it's afternoon or evening, e.g. 1:00 pm is the same as 13:00 on a 24-hour clock.
6) When it gets to midnight, the 24-hour clock goes from 23:59 to 00:00.

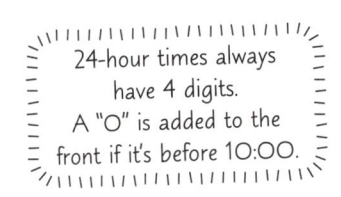

24-hour times always have 4 digits. A "0" is added to the front if it's before 10:00.

11+ **Example** Questions

EXAMPLE: Which of the following 24-hour times is the same as ten to three in the afternoon?

   A 15:10   B 02:50   C 15:50   D 14:50   E 03:50

1) "Ten to three" in the afternoon in 12-hour time is 2:50 pm.
2) Because it's in the afternoon, you add 12 hours to convert it to the 24-hour clock.
   2:50 + 12 hours = 14:50. So the answer is D.

Section Six — Units and Measures

Time

More 11+ Example Questions

EXAMPLE: Jevan spent 45 minutes weeding and then 52 minutes mowing the grass. How long did he spend gardening?

    A 1.37 hours   B 1 hour 37 minutes   C 137 hours
    D 9.7 hours   E 97 hours

1) Add the numbers of minutes together to get the total. ⟶ 45 + 52 = 97 minutes

2) Convert this to hours and minutes.

    There are 60 minutes in one hour. If you subtract 60 from 97 you're left with 37 minutes (97 − 60 = 37). So 97 minutes = 1 hour and 37 minutes — the answer is B.

1.37 hours is not the same as 1 hour 37 minutes because there are 60 minutes in 1 hour and not 100.

EXAMPLE: Lorna was born on Saturday 8th March. What day of the week was Chizoba born on if she was born on 4th May the same year?

1) First, find how many days there are between the two dates. You can do this in short, easy stages — write down the numbers of days in each month between the dates.

    31 − 8 = 23 days   30 days   4 days

    8th March ⟶ 31st March ⟶ 30th April ⟶ 4th May

Now add up the number of days: 23 + 30 + 4 = 57 days

2) There are 7 days in a week, so every 7th day after 8th March will be a Saturday too. Find the multiple of 7 which is closest to 57.

    8 × 7 = 56. So the 56th day after 8th March is a Saturday.

3) Now work out the day that 4th May falls on.

    There are 57 days between 8th March and 4th May, and the 56th day is a Saturday. So 4th May must be a Sunday.

EXAMPLE: To get to work one day, Elise walks for 12 minutes to get to the bus stop, then waits 6 minutes for her bus. The bus journey takes 18 minutes, then she walks for another 3 minutes to get to her office. She arrives at the office at 8:24 am. What time did she set off?

1) Add up the time Elise spends on each stage of her journey.

    12 + 6 + 18 + 3 = 39 minutes

2) Now find the time that is 39 minutes before 8:24 am.

    There are 24 minutes between 8 am and 8:24 am. This leaves 39 − 24 = 15 minutes of journey time before 8 am, so Elise set off at 7:45 am.

You could work this out by counting back — i.e. count back 3 minutes from 8:24 am, then count back another 18 minutes, then 6, then 12.

Section Six — Units and Measures

Time

EXAMPLE: Hannah needs to get to Millham by 2 pm. What is the latest that she can get a bus from Dale Street?

Ulverstown	1254	1314	1334	1404
Dale Street	1259	1319	1339	1409
Railway Station	1308	1327	1348	1417
Canal Foot		1340		1430
Millham	1324	1347	1404	1437
Daltown	1345	1411	1425	1511

Times in timetables are often written without a colon, so 1254 is the same as 12:54.

1) Hannah needs to get to Millham by <u>2 pm</u>, but the timetable is in <u>24-hour clock time</u>. Convert 2 pm to the 24-hour clock.
   It's in the afternoon, so add 12 hours: 2 pm = 2 + 12 = 14:00

2) Now find the row for <u>Millham</u>. This lists the times that buses arrive there.

3) Find the <u>latest time</u> before 14:00 that Hannah can arrive at Millham.
   The bus that arrives at 14:04 is too late. The one before gets in at 13:47.

4) Look <u>up the column</u> to find when this bus leaves Dale Street.
   It leaves Dale Street at 13:19.

Practice Questions

1) Some children's birthdays are given below. Which child is youngest?
   Meg — 14th May 2009   Fred — 16th March 2009   Geeta — 1st February 2008
   Jim — 28th December 2008   Max — 13th October 2009

2) Kerry completes one page of her Maths book each day, starting on 1st September. If there are 154 pages, in which month will she finish her book?

3) Jamie starts his homework at 4:53 pm. If he finishes it at 7:15 pm, how long did it take?
   A 2.22 hours
   B 202 minutes
   C 22 hours 2 minutes
   D 2 hours 22 minutes
   E 3 hours 38 minutes

Make sure you're happy with both 12-hour and 24-hour times...

The method used to find the difference between two dates can be used to find the difference between two times. E.g. to find the number of minutes between 9:46 am and 11:31 am:

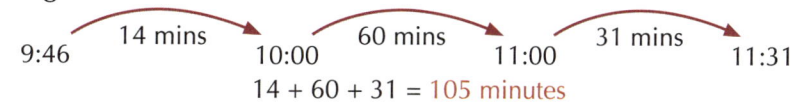

9:46 —14 mins→ 10:00 —60 mins→ 11:00 —31 mins→ 11:31

14 + 60 + 31 = **105 minutes**

Section Six — Units and Measures

Practice Questions

Now you've finished the Units and Measures section, check how much has sunk in with these Practice Questions.

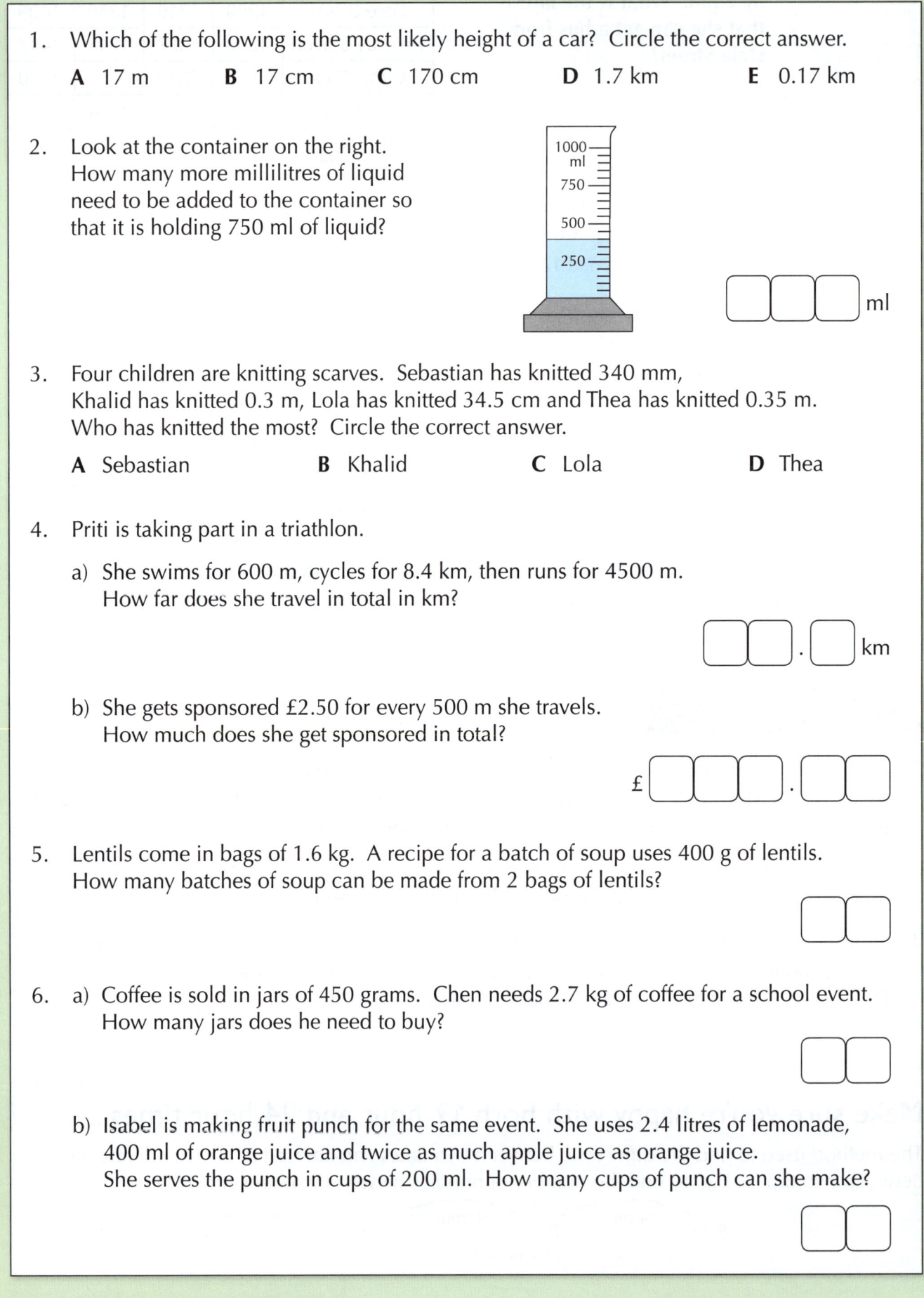

1. Which of the following is the most likely height of a car? Circle the correct answer.

   A 17 m   B 17 cm   C 170 cm   D 1.7 km   E 0.17 km

2. Look at the container on the right. How many more millilitres of liquid need to be added to the container so that it is holding 750 ml of liquid?

   ☐☐☐ ml

3. Four children are knitting scarves. Sebastian has knitted 340 mm, Khalid has knitted 0.3 m, Lola has knitted 34.5 cm and Thea has knitted 0.35 m. Who has knitted the most? Circle the correct answer.

   A Sebastian   B Khalid   C Lola   D Thea

4. Priti is taking part in a triathlon.

   a) She swims for 600 m, cycles for 8.4 km, then runs for 4500 m. How far does she travel in total in km?

   ☐☐.☐ km

   b) She gets sponsored £2.50 for every 500 m she travels. How much does she get sponsored in total?

   £☐☐☐.☐☐

5. Lentils come in bags of 1.6 kg. A recipe for a batch of soup uses 400 g of lentils. How many batches of soup can be made from 2 bags of lentils?

   ☐☐

6. a) Coffee is sold in jars of 450 grams. Chen needs 2.7 kg of coffee for a school event. How many jars does he need to buy?

   ☐☐

   b) Isabel is making fruit punch for the same event. She uses 2.4 litres of lemonade, 400 ml of orange juice and twice as much apple juice as orange juice. She serves the punch in cups of 200 ml. How many cups of punch can she make?

   ☐☐

Section Six — Units and Measures

Practice Questions

7. A digital watch shows the time 16:04. The watch is running 12 minutes fast. What is the correct time in the 12-hour clock? Circle the correct answer.

   A 16:16   B 15:52   C 4:52 pm   D 3:52 pm   E 4:16 pm

8. A netball tournament starts at 9:45 am and finishes at 1:20 pm. How long does it last for in hours and minutes?

   ☐☐ hours ☐☐ minutes

9. Isla's birthday is on 14th July. Rory's birthday is 20 days before Isla's. What date is Rory's birthday?

   A 22nd June   B 23rd June   C 24th June   D 25th June

10. Esme takes 5 minutes and 24 seconds to complete a puzzle. How long is this in seconds?

    ☐☐☐ seconds

11. Look at this train timetable.

North River	1118	1147	1203	1225	1241	1308
South Path	1136	1205	1221	1243	1259	1326
East Water	1202	1231	1247	1309		1352
West Mile	1219		1304		1342	1409

    a) How long is the train journey from North River to East Water?

    ☐☐ mins

    b) Jiya needs to be in West Mile by 1:30 pm. What is the latest that she can catch a train from South Path?

    ☐☐ : ☐☐

    c) Kofi has a piano lesson in North River. The lesson starts at 11:15 am and lasts for 35 minutes. The train station is 15 minutes away from his piano teacher's house. What is the earliest time Kofi can arrive at East Water?

    ☐☐ : ☐☐

    d) Mr Adams lives 8 minutes away from the East Water train station. If he leaves his house at 11:55 am, how long will he have to wait for the next train?

    ☐☐ mins

Section Six — Units and Measures

Section Seven — Mixed Problems

Mixed Problems

Some questions test your knowledge of more than one topic, so you might have to read a pie chart and work out some angles. The questions on these pages are examples, but you could be tested on any combination of topics.

11+ Example Questions

EXAMPLE: A cruise ship travels 30 $\frac{1}{2}$ kilometres every hour.
It left port at 7 pm on Monday and arrived at its destination at 1 am on Tuesday.

How far did it travel?

1) Work out how many <u>hours</u> the cruise ship was <u>travelling</u> for.

   On Monday the ship travelled for 5 hours between 7 pm and 12 am.
   On Tuesday the ship travelled for 1 hour between 12 am and 1 am.
   5 + 1 = 6 hours.

2) Now <u>multiply</u> 6 hours by 30$\frac{1}{2}$ kilometres.

   Use partitioning to find 6 × 30$\frac{1}{2}$. Partition 30$\frac{1}{2}$ into 30 and $\frac{1}{2}$.
   6 × 30 = 180, and 6 × $\frac{1}{2}$ = 3 (it's the same as half of 6).
   Add together your results: 180 + 3 = **183 km**.

3) The ship travelled **183 kilometres**.

EXAMPLE: Penny packs 10 identical candles into a cuboid box. Each candle has a volume of 240 cm³. The box is 30 cm long, 20 cm wide and 5 cm high.

What fraction of the volume of the box is taken up by the candles?

A $\frac{1}{4}$ B $\frac{4}{5}$ C $\frac{3}{4}$ D $\frac{2}{5}$ E $\frac{3}{8}$

1) First, multiply to find the <u>total volume</u> of <u>10</u> candles.

   The volume of one candle is 240 cm³,
   so the volume of 10 candles is 10 × 240 = 2400 cm³.

2) Then, calculate the volume of the <u>box</u>.

   Volume of a cuboid = length × width × height,
   so the volume of the box = 30 × 20 × 5 = 3000 cm³.

3) Finally, write the <u>volume of the candles</u> as a fraction of the <u>volume of the box</u>.

   You need to simplify the fraction so it matches one of the options.
   $\frac{2400}{3000} = \frac{24}{30} = \frac{4}{5}$ — the answer is **B**.

Mixed Problems

EXAMPLE: Dylan has some shapes which have areas *q* and *r*.

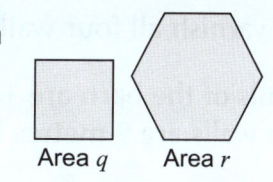

Area *q*   Area *r*

He cuts some of his shapes in half and makes a pattern.

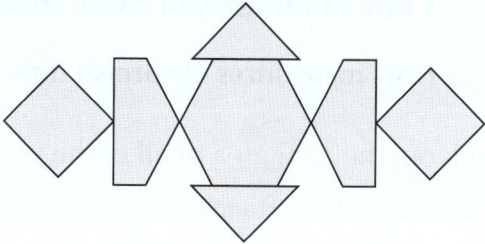

What is the area of the pattern?

A $2q + 3r$ B $3q + r$ C $3q + 2r$
D $3q + 4r$ E $4q + 4r$

Have a look back at pages 43-46 for more on algebra.

1) Work out what shapes make up the <u>pattern</u>.

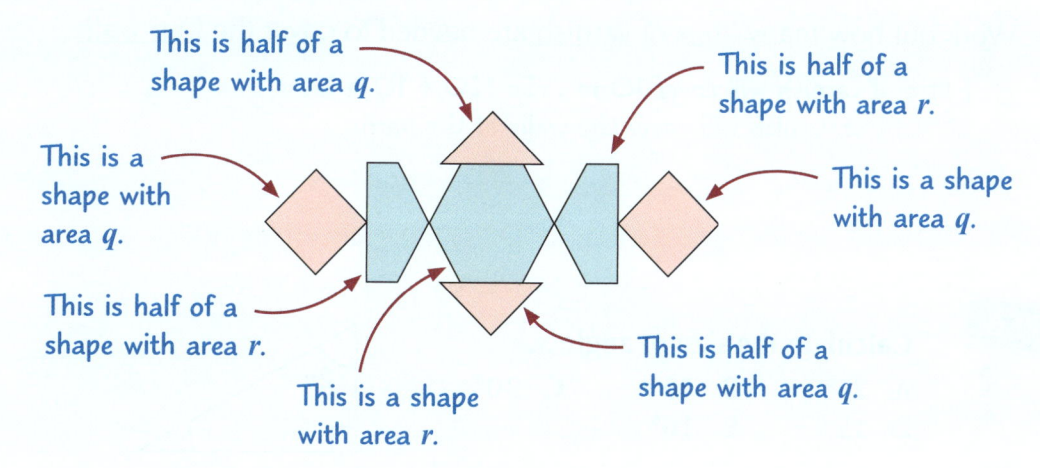

   - This is half of a shape with area *q*.
   - This is half of a shape with area *r*.
   - This is a shape with area *q*.
   - This is a shape with area *q*.
   - This is half of a shape with area *r*.
   - This is half of a shape with area *q*.
   - This is a shape with area *r*.

2) Now <u>add together</u> all of the <u>areas</u>.

   There are two whole shapes and two half shapes with area *q*: $2 + \frac{1}{2} + \frac{1}{2} = 3$.
   The pattern has a total of 3 shapes with area *q*, so these shapes have an area of $3q$.

   There is one whole shape and two half shapes with area *r*: $1 + \frac{1}{2} + \frac{1}{2} = 2$.
   The pattern has a total of 2 shapes with area *r*, so these shapes have an area of $2r$.

   The total area of the pattern is the areas of the shapes added together, $3q + 2r$.

3) So the <u>answer</u> is C.

TEST TIP

Always read mixed problem questions really carefully...

These questions can look quite difficult, but you just need to take your time with them. Work out what steps you need to follow to get to the answer before you start answering the question.

Section Seven — Mixed Problems

Mixed Problems

EXAMPLE: Cliff wants to varnish all four walls of his barn.

Two of the walls of the barn are 15 metres long and 2.5 metres high. The other two walls are 9 metres long and 2.5 metres high.

1 litre of varnish will cover 10 square metres.

How many litres of varnish does he need?

1) Work out the total area of all of the walls.

The area of a rectangle = length × height
Two of the walls are 15 m by 2.5 m, so the area of each wall is:
15 × 2.5 = (15 × 2) + (15 × 0.5) = 30 + 7.5 = 37.5 m²
The other two walls are 9 m by 2.5 m, so the area of each wall is:
9 × 2.5 = (9 × 2) + (9 × 0.5) = 18 + 4.5 = 22.5 m²
Add up the area of each wall:
37.5 + 37.5 + 22.5 + 22.5 = 75 + 45 = 120 m²

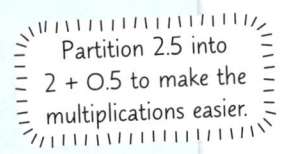

Partition 2.5 into 2 + 0.5 to make the multiplications easier.

2) Work out how many litres of varnish are needed to cover the four walls.

1 litre of varnish will cover 10 m². So 120 ÷ 10 = 12.
12 litres of varnish will cover the walls of the barn.

EXAMPLE: Calculate the size of angle x.

A 25°   B 40°   C 30°
D 15°   E 10°

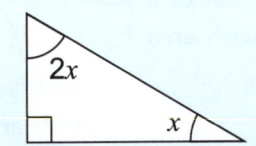

1) Use the information you have to make an equation.

Angles in a triangle add up to 180°.
One of the angles is a right angle (90°) so the other two angles must add up to 180° − 90° = 90°.
$2x + x = 90°$
So $3x = 90°$.

2) Use your equation to find the size of angle x.

Find x when $3x = 90°$.

$3x = 90°$
÷3   ÷3
$x = 30°$

The opposite of × 3 is ÷ 3, so divide both sides by 3.
That gives you the answer — x is 30°. **C** is correct.

Section Seven — Mixed Problems

Mixed Problems

EXAMPLE: Jason's class conducted a survey. They asked the teachers who drove to school how many passengers they took with them.

They collected their results in a bar chart.

What percentage of the teachers travelled with 3 passengers?

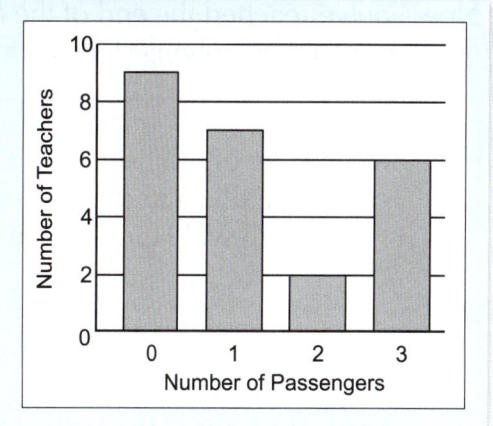

1) First work out <u>how many teachers</u> took part in the <u>survey</u>.

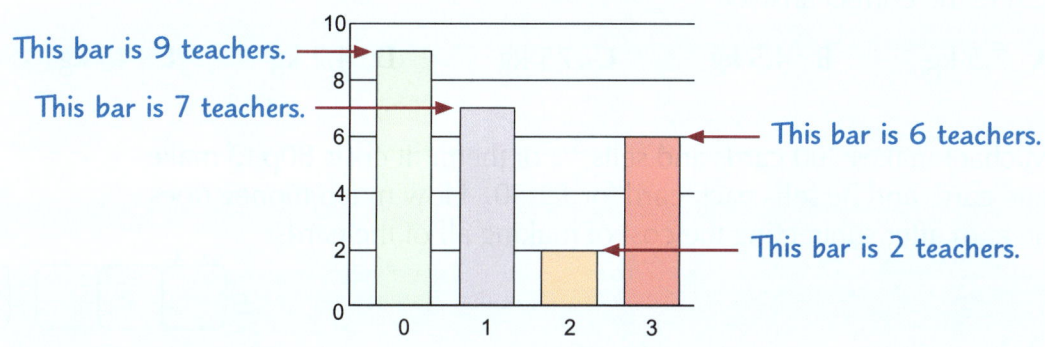

   This bar is 9 teachers.
   This bar is 7 teachers.
   This bar is 6 teachers.
   This bar is 2 teachers.

   The total number of teachers is 9 + 7 + 2 + 6 = 24.

2) Now you can work out the <u>percentage</u> of <u>teachers</u> who travelled with <u>3 passengers</u>.

   6 teachers out of a total of 24 travelled with 3 passengers. This gives you the fraction $^6/_{24}$. This fraction can be simplified to $^1/_4$.

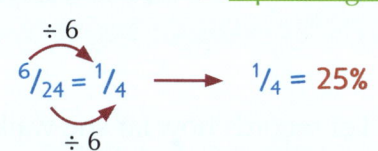

   $^6/_{24} = ^1/_4$ ÷ 6 → $^1/_4$ = 25%

3) The <u>percentage</u> of <u>teachers</u> who travelled with <u>3 passengers</u> is <u>25%</u>.

Practice Questions

1) A swimming pool is 10 metres long, 10 metres wide and 1.6 metres deep. It costs 25p to fill 1 m³ of the pool with water. What is the cost of filling the pool to the top?

2) Mr O'Brian recorded the colour of the flowers in his garden in the pie chart shown. What percentage of his flowers were red?

   A 5% **B** 12.5% **C** 25% **D** 42% **E** 54%

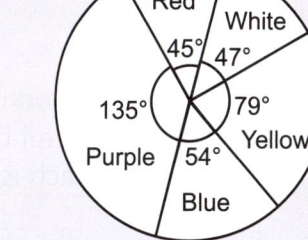

Revise any bits you find tricky...

REVISION TIP Mixed question problems are a good way of seeing which topics you know really well. If there are any bits you're getting stuck on, go back and practise those topics a bit more.

Section Seven — Mixed Problems

Practice Questions

Now you've reached the end of the Mixed Problems section, test your problem-solving skills with these Practice Questions.

1. A 5 kg bag of fertiliser costs £7 and covers 30 m². Horace needs enough fertiliser to cover his garden, which is 13 m long and 8 m wide. How much will Horace have to spend on fertiliser?

   £ ☐☐☐

2. A full sack of flour leaks 10 g of flour every second. After $7\frac{1}{2}$ minutes, all of the flour has leaked out of the sack. How much flour was in the sack originally, in kilograms? Circle the correct answer.

   A 7.5 kg   **B** 4.5 kg   **C** 75 kg   **D** 4.2 kg   **E** 45 kg

3. Michael makes 300 cards and sells $\frac{3}{5}$ of them. It costs 80p to make one card, and he sells each card for £2.50. How much money does he earn after subtracting the cost of making all of the cards?

   £ ☐☐☐.☐☐

4. A regular pentagon and a regular octagon have the same perimeter. Each side of the pentagon is 16 cm long. How long is each side of the octagon?

   ☐☐ cm

5. Lei records how far she walks on five days and puts the distances on a line graph.

   a) What is the mean distance she walks each day?

      ☐.☐ km

   b) What percentage of the total distance does she walk on Monday?

      ☐☐ %

6. A cleaning solution is made from bleach and water in the ratio 1 : 8. Kevin has a 750 ml bottle of bleach. He makes 2.7 litres of cleaning solution. How much bleach is left in the bottle?

   ☐☐☐☐ ml

7. Imogen buys a bag of sweets and eats 5% of the bag each day. How many days will it take her to eat $\frac{3}{4}$ of the bag?

   ☐☐

Practice Questions

8. Chinelo draws a shape on a coordinate grid. The corners of the shape have coordinates (x, y), (x + 2, y), (x, y − 6) and (x + 2, y − 6). What type of shape has she drawn? Circle the correct answer.

   A Square   **B** Rectangle   **C** Parallelogram   **D** Trapezium

9. Caroline runs 15 km to raise money for charity. She is sponsored £5 per kilometre for the first 10 km, then £8 for each kilometre after that. What is the mean amount she is sponsored per kilometre for her run? Circle the correct answer.

   A £6.50   **B** £6   **C** £9   **D** £5   **E** £7

10. Some items for sale at a cafe are shown on the right.

Menu	
Coffee	£1.80
Tea	£1.50
Brownie	£2.30
Cookie	£1.60

    a) Linda has a £20 note. She buys a coffee, a tea and a brownie. What percentage of £20 does she have left?

    ☐☐ %

    b) Annabel and Tamal buy two coffees, a brownie and a cookie. They share the cost in the ratio 2 : 1. How much does Annabel pay?

    £ ☐.☐☐

11. What fraction of the whole numbers from 1 to 20 are prime? Circle the correct answer.

    A $\frac{1}{8}$ **B** $\frac{1}{4}$ **C** $\frac{2}{5}$ **D** $\frac{8}{10}$ **E** $\frac{9}{20}$

12. Look at the diagram below. What is the value of p?

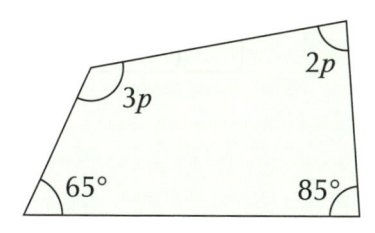

    (Quadrilateral with angles $3p$, $2p$, $85°$, $65°$)

    ☐☐ °

13. Tafsir planted a flower on 5th May. It was 5 cm tall when it was planted, and it grew 4 mm each day. How tall was the flower on 16th June?

    ☐☐.☐ cm

Section Seven — Mixed Problems

Mixed Practice Tests

If you want to attempt each mixed practice test more than once, you will need to print **multiple-choice answer sheets** for these questions from our website — go to www.cgpbooks.co.uk/11plusanswersheets. If you'd prefer to answer them in standard write-in format, either write your answers in the spaces provided or circle the **correct answer** from the options **A** to **E**.

Give yourself **7 minutes** to complete this test. Write down your score in the box at the end.

Test 1

1. How many lines of symmetry does a regular octagon have?

2. What is 4030 ml in litres?

   A 4.3 litres   B 40.3 litres   C 43 litres   D 4.03 litres   E 403 litres

3. Winston was born in MMIX. The church in his village was built 352 years before he was born. In what year, in digits, was the church built?

4. Megan calls her friend at 4:55 pm. The phone call lasts for 37 minutes. At what time does the call end? Give your answer using the 24-hour clock.

5. Round 23 486 to the nearest thousand.

6. 1452 ÷ 12 = 121. What is 1452 ÷ 4?

7. What is the area of the shape on the right?

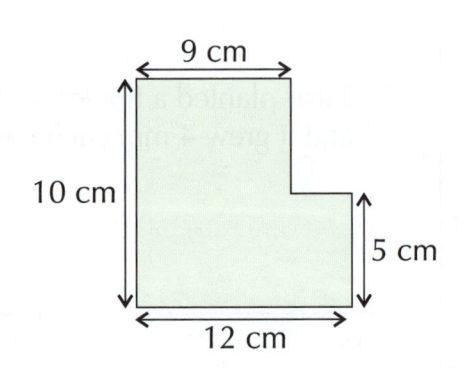

   ☐☐☐ cm²

Mixed Practice Tests

8. The table below shows the different types of cake sold at a cafe in one day.

	Large cakes	Small cakes	Total
Lemon	4		
Chocolate		7	
Vanilla	3		12
Total	10		30

a) What percentage of the total number of cakes sold weren't vanilla?

☐☐ %

b) How many small lemon cakes did they sell?

☐☐

c) The cafe owner asks his customers if they prefer tea, coffee or hot chocolate. He puts the information in a pie chart. $^2/_5$ of the customers he asked said they prefer tea and 35% said they prefer coffee.
What angle represents 'hot chocolate' on the pie chart?

☐☐☐ °

d) Hasif buys 6 scones from the cafe. Each scone costs 80p. How much change will he get if he pays with a £5 note?

A £0.60   B 40p   C £1.20   D 80p   E 20p

e) The cafe served 39 meals at lunch time. All of the meals were served with either chips or salad, but not both. Which statement below could be true?

A Half of the meals were served with chips.

B Twice as many meals were served with salad than with chips.

C Four more meals were served with chips than with salad.

D Three quarters of the meals were served with chips.

E Twelve more meals were served with salad than with chips.

Total (out of 12): ☐

Mixed Practice Tests

Give yourself **7 minutes** to complete this test. Write down your score in the box at the end.

Test 2

1. Which of the following numbers is the smallest?

   A 0.95   B 1.18   C 0.8   D 1.2   E 0.76

2. What is the smallest multiple of 9 that is also a cube number?

3. A box of 100 pencils costs £8. How much would it cost to buy 2400 pencils?

4. 393, 404, 415, ☐, 437, ...

   What number should go in the box in the sequence above?

5. The square on the coordinate grid on the right is translated so that the new coordinates of P are (−1, 2). What are the new coordinates of point S?

   A (−2, 3)   B (2, 1)   C (1, 2)
   D (3, −2)   E (4, −2)

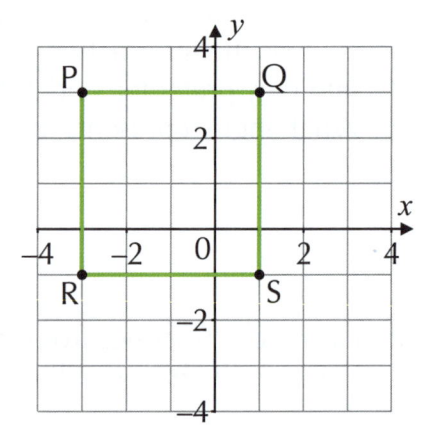

6. Tony and Julia share 36 sweets in the ratio 5 : 4. How many sweets does Julia get?

7. Olive builds the shape on the right out of cubes. Which shape below is the same as Olive's?

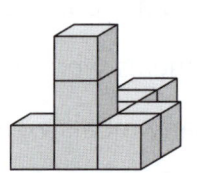

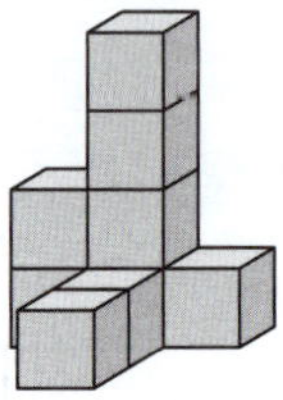

   A 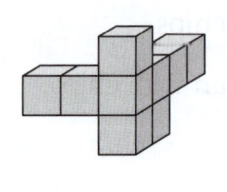   B 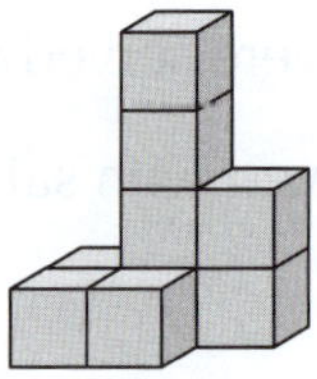   C 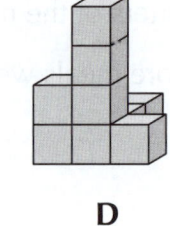   D 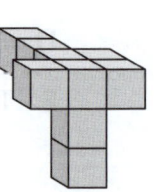   E

Mixed Practice Tests

Mixed Practice Tests

8. This pictogram shows where some Year 6 pupils went on their last holiday.

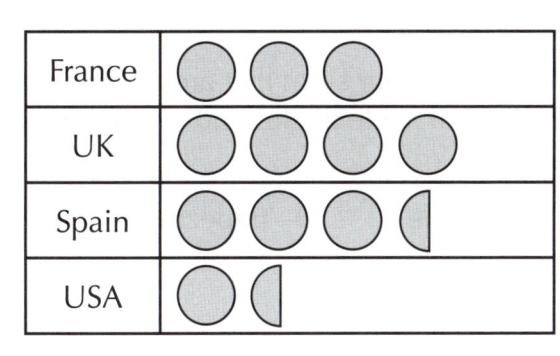

France	◯ ◯ ◯
UK	◯ ◯ ◯ ◯
Spain	◯ ◯ ◯ ◖
USA	◯ ◖

Key: ◯ = 2 pupils

a) How many more pupils went to France or Spain than went to the UK or USA?

b) What fraction of the pupils went to the USA on their last holiday?

   A $1/5$ **B** $3/12$ **C** $1/3$ **D** $1/2$ **E** $1/8$

c) One day in February, the temperature in San Francisco is 12 °C.
On the same day, the temperature in Chicago is –4 °C.
How much warmer is it in San Francisco than in Chicago?

   °C

d) Elsie has £271.42 in her savings. She gets £34.50 for her birthday, and then she spends £214.95 on plane tickets to Spain. How much money does she have left?

£

e) Whilst on holiday, Nasim wants to hire a rowing boat.
Hiring a rowing boat costs £8, and then £5 for each hour.
What is the cost, in pounds, of hiring a rowing boat for H hours?

   A $5 + 8H$ **B** $8 + 5H$ **C** $5 \times (8 + H)$ **D** $5 - 8H$ **E** $8 - 5H$

Total (out of 12):

Mixed Practice Tests

Give yourself **7 minutes** to complete this test. Write down your score in the box at the end.

Test 3

1. Bernie describes a shape. He says, "It has four sides that are all the same length, two pairs of parallel sides, a pair of equal acute angles and a pair of equal obtuse angles." What is Bernie's shape?

    A Square   B Kite   C Rectangle   D Trapezium   E Rhombus

2. What is 25% of 48?

3. Kyle has three parcels to deliver. The first parcel weighs 3.78 kg, the second parcel weighs 2.15 kg and the third parcel weighs 4.5 kg. What is the total weight of the three parcels?

    ☐☐.☐☐ kg

4. Sally measures the lengths of some keys.
    The lengths are 6 cm, 8 cm, 9.5 cm, 5 cm and 6.5 cm.
    What is the mean length of the keys?

    A 7.2 cm   B 8.5 cm   C 7 cm   D 6.8 cm   E 9 cm

5. What is 32 × 77 + 68 × 77?

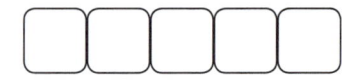

6. Eleanor makes salad dressing by mixing olive oil and vinegar in the ratio 3 : 2. She has 800 ml of vinegar. How many litres of salad dressing can she make?

    A 1.2 litres   B 2.4 litres   C 2 litres   D 4 litres   E 3.2 litres

7. This line chart shows the average daily sales of ice cream at an ice cream van from 2015 to 2019. Why is this graph misleading?

    A The horizontal axis doesn't go up in even steps.

    B The graph only shows data from five years.

    C We don't know what flavour ice creams were sold.

    D The vertical axis doesn't start from zero.

    E We don't know the exact number of ice creams sold each day.

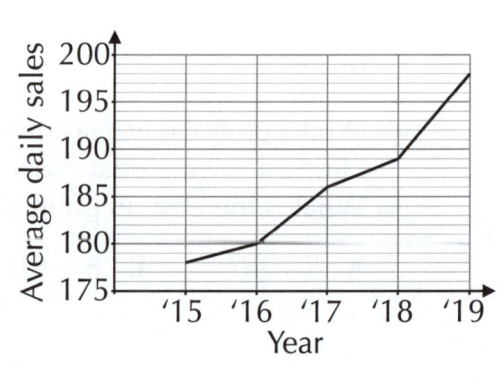

Mixed Practice Tests

Mixed Practice Tests

8. A bus timetable is shown below.

Angelby	1108	1234	1417
Bagthorpe	1125	1251	1434
Castleton	1147	1313	1456
Donford	1208	1334	1517

a) How long does the bus journey from Bagthorpe to Donford take?

☐☐ minutes

b) Greg wants to catch a bus from Angelby to Castleton. He needs to be in Castleton by 2:45 pm. It takes 12 minutes to get to the Angelby bus stop from his house. What is the latest time he can leave home to arrive in Castleton on time?
Give your answer using the 24-hour clock.

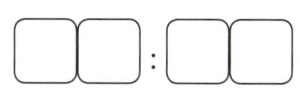

☐☐ : ☐☐

c) The bus company's logo is shown on the right.
What fraction of the logo is shaded?

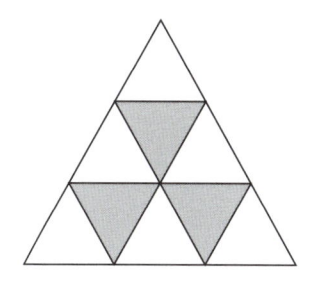

A $\frac{1}{4}$ B $\frac{1}{2}$ C $\frac{3}{8}$ D $\frac{2}{5}$ E $\frac{1}{3}$

d) A bus is 15 m long, rounded to the nearest metre.
What is the shortest possible length of the bus?

A 14.4 m   B 14.55 m   C 15.5 m   D 14.5 m   E 14 m

e) To get to school, Nick walks 660 m to the Castleton bus stop, and then travels 5.7 km on the bus. How far is Nick's journey to school, in kilometres?

☐☐.☐☐ km

Total (out of 12): ☐

Mixed Practice Tests

Give yourself **7 minutes** to complete this test. Write down your score in the box at the end.

Test 4

1. Five people record their scores on a video game.

Name	Jemma	Luke	Halima	Suzy	Patrick
Score	1831	1673	1828	1839	1799

   Who got the highest score?

   A Jemma   **B** Luke   **C** Halima   **D** Suzy   **E** Patrick

2. What is 37.2 − 24.83?

   ☐☐.☐☐

3. 40 pupils voted for their favourite day of the week. The results are shown in the bar chart, but the bar for Thursday is missing. How many pupils voted for Thursday?

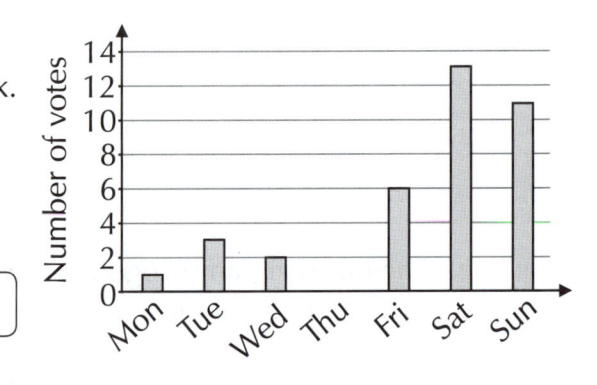

   ☐☐

4. A model train is made up of 8 identical carriages. Each carriage is 7.3 cm long. What is the total length of the model train?

   ☐☐.☐ cm

5. What is the size of angle *x* in the diagram on the right?

   A 76°   **B** 72°   **C** 108°
   D 104°   **E** 88°

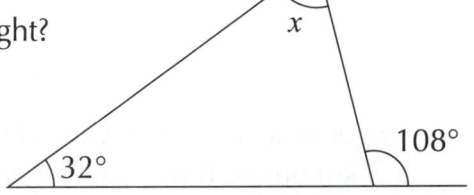

6. Look at the table on the right. Which number could go in the shaded section?

   A 4   **B** 12   **C** 1
   D 7   **E** 2

	Prime	Not prime
Factor of 12	?	6
Not a factor of 12	5	9

Mixed Practice Tests

7. Imani cuts four identical equilateral triangles and a square out of some card. She uses the shapes to make the star shown on the right. The star has a perimeter of 32 cm. What is the area of the square piece of card?

☐☐ cm²

8. Some children are making biscuits to sell at their school fair.

   a) Leah's recipe uses the ingredients on the right to make biscuit dough. Each biscuit uses 30 g of dough. She eats 5 of the biscuits before the fair. How many biscuits does she have left to sell?

   Ingredients
   Flour   360 g
   Butter 180 g
   Sugar   120 g

   ☐☐

   b) Write the ratio of butter to sugar in the recipe above in its simplest form.

   ☐☐ : ☐☐

   c) Bradley is using the same recipe as Leah. He has 600 grams of sugar. How many kilograms of flour does he need if he makes as many biscuits as he can?

   ☐☐.☐☐ kg

   d) Bradley packs his biscuits into a cuboid-shaped box that is 20 cm long and 15 cm wide. The box has a volume of 7500 cm³. What is the height of the box?

   ☐☐☐ cm

   e) Class 6A makes 729 biscuits between them. They sell them in packs of 12. They fill as many packs as they can. How many biscuits do they have left over?

   ☐☐

Total (out of 12): ☐

Mixed Practice Tests

There are **multiple-choice answer sheets** for these questions on our website — go to www.cgpbooks.co.uk/11plusanswersheets. If you want to attempt each test-style paper more than once, you will need to print a separate answer sheet for each attempt. If you'd prefer to answer the questions in write-in format, write directly on the test.

11+ Test-Style Paper 1
For Ages 10-11
Numerical Reasoning
For the CEM Test

Read the following:

Do not start the test until you are told to do so.

1. This test can be taken in either multiple-choice or write-in format.

2. If you are taking it as a multiple-choice test, you should mark your answer to each question in pencil on the answer sheet you've printed from www.cgpbooks.co.uk/11plusanswersheets. Mark the correct box quickly and neatly using a horizontal line.

3. If you are taking it as a write-in test, you should write your answer to each question in pencil on the paper. Write your answer carefully in the space provided or, if there is a range of options, mark the correct box quickly and neatly using a horizontal line.

4. If you make a mistake, rub it out and mark your new answer clearly.

5. You will have a total of 34 minutes to complete the test.

6. This paper includes examples showing you how to answer the questions. You may refer to these examples at any time as you work through the test.

7. Do as many questions as you can. For some questions you will be given a range of options — if you get stuck on one of these questions, choose the answer that you think is most likely to be correct, then move on to the next question. If you get stuck on a question for which no options are given, leave it and move on to the next question. If you have time at the end of the test, go back and have another go at the questions you could not answer.

8. You should do any rough working on a separate piece of paper.

Work carefully, but go as quickly as you can.

Test-Style Paper 1

Example Read these example questions. You may return to these examples at any time as you work through this test.

1) Which of the following numbers is not prime?   7 □   13 □   27 ■   31 □

2) Joey's pet lizard is 26.4 cm long. Aleena's lizard is 32 mm longer. How long is Aleena's lizard in centimetres?

  `2` `9` . `6` cm

⚠️ **Wait until you are told to go on** ⚠️

You have 34 minutes to complete this test

This test contains single-part and multi-part questions.
There are **21** questions in this test

1) Tanya is researching some local towns for a Geography project. She records the population of each town in the table below.

Town	Pondham	Setford	Thekeston	Bollenby
Population	29 157	28 891	29 086	29 172

a) Which of the towns has the largest population?

Pondham □   Setford □   Thekeston □   Bollenby □

b) What is the population of Thekeston to the nearest ten thousand?

c) Setford was founded in MDCXIV. Pondham was founded 100 years later. In what year was Pondham founded? Give your answer in digits.

Go to the next question ➡️

Test-Style Paper 1

2) The prices of some items sold at a sewing shop are shown below.

Plain fabric	£4.50 per metre
Flowery fabric	£6.10 per metre
Thread	£1.50 per spool
Sewing needles	£2.80 per pack

a) Janine buys three metres of flowery fabric and a spool of thread. She pays with a £20 note. How much change does she get?

☐☐ p

b) The shop makes £45 one day from selling spools of thread. How many spools of thread did they sell that day?

☐☐☐

c) There is a 15% discount on purchases of more than £20. Harry spends £24. What is the total cost after the discount?

£ ☐☐ . ☐☐

3) Exercise books come in packs of 10. Each pack costs £3.80.

a) How much does one exercise book cost?

☐☐☐ p

b) An exercise book has 120 pages. How many pages are there in 5 packs of exercise books?

☐☐☐☐☐

c) A school orders 300 exercise books. What is the total cost of their order?

£ ☐☐☐☐ . ☐☐

Test-Style Paper 1

4) Look at the Venn diagram below.

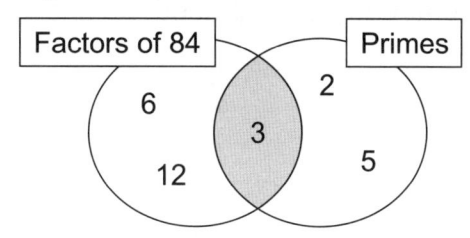

[Venn diagram: Factors of 84 circle contains 6, 12; overlap (shaded) contains 3; Primes circle contains 2, 5]

a) Which number has been put in the wrong section?

    2 ☐   3 ☐   5 ☐   12 ☐   6 ☐

b) What is the biggest number that can go in the shaded section? ☐☐

5) Niall times how long his paper round takes each weekday morning over one week. He records his data in a bar chart.

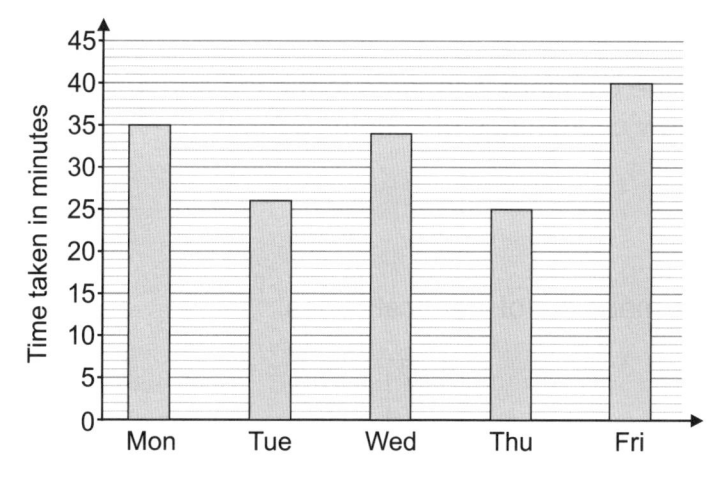

[Bar chart — Time taken in minutes: Mon 35, Tue 26, Wed 34, Thu 25, Fri 40]

a) How many minutes longer did the paper round take on Friday than on Tuesday? ☐☐ minutes

b) On Wednesday, Niall finished his paper round at 7:13 am. What time did he begin his paper round? ☐☐ : ☐☐ am

c) What is the mean time it took him to do his paper round? ☐☐ minutes

Go to the next question

Test-Style Paper 1

6) Saira and Lyle are playing a game where they make shapes by placing counters on a grid. Three counters have already been placed, as shown below.

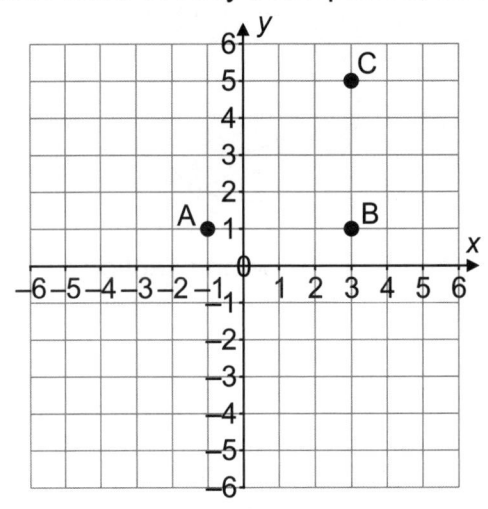

a) Saira places another counter. The four counters make a square.
Which of these could be the coordinates of the fourth counter?

(1, 5)   (1, –5)   (–1, 5)   (–1, –5)   (5, –1)
 ☐   ☐   ☐   ☐   ☐

b) Lyle translates the counters 2 squares to the left and 4 squares down.
What are the new coordinates of counter C?

(☐ , ☐)

7) The shape below is made out of identical cubes.

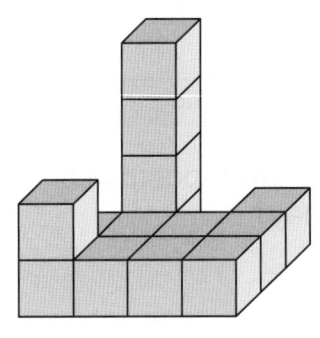

a) Which of the following is a side elevation of the shape?

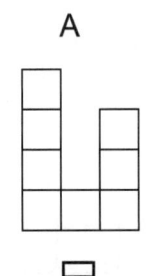

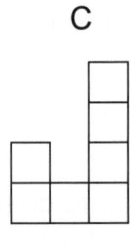

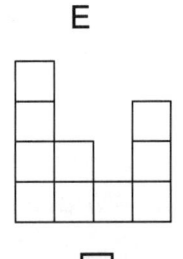

A   B   C   D   E
☐   ☐   ☐   ☐   ☐

b) Each cube has a side length of 2 cm.
What is the volume of the shape?

☐☐☐ cm³

Test-Style Paper 1

⑧ A sculpture is made of three separate pieces of stone.
The total height of the sculpture is 1.08 m. The first piece is 48 cm tall
and the second piece is 340 mm tall. How tall is the third piece, in cm?

☐☐ cm

⑨ What is the name of the new shape made
by reflecting this shape in the mirror line?

mirror line

Pentagon   Hexagon   Trapezium   Heptagon
   ☐   ☐   ☐   ☐

⑩ Carol sold raffle tickets for 4 weeks to raise money for charity.
She sold 339 tickets in Week 1, 627 in Week 2 and 484 in Week 3.

a) By the end of Week 4, she had sold 1800 tickets.
How many tickets did she sell in Week 4?

☐☐☐☐

b) She raised £2700 from selling raffle tickets.
How much did she sell each raffle ticket for?

£☐☐.☐☐

c) Carol spent £95 on the main raffle prize, and £15 each on 5 runner-up prizes.
She donated the rest of the money to charity. How much money did she donate?

£☐☐☐☐

Go to the next question ⇨

Test-Style Paper 1

11) Part of a train timetable is shown below.

Lakestone	1156	1245	1313	1402
Hartbridge	1209	1258	1326	1415
Wetherton	1232	1321	1349	1438
Ternslow	1258	1347	1415	1504

a) How long does it take to get from Lakestone to Wetherton?

☐☐ minutes

b) Deeva lives in Wetherton. It takes her 14 minutes to get to the station. She needs to be in Ternslow by 2 pm. What is the latest time that she can leave her house to arrive in Ternslow on time? Give your answer using the 24-hour clock.

☐☐ : ☐☐

Bert gets the 13:26 train from Hartbridge to Wetherton, then cycles to Ternslow.

c) He arrives in Ternslow at 15:19. How long does he spend cycling?

☐☐☐ minutes

d) He cycles 30 km per hour. How many kilometres does he cycle from Wetherton to Ternslow?

☐☐☐ km

12) Rachel asks some people in an office whether they like milk and sugar in their tea. She records their answers in the table below.

	Milk	No milk
Sugar	9	2
No sugar	14	3

a) How many more people like milk than don't like milk in their tea?

☐☐

b) What fraction of the people asked like milk and no sugar in their tea?

$\frac{1}{3}$ ☐ $\frac{2}{3}$ ☐ $\frac{1}{2}$ ☐ $\frac{1}{4}$ ☐ $\frac{7}{25}$ ☐

Test-Style Paper 1

13 A bag contains 76 marbles, which are either red or green.
There is a square number of red marbles and a cube number of green marbles.
How many red marbles are there in the bag?

14 A rectangular piece of card is cut into triangles along the dotted lines.

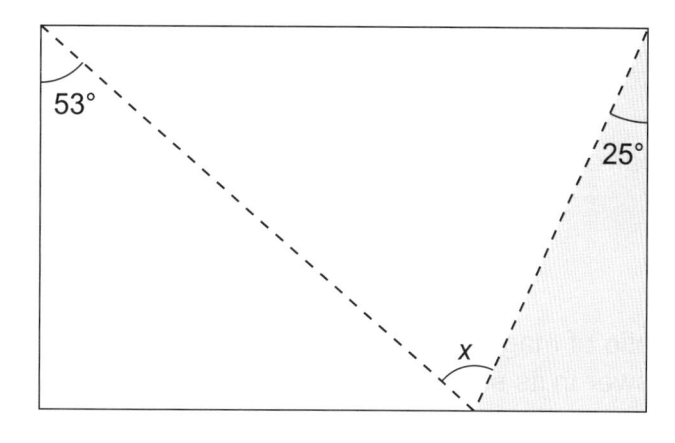

a) What type of triangle is the shaded triangle?

    Isosceles   Right-angled   Equilateral   Can't tell

b) What is the size of angle x?

15 Jeremy goes ice skating with four friends. For each person, ice skating costs £7 per hour, plus £4 to hire the ice skates. Everyone in the group hires ice skates.

a) Which of the following is the correct formula to work out the cost of one person going ice skating for h hours, in pounds?

    $7 + 4h$ $7h + 4$ $7h - 4$ $4 + 7 + h$ $4 - 7h$

b) The ice skating rink offers £15 off the total cost for groups of 4 or more. How much would it cost in total for Jeremy and his four friends to all go ice skating for two hours?

£

Go to the next question

Test-Style Paper 1

16) Wei records the number of different types of birds she sees in her garden one day.

Sparrow	◇ ◇ ◇
Magpie	◇ ◁
Blackbird	◇ ◸
Robin	◇ ◇ ◇

Key: ◇ = 4 birds

a) How many sparrows and blackbirds did she see in total?

☐☐

b) What is the ratio of magpies to robins that Wei saw?
Give your answer in its simplest form.

☐ : ☐

Wei opens a new bag of bird seed on Tuesday. She feeds the birds 150 g of seed each day. She uses the last 150 g in the bag on Sunday.

c) How many kilograms of bird seed were in the bag?

☐☐ . ☐ kg

17) Matt is following a recipe for vegetable soup.
1.2 kg of onions are needed to make 8 portions of soup.

a) How many grams of onions does Matt need to make 12 portions of soup?

☐☐☐☐ g

b) The ratio of onions to carrots in the recipe is 3 : 4.
How many kilograms of carrots does Matt need to make 4 portions of soup?

☐☐ . ☐ kg

Test-Style Paper 1

18 What is (5 − 2)³ + 8 × 2?

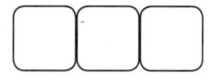

19 Hiram asked some Year 6 pupils how they travelled to school that morning.
He displays their answers on this pie chart.

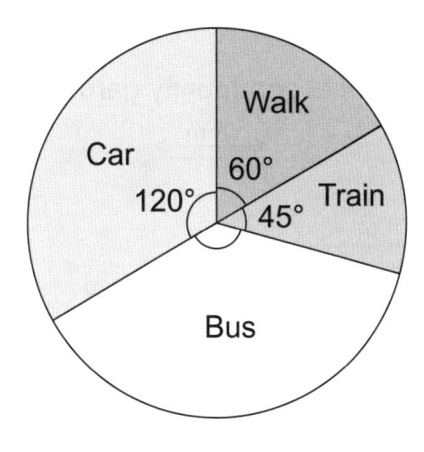

a) What is the angle of the 'bus' sector?

b) What fraction of the pupils got the train to school?

| ¼ | ⅖ | ⅓ | ⅛ | ⅙ |

c) 12 pupils said they walked to school.
How many Year 6 pupils did he ask in total?

d) 25% of the pupils who travelled by car came in a blue car.
How many pupils came in a blue car?

Go to the next question

Test-Style Paper 1

20 The *n*th term rule for a sequence is 7*n* + 1.

a) Which of the following numbers is not in the sequence?

36   22   76   43   64

b) What is the 20th term in the sequence?

21 Toshiko sketches a plan of her local community garden, shown in the diagram below.

a) What is the area of the community garden, including the pond?

☐☐☐ m²

b) Fencing costs £8 per metre. How much would it cost to put a fence around the entire perimeter of the garden?

£ ☐☐☐

The pond in the community garden has a volume of 6 m³.
It is filled with a hosepipe at a rate of 0.2 m³ of water every minute.
The hosepipe is turned off when the pond is full.

c) How long does it take to fill the pond?

☐☐☐ minutes

d) The pond is empty when the hosepipe is turned on at 1:35 pm.
What time is the hosepipe turned off? Give your answer using the 24-hour clock.

☐☐ : ☐☐

This is the end of the test.

Test-Style Paper 1

133

CGP

There are **multiple-choice answer sheets** for these questions on our website — go to www.cgpbooks.co.uk/11plusanswersheets. If you want to attempt each test-style paper more than once, you will need to print a separate answer sheet for each attempt. If you'd prefer to answer the questions in write-in format, write directly on the test.

11+ Test-Style Paper 2
For Ages 10-11
Numerical Reasoning
For the CEM Test

Read the following:

Do not start the test until you are told to do so.

1. This test can be taken in either multiple-choice or write-in format.

2. If you are taking it as a multiple-choice test, you should mark your answer to each question in pencil on the answer sheet you've printed from www.cgpbooks.co.uk/11plusanswersheets. Mark the correct box quickly and neatly using a horizontal line.

3. If you are taking it as a write-in test, you should write your answer to each question in pencil on the paper. Write your answer carefully in the space provided or, if there is a range of options, mark the correct box quickly and neatly using a horizontal line.

4. If you make a mistake, rub it out and mark your new answer clearly.

5. You will have a total of 34 minutes to complete the test.

6. This paper includes examples showing you how to answer the questions. You may refer to these examples at any time as you work through the test.

7. Do as many questions as you can. For some questions you will be given a range of options — if you get stuck on one of these questions, choose the answer that you think is most likely to be correct, then move on to the next question. If you get stuck on a question for which no options are given, leave it and move on to the next question. If you have time at the end of the test, go back and have another go at the questions you could not answer.

8. You should do any rough working on a separate piece of paper.

Work carefully, but go as quickly as you can.

Test-Style Paper 2

Example — Read these example questions. You may return to these examples at any time as you work through this test.

1) Which of the following numbers is not prime?   7 ☐   13 ☐   27 ■   31 ☐

2) Joey's pet lizard is 26.4 cm long. Aleena's lizard is 32 mm longer. How long is Aleena's lizard in centimetres?   2 9 . 6 cm

⚠ **Wait until you are told to go on** ⚠

You have 34 minutes to complete this test

This test contains single-part and multi-part questions.
There are **22** questions in this test

1) Emmett sets off on a 12.8 km walk.

a) How long is the walk in metres?   ☐☐☐☐☐ m

After he has walked 7.52 km, he stops to have lunch.

b) How much further does he have left to walk in kilometres?   ☐☐.☐☐ km

c) Emmett started his walk at 10:40 am. He walked for 2 hours and 43 minutes in total, and stopped for 45 minutes to have lunch. What time did he finish his walk? Give your answer using the 24-hour clock.

☐☐:☐☐

Test-Style Paper 2

② At a village fair, each person guesses how many jelly beans are in a jar.
The four closest guesses are shown in the table below.

Name	Zara	Jaleel	Maggie	David
Guess	3265	3782	3249	3519

a) Which of the following people guessed the smallest number of jelly beans?

　　Zara　　　　Jaleel　　　　Maggie　　　　David
　　☐　　　　　☐　　　　　　☐　　　　　　☐

There are exactly 3672 jelly beans in the jar.

b) How far away was David's guess from the actual number of jelly beans?

c) Jaleel wins the jar of jelly beans. He splits the beans into 18 equal piles.
How many jelly beans are in each pile?

③ Look at the set of numbers below.

| 8 | 5 | 18 | 10 | 15 | 9 | 1 | 13 |

a) How many of the numbers in the set are prime?

b) What is the biggest number in the set that is a factor of both 60 and 90?

c) How many numbers in the set are either square or cube numbers?

Go to the next question

Test-Style Paper 2

4) Paloma measured the temperature in her greenhouse throughout a summer day. She recorded the temperatures on this line graph.

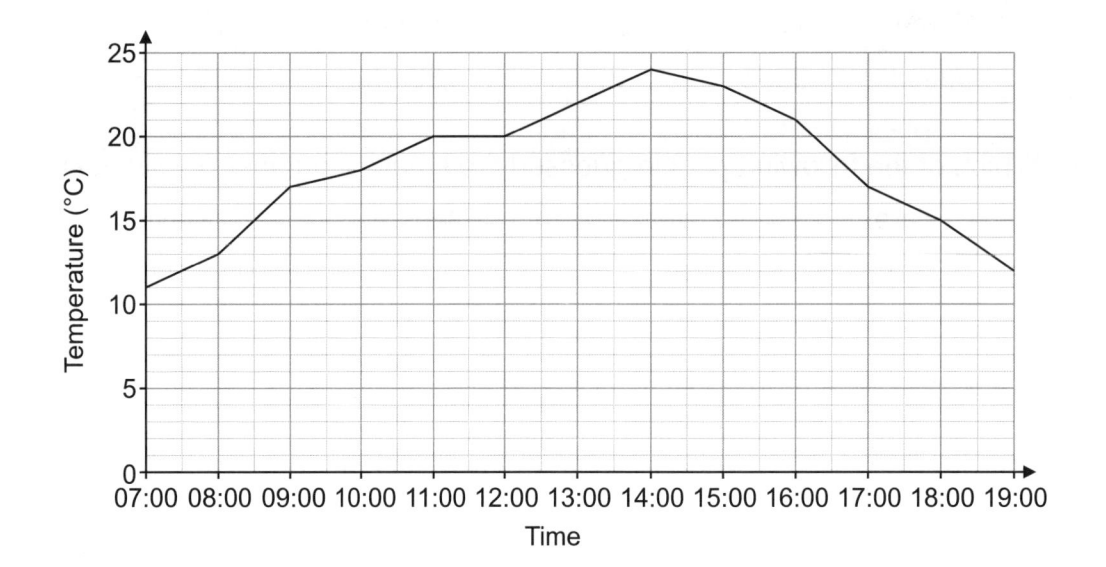

a) What is the difference between the highest and lowest temperatures?

☐☐ °C

b) For how many hours was the temperature in the greenhouse at least 17 °C?

☐☐ hours

c) Paloma measured the temperatures in the greenhouse again on a winter day. The temperature at 6 pm on the winter day was 19 °C colder than at 6 pm on the summer day. What was the temperature at 6 pm on the winter day?

–4 °C   3 °C   4 °C   –3 °C   –5 °C
☐   ☐   ☐   ☐   ☐

5) Which of these amounts is the largest?

½ of 30   25% of 40   ⅘ of 25   50% of 20   ¼ of 60
☐   ☐   ☐   ☐   ☐

Test-Style Paper 2

6) Eli and Olivia pick blackberries to make some fruit pies.
Eli picks 1456 g of blackberries and Olivia picks 2371 g.

a) How many grams of blackberries did they pick in total?

☐☐☐☐ g

Each fruit pie also uses 480 g of apples.

b) How many kilograms of apples do they need to make three fruit pies?

☐ . ☐☐ kg

c) Each of the three pies is cut into 8 equal slices.
Olivia has two slices of pie, Eli has three slices and Eli's sister has one slice. What percentage of the three pies is left?

☐☐ %

7) Four members of a running club record how long it took them to run 5 kilometres, rounded to the nearest minute.

Name	Marie	Kazuo	Lyla	Jon
Time (minutes)	26	24	22	32

a) What is the shortest possible time it could have taken Lyla to run 5 km?

☐☐ minutes ☐☐ seconds

b) What was the mean time taken to complete the 5 km run?

☐☐ minutes

Kazuo runs in a charity race. For every 250 m he runs, Marie sponsors him £1.20, Lyla sponsors him £1.30 and Jon sponsors him £1.50.

c) How much do they sponsor Kazuo per kilometre in total?

£ ☐☐ . ☐☐

d) He raises £320 from their sponsorship. How many kilometres does Kazuo run?

25 km   5 km   32 km   16 km   20 km
 ☐   ☐   ☐   ☐   ☐

Go to the next question ➡

Test-Style Paper 2

8) Miss Shaw has a 2 litre bottle of PVA glue. She fills x identical pots with glue.

a) Each pot holds 80 ml of glue. Which of the following is the correct expression for the amount of glue left in the bottle in millilitres?

$8x - 2000$ ☐ $2 - 80x$ ☐ $2000 - 80x$ ☐ $80x - 2000$ ☐ $2000 - 80 - x$ ☐

b) Miss Shaw fills 15 pots with glue. How much glue is left in the bottle in litres?

☐.☐☐ litres

9) Jasmine draws a shape on the coordinate grid below.

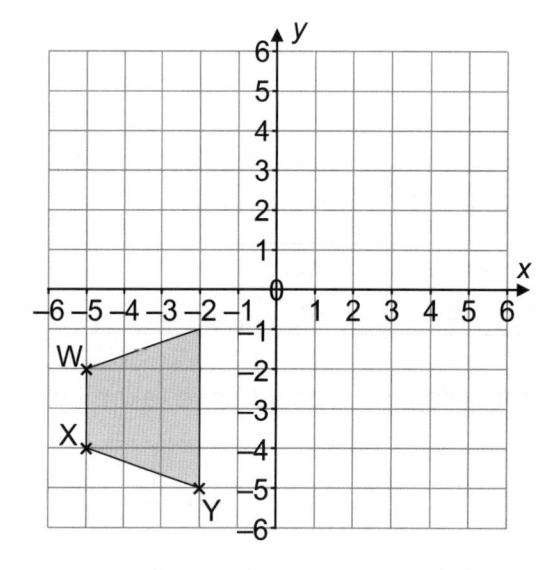

a) How many lines of symmetry does the shape have?

☐

b) She reflects the shape in the x-axis.
What are the coordinates of W after the reflection?

$(-5, 2)$ ☐ $(1, -5)$ ☐ $(5, -2)$ ☐ $(-2, 5)$ ☐ $(1, -2)$ ☐

c) She then translates the original shape. After the translation, Y has coordinates $(3, -4)$. What are the coordinates of X after the shape has been translated?

$(0, 3)$ ☐ $(-2, -4)$ ☐ $(5, 1)$ ☐ $(-4, 1)$ ☐ $(0, -3)$ ☐

Test-Style Paper 2

10) A sequence begins 3, 7, 10, 17, 27...
What is the seventh term in the sequence?

11) 618 × 14 = 8652

What is 618 × 7?

12) Logan cooks breakfast for the guests at a hotel.

a) One morning, he uses 135 eggs to make scrambled eggs. Each portion uses 3 eggs. How many portions of scrambled eggs does he make?

b) A tray of 12 eggs costs £1.80.
How much would it cost to buy 2400 eggs?

Part of the breakfast menu at the hotel is shown below.

MENU	
Waffles	£4.00
Pancakes	£5.00
Scrambled eggs	£5.50
Omelette	£5.75
Coffee	£2.00

c) Annie's table order three pancakes, one omelette and three cups of coffee. What is the cost of the order rounded to the nearest whole pound?

d) Gregor and Noah's breakfast costs £21 in total.
They split the cost in the ratio 2:1. How much does Gregor pay?

Go to the next question

Test-Style Paper 2

13) The design on the right is made out of five tiles.
Four of the tiles are identical regular hexagons.

a) What shape is the grey tile?

Trapezium   Square   Rhombus   Pentagon
☐   ☐   ☐   ☐

b) The perimeter of the design is 48 cm.
What is the perimeter of the grey tile?

☐☐ cm

c) A grey tile costs ⅓ as much as a hexagon tile.
Each hexagon tile costs £3.60. What is the total cost of the design?

£☐☐.☐☐

Douglas uses the hexagon tiles to make the first three patterns in a sequence.

Pattern 1   Pattern 2   Pattern 3

d) How many tiles are there in the fifth pattern in the sequence?

☐☐

14) Geraint writes down how many acorns he finds each day for 5 days.

Day	Monday	Tuesday	Wednesday	Thursday	Friday
Acorns	7	?	6	5	8

The number for Tuesday is missing, but the mean number of acorns
he found each day was 6. How many acorns did he find on Tuesday?

☐☐

15) Peggy thinks of a number. She multiplies it by 7 and then adds 11.
The result is 74. What was Peggy's original number?

☐☐

Test-Style Paper 2

16 Samira makes a flower out of 4 identical right-angled triangles, shown below. Each triangle has a width of 5 cm and a vertical height of 12 cm.

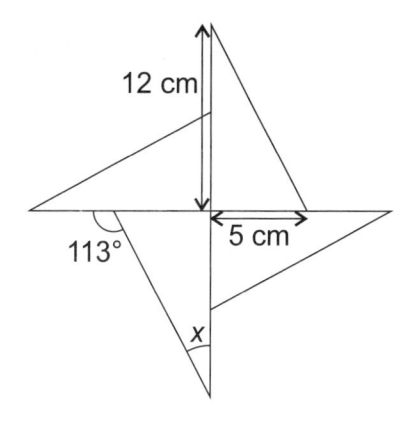

a) What is the total area of the flower? ☐☐☐ cm²

b) What is the size of angle x? ☐☐☐ °

17 Clara is packing pieces of toffee into a cuboid box. Each piece is a cube with 2 cm long sides. She packs as many pieces of toffee as she can into the box, and then removes 10 pieces. How many pieces of toffee are left in the box?

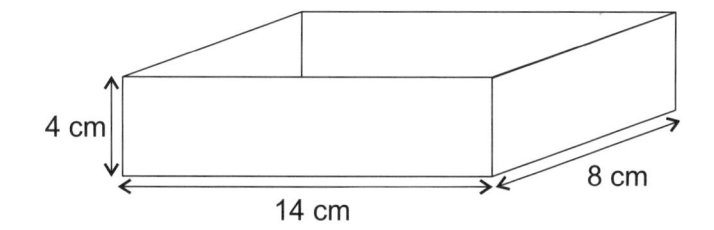

☐☐☐

18 Which of these expressions is the same as 3(a − 5)?

3a − 5   a + 15   3a − 15   3a + 12   a − 15
  ☐   ☐   ☐   ☐   ☐

Go to the next question

Test-Style Paper 2

19) A car park has 200 parking spaces. At 9 am, $\frac{2}{5}$ of the parking spaces are being used. By 10 am, another $\frac{3}{20}$ of the parking spaces are being used.

a) What fraction of the parking spaces are free at 10 am? $\frac{9}{20}$ ☐ $\frac{21}{100}$ ☐ $\frac{7}{10}$ ☐ $\frac{11}{20}$ ☐

b) Two hours later, there are 40 more cars parked. How many spaces are being used now? ☐☐☐

Each parking space is 2.5 m wide, and there is a 20 cm gap between each space, as shown in the diagram. There are 8 parking spaces in each row.

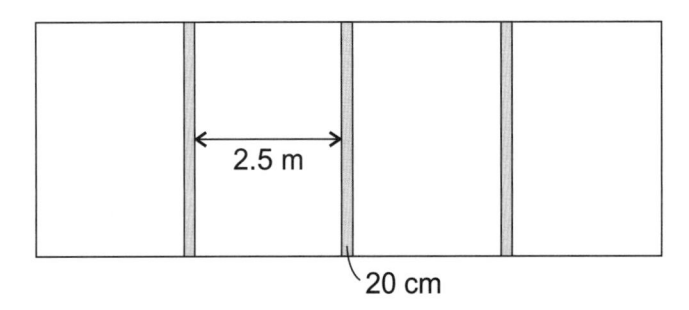

c) How long is each row of parking spaces? ☐☐.☐ m

20) Carys sees the chart below in a newspaper. Why is the chart misleading?

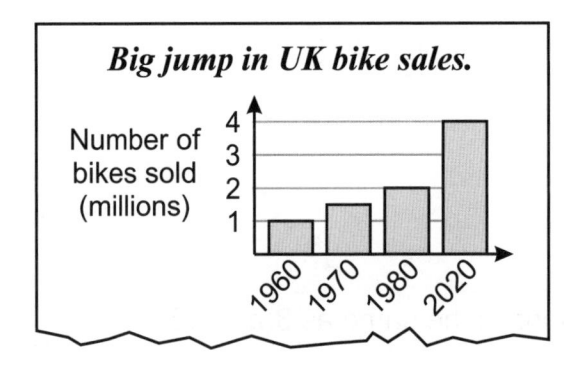

Big jump in UK bike sales.

☐ A: It doesn't show the number of bikes sold in other countries.
☐ B: The graph shows no data from before 1960.
☐ C: The scale on the horizontal axis is uneven.
☐ D: The number of bikes should be written in thousands.
☐ E: A line graph would be a better way to show the data.

21) Howard asked 60 people how many cats they own.
He records their answers on this pie chart.

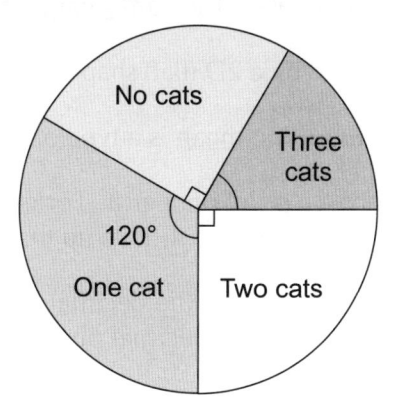

a) What is the angle of the 'three cats' sector?

b) What fraction of the people asked own fewer than two cats?

7/10   3/8   5/6   7/12   1/3

Abigail and Hamza buy the same cat food. Abigail's cats eat a bag of cat food every six days and Hamza's cats eat a bag every eight days.

c) They both open a new bag of cat food on the same day.
How many days will it be before they next open a new bag on the same day?

d) They both open a new bag of cat food on 14th June.
What is the next date that they will both open a new bag on the same day?

22nd June   8th July   28th June   28th July   16th July

22) Which of the following nets would fold up to make a cube with the shaded faces on opposite sides?

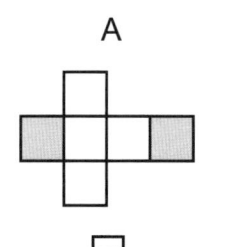

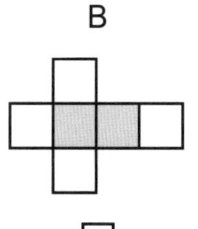

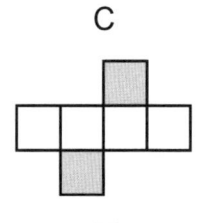

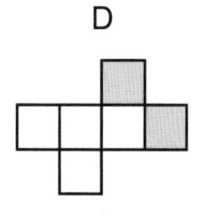

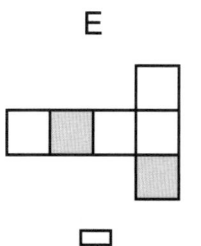

A   B   C   D   E

This is the end of the test.

Test-Style Paper 2

Glossary

acute angles	Angles that measure less than 90°. They are smaller than right angles.
area	The amount of space covered by a 2D (flat) shape. It is measured in square units (e.g. cm^2).
average	A typical (or 'normal' value). The mean is a type of average.
coordinates	They tell you the position of a point on a grid. For example, (3, 4) means 3 units along the horizontal x-axis and 4 units up the vertical y-axis.
decimal places	The places in a number to the right of the decimal point. For example, the number 4.56 has 2 decimal places.
degrees, °	The units used to measure angles. For example, a right angle measures 90°.
denominator	The bottom number of a fraction.
equivalent	Something that has the same value. For example, ½ and ²⁄₄ are equivalent fractions.
estimate	An estimate is a sensible guess at the answer. You can use rounding to help you estimate answers.
factor	A whole number that divides exactly into another whole number. For example, the factors of 6 are 1, 2, 3 and 6.
frequency	How many times something appears in a set of data.
mass	Mass is what most people mean when they say 'weight'. A brick has a greater mass than a loaf of bread. Mass is measured in grams or kilograms.
multiple	Multiples are the numbers in a times table that goes on forever. For example, the multiples of 4 are 4, 8, 12, 16...
numerator	The top number of a fraction.
obtuse angles	Angles that measure more than 90° but less than 180°. They're bigger than right angles.
parallel	Parallel lines, faces and edges are always the same distance apart. They will never meet or cross.
perimeter	The distance around the outside of a shape.
perpendicular	Lines, faces or edges that meet each other at right angles (or would meet at right angles if you extended them) are perpendicular.
polygon	A 2D (flat) shape with straight sides.
prime	A prime number is a number that has exactly two factors: 1 and itself. For example, 2, 3, 5 and 7 are all prime numbers.
prime factor	A factor of a larger number which is also a prime number. Any whole number that isn't prime can be split up into a set of prime factors. For example, 5 and 2 are the prime factors of 10.
ratio	A comparison between one part and another part. For example, if there were 4 girls and 1 boy on a bus, the ratio of boys to girls would be 1:4.
volume	The amount of space taken up by a 3D shape. It is measured in cubed units (e.g. cm^3).

Glossary

Answers

Section One — Working with Numbers

Page 6 — Place Value

1. **E** — All the numbers have the same units, so you need to look at the tenths. Four of the numbers have 4 in the tenths (Option B has 5, so it's not the answer), which means you need to look at the hundredths. E has the smallest number of hundredths, 3, so E is the answer.
2. **B** — A — incorrect, the numbers are 0.03 and 0.3 away from 7.
   B — correct, both numbers are 0.11 away from 7.
   C — incorrect, the numbers are 0.2 and 0.02 away from 7.
   D — incorrect, the numbers are 0.06 and 0.1 away from 7.
   E — incorrect, the numbers are 0.1 and 0.19 away from 7.

Page 8 — Rounding Up and Down

1. **D** — The 7 (in the ten thousands column) is being rounded. The 4 (in the thousands column) is less than 5 so 174 782 rounds down to 170 000.

Page 10 — Addition

1. **B** — Round each value to the nearest pound: £13.89 rounds up to £14.00. £3.35 rounds down to £3.00. £12.30 rounds down to £12.00. Add the rounded values together to estimate the answer: £14.00 + £3.00 + £12.00 = £29.00. The answer is either B or D. As you rounded down by 65p and up by 11p, the estimate is lower than the actual answer. So the actual answer must be B — £29.54. (You could also use a written method.)
2. **48.43 seconds** — Add the four numbers together using the column method:
   ```
     1 2 . 3 7
     1 1 . 8 8
     1 3 . 2 4
   + 1 0 . 9 4
   ─────────
     4 8 . 4 3
           2
   ```
   Their total time for the race was 48.43 seconds.

Page 12 — Subtraction

1. **E** — You need to subtract 48.28 from 75.63.
   Partition 48.28 into 40.00, 8.00, 0.20 and 0.08.
   75.63 − 40.00 = 35.63, then 35.63 − 8.00 = 27.63
   27.63 − 0.20 = 27.43, and 27.43 − 0.08 = 27.35
2. **Anita** — Use the rounding method to estimate the difference in scores for each person. Round each score to the nearest whole number:
   Joe: 62 − 58 = 4%   Holly: 64 − 60 = 4%
   Lucille: 63 − 63 = 0% Anita: 65 − 60 = 5%
   (Dave's score decreased between test 1 and test 2, so Dave is not included.) As no one else's score increased by around 5%, Anita is the correct answer.

Page 14 — Multiplying and Dividing by 10, 100 and 1000

1. **B** — Start by working out how many books of tickets were sold. Divide the number of tickets sold by the number of tickets in a book: 1000 ÷ 10 = 100 books. Then divide the amount of money made by the number of books sold to find the cost of each book: 375 ÷ 100 = £3.75.
2. **0.0042** — 4.2 ÷ 10 = 0.42. The number that fills in the blank should equal 0.42 when it's multiplied by 100. So, divide 0.42 by 100 to find the missing number. 0.42 ÷ 100 = 0.0042.

Page 17 — Multiplication

1. **27 650** — 350 is 100 times larger than 3.5. 79 is 10 times larger than 7.9. So, the answer to 350 × 79 will be 1000 (100 × 10) times larger than 27.65. 27.65 × 1000 = 27 650.

2. **A** — Round the cost of the toy robot up to £5.50, then multiply by 6. Partition £5.50 to make the multiplication easier: (£5.00 × 6) + (£0.50 × 6) = £30 + £3 = £33. Then subtract the 6p that you rounded up by to get the answer: £33 − £0.06 = £32.94
3. **D** — Estimate the answer by rounding each value to the nearest whole number and then multiplying the rounded values together. 6.9 rounds up to 7, 8.2 rounds down to 8. 8 × 7 = 56, so the answer is around 56. The only realistic option is option D, 56.58.
4. **954** — Use written multiplication to find the answer:
   ```
         5 3
   ×     1 8
   ─────────
       4 2₂4
   +   5 3 0
   ─────────
       9 5 4
   ```

Page 20 — Division

1. **2.2** — First, convert the decimal into a whole number: 8.8 × 10 = 88. Then do the division: 88 ÷ 4 = 22. You multiplied 8.8 by 10 at the beginning, so divide your answer by 10 now: 22 ÷ 10 = 2.2.
2. **11** — Divide 14.50 by 1.30 to see how many lots of 1.30 there are in 14.50. Partition 14.50 into numbers that are easier to work with. Find a number that's close to 14.50 and is a multiple of 1.30 — there are 10 lots of 1.30 in 13.00, which leaves you with 1.50 left over. This is enough to buy 1 more soft toy (1.50 − 1.30 = 0.20). The total number of toys you can buy is 10 + 1 = 11.
3. **C** — The answer to 19 200 ÷ 4 will be four times larger than the answer to 19 200 ÷ 16 (because 4 is four times smaller than 16). So, multiply 1200 by 4 to find the answer to 19 200 ÷ 4. 1200 × 4 = 4800.
4. **33** — You need to divide 264 by 8. Split 264 into two smaller numbers that are easier to divide — e.g. 64 and 200. 64 ÷ 8 = 8 and 200 ÷ 8 = 25. Add the answers together to find the final answer: 8 + 25 = 33 levels
5. **£112** — Divide £1680 by 15 using long division.
   ```
         0 1 1 2
      15│1 6 8 0
       − 1 5
         ─────
           1 8
         − 1 5
           ───
             3 0
           − 3 0
             ───
               0
   ```

Page 22 — Mixed Calculations

1. **18** — Follow BODMAS to do the calculations in the correct order.
   6 + 4 × 3² ÷ (16 − 13) = 6 + 4 × 3² ÷ 3
   = 6 + 4 × 9 ÷ 3 = 6 + 36 ÷ 3 = 6 + 12 = 18.
2. **14 610** — 1.7 and 8.3 are both multiplied by 1450.
   Add 1.7 and 8.3 together and multiply the total by 1450:
   1.7 + 8.3 = 10, so 10 × 1450 = 14 500.
   Then you need to add on 110: 14 500 + 110 = 14 610

Pages 23-26 — Practice Questions

1. **C** — All the numbers have the same ten thousands, so look at the thousands. B has 3 thousands and the rest have 4, so it can't be B. Look at the hundreds — D has 2 hundreds and the others have 3, so D isn't the answer. Then look at the tens — C has 5 tens and A has 2 tens, so the answer is C.
2. **130** — There are ten divisions between 100 and 150. The difference between 100 and 150 is 50, so each division is worth 50 ÷ 10 = 5. The arrow is pointing to the 6th division to the right of 100, so it is pointing at 100 + (6 × 5) = 130.
3. **C** — 4.7 is 0.3 away from 5. 5.35 is 0.35 away from 5. 5.15 is 0.15 away from 5. 4.8 and 5.2 are both 0.2 away from 5. 0.15 is the smallest, so the answer is C.

4 a) **20** — The 1 (in the tens column) is being rounded. The 9 (in the ones column) is more than 5, so 19.21 rounds up to 20.
   b) **19** — The 9 (in the ones column) is being rounded. The 2 (in the tenths column) is less than 5, so 19.21 rounds down to 19.

5 **60 000** — The 5 (in the ten thousands column) is being rounded. The digit in the thousands column is 5, so 55 300 rounds up to 60 000.

6 **550 000** — The number will be smaller than 600 000, so the answer will have 5 hundred thousands. The digit in the ten thousands column has to be the smallest digit that rounds up, which is 5, so the answer is 550 000.

7 **5622** — 999 is 1 less than 1000. 4623 + 1000 = 5623, so subtract 1 to find 4623 + 999 = 5623 − 1 = 5622.

8 **C** — 8.9 is 0.1 less than 9 and 7.9 is 0.1 less than 8. So 8.9 + 7.9 is 0.1 + 0.1 = 0.2 less than 9 + 8. 9 + 8 = 17, so 8.9 + 7.9 = 17 − 0.2 = 16.8 cm — option C.

9 **28.2** — Add up the four numbers using the column method. Write 7 as 7.0.
```
    8 . 4
    9 . 1
    7 . 0
  + 3 . 7
  -------
   28 . 2
      1
```
So her total score was 28.2.

10 **B** — Partition 6.78 into 6.00, 0.70 and 0.08. 90 − 6.00 = 84.00, then 84.00 − 0.70 = 83.30 and 83.30 − 0.08 = 83.22.

11 **5330** — Subtract using the column method.
```
    7 4 5 0
  − 2 1 2 0
  ---------
    5 3 3 0
```

12 a) **A** — Add up the three numbers using the column method.
```
    2 . 1 8
    4 . 6 5
  + 3 . 2 2
  ---------
   10 . 0 5
     1 1
```
So they have £10.05 in total.

   b) **£1.43** — You need to subtract £3.22 from £4.65. Partition £3.22 into £3.00, £0.20 and £0.02. £4.65 − £3.00 = £1.65, then £1.65 − £0.20 = £1.45 and £1.45 − £0.02 = £1.43. So Josh has £1.43 more than Tammy.

13 **£6.51** — First, subtract £22.99 from £50. £22.99 is £0.01 less than £23, so £50 − £22.99 = £50 − £23 + £0.01 = £27 + £0.01 = £27.01. Now partition £20.50 into £20.00 and £0.50 and subtract from £27.01. £27.01 − £20.00 = £7.01, then £7.01 − £0.50 = £6.51. So Monib has £6.51 left.

14 a) **8022** — 4578 tickets were sold for show 1 and 3444 tickets were sold for show 3. Add these numbers with the column method.
```
    4 5 7 8
  + 3 4 4 4
  ---------
    8 0 2 2
      1 1 1
```

   b) **1013** — First, find the number of tickets sold for shows 2 and 3 combined. Partition 2018 (the tickets sold for show 2) into 2000, 10 and 8 then add to 3444 (the tickets sold for show 3). 3444 + 2000 = 5444, then 5444 + 10 = 5454 and 5454 + 8 = 5462. Then subtract this from 6475 (the tickets sold for show 4) using the column method.
```
    6 4 7 5
  − 5 4 6 2
  ---------
    1 0 1 3
```
So 1013 more tickets were sold for show 4.

15 **D** — To divide by 100, move the digits two places to the right. 1468 ÷ 100 = 14.68, so the answer is option D.

16 **C** — The opposite of multiplication is division, so divide 57 840 by 1000 to find the missing number. To divide by 1000, move the digits three places to the right. 57 840 ÷ 1000 = 57.84.

17 **£127.00** — Multiply the number of bars by the cost of each bar. To multiply by 100, move the digits two places to the left. 100 × £1.27 = £127.

18 **A** — You would need to divide the mass of the first pile by 100 to work out the mass of the second pile. You need to multiply the mass of the second pile by 10 to work out the mass of the third pile. Combining these statements tells you that you would have to divide the mass of the first pile by 100 then multiply by 10 to find the mass of the third pile. Dividing by 100 then multiplying by 10 is the same as dividing by 10, so the third pile is 10 times lighter than the first pile.

19 **120** — First, work out the total number of marbles he buys: 12 × 100 = 1200. Then divide by the number of boxes to work out how many marbles are in each box: 1200 ÷ 10 = 120 marbles.

20 **168** — First, work out the number of fish they eat in total in a day. 6 × 4 = 24 fish. There are 7 days in a week, so multiply by 7 to find the total number of fish they eat in a week.
```
      2 4
    ×   7
    -----
    1 6 8
      2
```

21 **C** — All of the options are multiplications, so compare the numbers in each option. Smaller numbers in the calculation will give a smaller answer. The smallest numbers in the options are 5.43 and 7.9, which are both in option C, so it gives the smallest answer.

22 **300 m** — Multiply the number of metres it rises each second by the number of seconds: 1.5 × 200 = 1.5 × 2 × 100 = 3 × 100 = 300 m

23 **D** — 3 is 3 times smaller than 9, so the missing number needs to be 3 times larger than 120 for the two multiplications to be equal. 120 × 3 = 360, so the missing number is 360 — option D.

24 **C** — There are 12 months in a year, so multiply the distance she runs each month by 12. Partition 12 into 10 and 2. 140 × 10 = 1400, then 140 × 2 = 280. So she runs 1400 + 280 = 1680 km in a year.

25 **560** — You need to multiply the number of pencils Padma has by 5 and then by 4 to find the number of pencils Una has. Multiplying by 5 and then by 4 is the same as multiplying by 5 × 4 = 20, so multiply 28 by 20. 20 = 2 × 10, so 28 × 20 = 28 × 2 × 10 = 56 × 10 = 560 pencils.

26 **C** — You could find the missing number by dividing 182 by 26, but it is easier to use the fact that multiplication is the opposite of division to work out which number multiplies with 26 to give 182. Try the answer choice in the middle first so that you can narrow down the other options if that one is wrong.
```
      2 6
    ×   7
    -----
    1 8 2
      4
```
Since 26 × 7 = 182, the missing number is 7 — option C.

27 **120 cm** — You need to work out 480 ÷ 4. Since 480 is 10 times larger than 48, 480 ÷ 4 is 10 times larger than 48 ÷ 4 = 12. 12 × 10 = 120, so each piece is 120 cm long.

28 **E** — 48.65 is 100 times smaller than 4865, so 48.65 ÷ 7 will be 100 times smaller than 4865 ÷ 7. So 48.65 ÷ 7 = 695 ÷ 100 = 6.95.

29 **865** — Use short division to work out 4325 ÷ 5:
```
      0 8 6 5
  5 ) 4 ⁴3 ³2 ²5
```
4325 ÷ 5 = 865, so there are 865 ants in each farm.

30 **£0.64** — Partition £3.20 into £3 and £0.20 = 20p before dividing by 5. £3 ÷ 5 = ³⁄₅ = ⁶⁄₁₀ = £0.60, and 20p ÷ 5 = 4p = £0.04. So each pastry was £0.60 + £0.04 = £0.64.

31 **D** — You need to be able to divide the total number of chairs by 11 or 12 without a remainder. One number that would work is 11 × 12 = 132 (since 132 ÷ 11 = 12 and 132 ÷ 12 = 11.) All of the options are larger than this, so try doubling it. 132 × 2 = 264 — option D. Since 264 is twice as large as 132, 264 ÷ 11 and 264 ÷ 12 will be twice as large as 132 ÷ 11 and 132 ÷ 12. So 264 ÷ 11 = 24 and 264 ÷ 12 = 22. Both of these are whole numbers, so 264 could be the total number of chairs.

32 **205** — You need to be able to divide the number of comic books by 9 and get a remainder of 7. Find a number divisible by 9 close to 200. 9 × 11 = 99, so 9 × 22 = 9 × 11 × 2 = 99 × 2 = 198. Add 7 to get a number that gives a remainder of 7 when divided by 9. 198 + 7 = 205, which is between 200 and 210. So Leon has 205 comic books.

33 **9** — The rules of BODMAS tell you to work out brackets, then division, and finally subtraction:
42 ÷ 3 − (1 + 4) = 42 ÷ 3 − 5 = 14 − 5 = 9.

34 **C** — Follow the rules of BODMAS to calculate each expression.
A: 14 ÷ 2 + 3 − 1 = 7 + 3 − 1 = 10 − 1 = 9
B: 9 − 3 + 5 ÷ 2 = 9 − 3 + 2.5 = 6 + 2.5 = 8.5
C: 3 ÷ 2 + 3 × 2 = 1.5 + 3 × 2 = 1.5 + 6 = 7.5
D: (8 − 6) ÷ 2 + 5 = 2 ÷ 2 + 5 = 1 + 5 = 6
E: 3 × 1 + 12 − 9 = 3 + 12 − 9 = 15 − 9 = 6

35 **3800** — Since 28 and 72 are both multiplied by 38, you can add them together first. 28 + 72 = 100, then 100 × 38 = 3800.

36 **C** — Follow the rules of BODMAS to calculate each expression.
A: 90 + 30 ÷ 15 − 5 = 90 + 2 − 5 = 92 − 5 = 87
B: 90 − 30 ÷ 15 + 5 = 90 − 2 + 5 = 88 + 5 = 93
C: 90 ÷ 30 + 15 − 5 = 3 + 15 − 5 = 18 − 5 = 13
D: 90 + 30 − 15 ÷ 5 = 90 + 30 − 3 = 120 − 3 = 117
E: 90 − 30 + 15 ÷ 5 = 90 − 30 + 3 = 60 + 3 = 63

37 **30** — BODMAS tells you to start with the brackets. Use partitioning to find 80 × 2.5. Partition 2.5 into 2 and 0.5. 80 × 2 = 160 and 80 × 0.5 = 40. So 80 × 2.5 = 160 + 40 = 200. Now work out 6000 ÷ 200. You can simplify by dividing both numbers by 100 first. 6000 ÷ 200 = 60 ÷ 2 = 30.

Section Two — Number Knowledge

Page 28 — Types of Number

38 **19** — The person who works on the highest floor is Heather, on floor 15. The person who works on the lowest floor is Archie, on floor −4. To get from −4 to 0 you add 4. To get from 0 to 15 you add 15. 4 + 15 = 19

Page 31 — Factors, Multiples and Primes

1 **E** — A — false, 3 is a factor of 24 and is not a multiple of 2.
B — false, not all numbers ending in 3 are multiples of 3, e.g. 13.
C — false, 13 is a common factor of 13 and 52.
D — false, the highest common factor of 36 and 18 is 18.
E — true, 3 is a prime number and a multiple of 3.

2 **C** — 72 can be divided exactly by 4, 6, 8 and 9.
72 ÷ 4 = 18, 72 ÷ 6 = 12, 72 ÷ 8 = 9, 72 ÷ 9 = 8.
But 72 doesn't divide exactly by 7.

Page 34 — Fractions

1 **D** — Lydia gave Gemma $2/5$ of her pie, so Lydia is left with $3/5$ of her pie. Rose gave Gemma $1/5$ of her pie, so Rose is left with $4/5$ and Gemma has $2/5 + 1/5 = 3/5$ of a pie. So Lydia and Gemma have the same amount of pie.

2 **C** — Alex's fraction of the apples is divided into 3 groups. So divide $2/3$ by 3: $2/3 ÷ 3 = 2/(3 × 3) = 2/9$

Page 36 — Ratio and Proportion

1 **1 : 2 orange cows to black and white cows** — Write the ratio out using the numbers in the question: 48 : 96. Simplify the ratio by dividing both sides by the same number, e.g. divide both 48 and 96 by 12 to give a ratio of 4 : 8, then divide 4 and 8 by 4 to give a ratio of 1 : 2. 1 : 2 is in its simplest form because it can't be divided.

2 **60** — Turn the proportion into a fraction: $5/7$ of the blocks are green. $1/7$ of 84 = 84 ÷ 7 = 12, so $5/7$ of 84 = 12 × 5 = 60 green blocks.

Page 39 — Percentages, Fractions and Decimals

1 **C** — There are 8 triangles in this shape and 2 are shaded in, so $2/8$ of the shape is shaded. You can simplify $2/8$ to $1/4$. $1/4$ is equal to 25%.

2 **B** — Reading off the chart, 20% of children chose pink as their favourite colour. 20% of 90 is the same as $2/10$ of 90. 90 ÷ 10 = 9. 9 × 2 = 18.

3 **A** — A — 25% of 4 is the same as $1/4$ of 4. 4 ÷ 4 = 1, 1 × 1 = 1
B — $3/4$ of 8. 8 ÷ 4 = 2. 2 × 3 = 6.
C — $2/5$ of 10. 10 ÷ 5 = 2. 2 × 2 = 4.
D — 10% of 25 is the same as $1/10$ of 25:
25 ÷ 10 = 2.5, 2.5 × 1 = 2.5
E — $2/6$ of 18. 18 ÷ 6 = 3. 3 × 2 = 6.

Pages 40-42 — Practice Questions

1 **D** — −14 °C would be furthest to the left if you wrote the numbers on a number line, so it has the lowest value.

2 **B** — Work out each calculation to see which one isn't true. 4^3 = 4 × 4 × 4 = 64 < 75, so A is correct. 9^2 = 9 × 9 = 81, so B is not correct. 3^3 = 3 × 3 × 3 = 27 > 20, so C is correct. 7^2 = 7 × 7 = 49 < 50, so D is correct. So the answer is B.

3 **8** — The number of gold coins must be either 1, 8 or 27 because these are the only cube numbers smaller than 44. If he had one gold coin, there would be 44 − 1 = 43 silver coins, but this isn't a square number. If he had 8 gold coins, he would have 44 − 8 = 36 silver coins. 36 = 6^2, so it's a square number, so he has 8 gold coins.

4 **B** — A — MXVI = 1000 + 10 + 5 + 1 = 1016.
B — MCIX = 1000 + 100 + 9 = 1109.
C — CMXC = 900 + 90 = 990.
D — DCCX = 500 + 100 + 100 + 10 = 710.
E — MLXI = 1000 + 50 + 10 + 1 = 1061.
So MCIX has the highest value.

5 **8** — The factors of 40 are 1, 2, 4, 5, 8, 10, 20 and 40. The factors of 72 are 1, 2, 3, 4, 6, 8, 9, 12, 18, 24, 36 and 72. The greatest number that appears in both lists is 8.

6 **E** — She shares the doughnuts between 6 people (herself and five others). They are shared equally, so everyone gets the same number of doughnuts. This means the number in the box must be a multiple of 6 — the only option that is a multiple of 6 is 18.

7 **37** — 39 isn't a prime number because it is a multiple of 3 (39 = 3 × 13). 38 isn't prime because it is a multiple of 2 (38 = 2 × 19). 37 is prime because its only factors are 1 and itself.

8 **7** — The factors of 35 are 1, 5, 7 and 35. The factors of 84 are 1, 2, 3, 4, 6, 7, 12, 14, 21, 28, 42 and 84. The only prime number that appears in both lists is 7.

9 **45** — The first few multiples of 9 are 9, 18, 27, 36, 45, 54... The first few multiples of 15 are 15, 30, 45, 60... The smallest number that appears in both of the lists is 45.

10 **E** — $10/25$ is the same as $2/5$. $12/30$, $4/10$ and $6/15$ are also the same as $2/5$ when the fractions are simplified. $30/50$ is the same as $3/5$, so E is not equivalent to $10/25$.

11 **E** — 2 is equivalent to $14/7$, so $2 3/7$ is $14/7 + 3/7 = 17/7$.

12 **A** — $5/6 ÷ 3 = 5/(6 × 3) = 5/18$

13 a) **B** — $2/5$, $1/3$ and $4/9$ are all less than $1/2$. $5/6$ is more than $1/2$, so this fraction is the biggest. So Beth has completed the most.

b) **D** — Add the two fractions together: $1/3 + 4/9 = 3/9 + 4/9 = 7/9$

c) **C** — Find equivalent fractions that have the same denominator, then subtract: $5/6 − 2/5 = 25/30 − 12/30 = 13/30$

14 **54** — $1 − 7/9 = 9/9 − 7/9 = 2/9$, so 12 pages is $2/9$ of the book. $1/9$ of the book is 12 ÷ 2 = 6 pages, so the book has 6 × 9 = 54 pages.

15 a) **4 : 1** — The ratio of pens to pencils is 24 : 6. Divide both numbers by 6 to simplify to 4 : 1.

b) **3** — Turn the proportion into a fraction: $1/8$ of the pens are ballpoint pens. There are 24 pens, so work out $1/8$ of 24. 24 ÷ 8 = 3, so there are 3 ballpoint pens.

16 **60 : 300** — There are 1 + 5 = 6 parts in total. 1 part is 360 ÷ 6 = 60 and 5 parts is 5 × 60 = 300, so the answer is 60 : 300.

17 a) **A** — The ratio of people to inflatables in the pool is 4 : 3. There are 3 × 4 = 12 inflatables, so there will be 4 × 4 = 16 people.

b) **60** — There are 4 × 20 = 80 people, so there will be 3 × 20 = 60 inflatables.

18 **7 : 3** — Count the squares in the diagram. Side a is 7 squares long and side b is 3 squares long, so the ratio is 7 : 3.
19 **144 g** — Find out the mass of each screw: 180 g ÷ 20 = 9 g. He has used 4 screws, so the mass of the screws he has used is 4 × 9 g = 36 g. So the mass of the remaining screws is 180 g – 36 g = 144 g.
20 **0.85** — $^{17}/_{20}$ is equivalent to $^{(17 \times 5)}/_{(20 \times 5)} = ^{85}/_{100}$, which is 0.85.
21 **30%** — There are 20 triangles in the rectangle. 6 of the triangles are shaded, so $^6/_{20} = ^3/_{10}$ = 30% of the rectangle is shaded.
22 **6%** — $^3/_{50}$ is equivalent to $^6/_{100}$, and $^6/_{100}$ = 6%.
23 **220** — They have 100% – 45% = 55% left. 50% of 400 = 400 ÷ 2 = 200. 5% of 400 = 400 ÷ 10 = 20. So 55% of 400 = 200 + 20 = 220.
24 **D** — 35% = $^{35}/_{100}$. Divide the numerator and denominator by 5 to simplify to $^7/_{20}$.
25 **48%** — $^7/_{25} = ^{28}/_{100}$ = 28%. Add up the percentages he has used: 28% + 24% = 52%. So there's 100% – 52% = 48% of the flour left.
26 **D** — 0.25 = 25% < 30%, so A is true. $^1/_5$ = 20% > 15%, so B is true. 0.9 = 90%, so C is true. $^4/_5$ = 0.8, so D is not true. $^3/_{10}$ = 0.3 > 0.25, so E is true.
27 **105** — Start by finding 10% of 2100. 10% = $^1/_{10}$, so 10% of 2100 = 2100 ÷ 10 = 210. 5% is half of 10%, so 5% of 2100 is 210 ÷ 2 = 105.

Section Three — Number Problems
Page 46 — Algebra
1 **£75** — The number of hours is 3 and the cost of the parts is £20. Put these values into the formula.
$C = 25 + 10h + p = 25 + 10 \times 3 + 20 = 25 + 30 + 20 = 75$
The cost of the electrician is £75.
2 **64** — Remove parts of the equation so that the x is left on its own.
$x \div 8 - 6 = 2$
First add 6 to both sides: $x \div 8 = 8$
Then multiply both sides of the equation by 8: $x = 64$
The value of x is 64.
3 **D** — Work out each part of the algebraic expression:
The width of the room is 3 metres. The length of the room is 4 × 3 = 12 metres (4 times the width). The height of the room is y metres. To calculate the volume, multiply the width, length and height together: Volume = $3 \times 12 \times y = 36y$

Page 49 — Number Sequences
1 **39** — The sequence is 4, 9, 15. The difference between the numbers is increased by one each time. The difference between 4 and 9 is 5, and 9 and 15 is 6. To find the fourth number you'd add 7, to find the fifth you'd add 8, and to find the sixth you'd add 9. 15 + 7 = 22. 22 + 8 = 30. 30 + 9 = 39.
2 **5n + 2** — The sequence increases by 5 for each term, so you need to multiply by 5 in the expression — 5n. For the first term, if you multiply by 5 you get 5 × 1 = 5. The actual number in the sequence is 7. Add 2 to your expression to get a sequence that works for the first term — 5n + 2. Test this to see if it works for the other terms:
2nd term: 5 × 2 + 2 = 12 — correct.
3rd term: 5 × 3 + 2 = 17 — correct
4th term: 5 × 4 + 2 = 22 — correct
5th term: 5 × 5 + 2 = 27 — correct

Page 53 — Word Problems
1 **E** — To get 42 tulips, Lena needs to buy 6 bunches of tulips (42 ÷ 7 = 6). To get 42 roses, Lena needs to buy 7 bunches of roses (42 ÷ 6 = 7). So 6 × £4.50 = £27 and 7 × £3.50 = £24.50. £27 + £24.50 = £51.50.
2 **£1.70** — You need to work out how much Benni spent:
£10 – £1.50 = £8.50. 5 sandwiches cost £8.50, so 1 sandwich costs £8.50 ÷ 5 = £1.70.

3 **£17.10** — Work out the profit that Simone makes on each bracelet. 50p – 20p = 30p. Then multiply this by the number she sells. The easiest thing to do here is to round the number she sells (57) up to an easier number (60), then do the multiplication. 30 × 60 can be worked out by finding 3 × 6 = 18, then add on the two zeros to give 1800p, or £18.00. Because you rounded the number sold up by three, you just need to subtract the cost of 3 bracelets (3 × 30p = 90p) from £18.00 to get the answer. £18.00 – 90p = £17.10.

Pages 54-56 — Practice Questions
1 **77** — Change n in the expression to 12, then follow BODMAS to work out the answer: 6 × 12 + 5 = 72 + 5 = 77.
2 **C** — Multiply both terms in the brackets by 3.
$(3 \times t) + (3 \times 4) = 3t + 12$.
3 **D** — The mugs can hold 7 × x = 7x ml and the glasses can hold 3 × y = 3y ml. So they can hold 7x + 3y ml in total — option D.
4 **6** — First, add 6 to both sides. This gives 5x = 30, so divide by 5 on both sides to find x = 30 ÷ 5 = 6.
5 a) **£25** — Change g in the formula to 4 and p to 3.
$B = 5 \times 4 + 3 + 2 = 20 + 3 + 2 = 25$, so it would cost £25.
b) **2** — Change p in the formula to 5 and B to 17, then work out the value of g. 17 = 5g + 5 + 2, so 17 = 5g + 7. Subtract 7 from both sides to get 10 = 5g, then divide both sides by 5 to get g = 10 ÷ 5 = 2.
6 **E** — First Sharla subtracts 5, so you need n – 5. She then divides by 2, but as division comes before subtraction in BODMAS, you need brackets to make sure the subtraction is done first: (n – 5) ÷ 2. Then, add 7 to get (n – 5) ÷ 2 + 7.
7 **B** — The numbers in the sequence increase by 5 between each term, so the rule for the sequence will begin 5n. For the first term, n = 1. So 5n = 5 × 1 = 5. The first term is 4, so you need to subtract 1 to get the expression to give the correct value. So, the expression for the nth term is 5n – 1.
8 **54** — For the 100th term, n = 100. Change n in the expression to 100: 100 ÷ 2 + 4 = 50 + 4 = 54, so the 100th term is 54.
9 **15** — To get from the third number to the fourth number, you add 8, and to get from the fourth number to the fifth, you add 8, so the rule for the sequence is 'add 8'. So the missing number is 7 + 8 = 15.
10 **199** — Start by finding the expression for the nth term. The numbers in the sequence increase by 4 between each term, so the rule for the sequence will begin 4n. For the first term, n = 1. So 4n = 4 × 1 = 4. The first term is 3, so you need to subtract 1 to get the expression to give the correct value. So the expression for the nth term is 4n – 1. For the 50th term, n = 50. Change n in the expression to 50: 4 × 50 – 1 = 200 – 1 = 199, so the 50th term is 199.
11 **13** — The first shape has 4 dots, the second shape has 7 dots and the third shape has 10 dots. The number of dots increases by 3 each time, so the next shape will have 10 + 3 = 13 dots.
12 a) **5** — Make a sequence by subtracting 7 each time:
79, 72, 65, 58, 51, 44... The sequence goes below 50 after 5 subtractions, so it takes 5 hours.
b) **23** — After 8 hours, he will have eaten 8 × 7 = 56 grapes. So there will be 79 – 56 = 23 grapes left.
13 **100 minutes** — £10 = 10 × 100 = 1000p. Half of this is 1000p ÷ 2 = 500p. So Chris needs to use 500p worth of call time to reduce his credit by half. At 5p per minute, that's 500 ÷ 5 = 100 minutes.
14 **8** — Do the operations in reverse. 70 – 6 = 64. Louise squares her number to get 64, and 8^2 = 8 × 8 = 64.
15 **20 weeks** — Alfie swims twice a week (Tuesdays and Thursdays) and 3.5 km each time he swims. So every week he swims 3.5 km × 2 = 7 km in total. Now divide 140 km by 7 km to find the answer: 140 ÷ 7 = 20 weeks.

16 **B** — The pineapple and watermelon cost £0.95 + £2.75 = £3.70. So Mac has £5 − £3.70 = £1.30 left over to spend on kiwi fruit. Convert to pence: 1.30 × 100 = 130p. At 15p each, 10 kiwi fruit cost 150p — this is too much. 9 kiwi fruit cost 15p × 9 = 135p, which is still too much, but 8 kiwi fruit cost 15p × 8 = 120p. So Mac buys 8 kiwi fruit and has 130p − 120p = 10p left.

17 **C** — £5 per hour for 3 hours comes to £5 × 3, then add on the fixed fee of £10 to get £5 × 3 + £10. The BODMAS rule says that multiplication comes before addition, so no brackets are needed.

18 **E** — A could be true (e.g. Tiana could have donated 18 jumpers and 9 T-shirts). This means that C could be true.
The amounts of each item add up to an odd number (27). So one amount must be odd and the other amount must be even. The difference between an even and an odd number is always odd. E says that the difference is even (8), so E cannot be true.
B could be true (e.g. Tiana could have donated 17 jumpers and 10 T-shirts) and D could be true (e.g. Tiana could have donated 16 T-shirts and 11 jumpers).

19 **£105** — The plumber charges £20 per hour, so they charge 3 × £20 = £60 for their time. Subtract this and the call-out fee from the total amount they charge to find the cost of the parts. £195 − £60 − £30 = £105.

20 **14** — 17 easy questions are worth a total of 17 × 3 = 51 points. That leaves 149 − 51 = 98 points from hard questions. Each hard question is worth 7 points, so Sanjay answered 98 ÷ 7 = 14 of them.

21 **E** — Four mugs cost £2.25 × 8. Partition £2.25 into £2 and £0.25. So £2.25 × 8 = (£2 × 8) + (£0.25 × 8) = £16 + £2 = £18. Now divide by 4: one mug costs £18 ÷ 4 = £4.50.

22 **D** — You're looking for a number that is 4 more than a multiple of 7. The first few multiples of 7 are 7, 14, 21 and 28. Add 4 to each: 7 + 4 = 11, 14 + 4 = 18, 21 + 4 = 25 and 28 + 4 = 32. So Aaron could have started with 25 carrots. You could also divide each option by 7. The number of carrots leaves a remainder of 4 when divided by 7. E.g. 25 ÷ 7 = 3 remainder 4.

Section Four — Data Handling

Page 58 — Data Tables

1 **B** — The number of children who own more than 15 DVDs is shown by the frequencies in the bottom two rows of the table. Find the total number of children by adding these frequencies together: 13 + 6 = 19.

2 **£6** — First find the total amount spent on senior citizen tickets by subtracting the cost of the adult tickets, child tickets and the booking fee from the "Amount to pay".
£212.50 − £2.50 − £32 − £160 = £18.
The table shows that three senior citizen tickets were bought, so divide £18 by 3 to find the cost of one ticket: £18 ÷ 3 = £6

Page 62 — Displaying Data

1 **36** — You know that 20° = 2 children, so 10° = 1 child. The whole pie chart is 360° and 360° ÷ 10° = 36, so there are 36 children in the class.

Page 64 — Analysing Data

1 **21** — Mean = (22 + 23 + 17 + 17 + 26) ÷ 5 = 105 ÷ 5 = 21.

Page 66 — Misleading Data

1 **C** — The headline suggests that sales of pencils have fallen by a massive amount. If you read the graph, the sales have only actually fallen from 500 million to 498 million. The graph makes it look like the sales have fallen more sharply because the axis doesn't start at zero — the drop isn't very big compared to the overall number of pencils sold.

Pages 67-70 — Practice Questions

1 a) **9** — 21 pupils chose swimming in total, and 12 of them were in Class A, so 21 − 12 = 9 were in Class B.

b) **C** — Work out how many pupils chose gymnastics in Class A: 28 − 12 − 6 = 10. So 10 + 12 = 22 pupils chose gymnastics, which is more than chose swimming (21) or cricket (10).

c) **53** — Add up the totals for each row: 21 + 10 + 22 = 53.

2 a) **D** — There are fewest symbols in the Purple Emperor row, so this is the least common type of butterfly.

b) **6** — There are 1½ more symbols in the Tortoiseshell row than in the Red Admiral row. Each symbol means 4 butterflies, so there are 4 × 1½ = 6 more Tortoiseshell butterflies.

c) **44** — There are 10 whole symbols and 2 half symbols, so 11 whole symbols in total. So there are 11 × 4 = 44 butterflies.

3 a) **30** — 100 books were borrowed on Tuesday and 70 books were borrowed on Monday. So 100 − 70 = 30 more books were borrowed on Tuesday.

b) **C** — The bar for Wednesday is significantly smaller than the others, and a similar number of books were borrowed on the other four days, so it's most likely that the library was only open for half a day on Wednesday.

c) **74** — Find the total number of books borrowed:
70 + 100 + 30 + 80 + 90 = 370.
There are five days, so divide the total by 5: 370 ÷ 5 = 74.

4 a) **$75** — Go up from £60 on the horizontal axis until you get to the green line. Then go across to the vertical axis and read off the value in dollars.

b) **£320** — From the graph, $100 is £80.
So 4 × $100 = $400 = 4 × £80 = £320.

c) **C** — From the graph, $25 = £20, so $27 will be just over £20, but not as much as £27. So the scarf costing £19 is the only possible option.

5 a) **B** — The angles in a pie chart add up to 360°, so subtract the angles you know from 360°: 360° − 90° − 90° − 120° = 60°

b) **60** — 120° is ⅓ of 360°, so 20 children is ⅓ of the total number of children. So multiply by 3 to find the total number of children: 20 × 3 = 60.

6 a) **3:25 pm** — There are 5 divisions between 0 cm and 10 cm, so one division is worth 10 ÷ 5 = 2 cm. Go across from 28 on the vertical axis until you get to the green line. Then go down to the horizontal axis and read off the time.

b) **D** — When the water was turned off, the depth doesn't change, so the green line will be flat. This happens between 3:10 pm and 3:20 pm.

c) **36 cm** — Go up from 3:30 pm on the horizontal axis until you get to the green line. Then go across to the vertical axis and read off the depth. It's two divisions below 40 cm, which is 36 cm.

7 **C** — The sector for irises is larger than the sector for lilies, so more children chose irises than lilies, so A is false.
The sector for tulips is larger than the sector for lilies, so more children chose tulips than lilies, so B is false.
Roses make up ¼ (90°) of the pie chart. ¼ of 72 is 72 ÷ 4 = 18, so C is true. The sectors for daisies and bluebells are different sizes, so D is false.
60° is ⅙ of 360°. ⅙ of 72 is 72 ÷ 6 = 12 (not 9), so E is false.

8 **£2.40** — The total she spent over the six months was 6 × £4.50 = (6 × £4) + (6 × £0.50) = £24 + £3 = £27.
Her total spend in the other 5 months was
£4.80 + £5.40 + £3.90 + £6.20 + £4.30 = £24.60.
So in the missing month she spent £27 − £24.60 = £2.40.

9 a) **11.0 °C** — Add up the temperatures: 11 + 9 + 8 + 10 + 12 + 13 + 14 = 77. There are 7 days, so divide the total by 7: 77 ÷ 7 = 11 °C.

b) **Saturday: 4 mph, Sunday: 10 mph** — The total for the 7 days is 9 × 7 = 63. Subtracting the values for Monday-Friday leaves 63 − 9 − 11 − 7 − 14 − 8 = 63 − 49 = 14.
Find two numbers that add up to 14 and have a difference of 6: 4 + 10 = 14, 10 − 4 = 6. The wind speed was greater on Sunday, so it was 4 mph on Saturday and 10 mph on Sunday.

10 **D** — Statements A-C and E are all true, but don't matter for the pictogram. Statement D does matter — the symbols are different in each row, so you can't tell how many of each type of house there are.

11 **D** — TJ got 25 votes and Leo got 22 votes. 25 isn't double 22, so A is false. Leo got 22 votes and Mai got 21 votes. 21 isn't $\frac{2}{3}$ of 22, so B is false. Mai got 21 votes and Amy got 20 votes. 20 isn't half of 21, so C is false. TJ got 25 votes and Amy got 20 votes. 20 is $\frac{4}{5}$ of 25, so D is true. Leo got 22 votes and Amy got 20 votes. 22 isn't three times 20, so E is false.

Section Five — Shape and Space

Page 72 — Angles

1 **D** — Angle c is smaller than a right angle, so it is less than 90°. This means that it must be either 10° or 45°. You can tell that it is about half of the size of a right angle, so the correct answer is option D — 45°.

2 **135°** — The total size of the angles on the circular compass is 360°. There are 8 compass points, so the size of the angle between each point is 360 ÷ 8 = 45°. South is three points away from north-east so the size of the angle between them is 45 × 3 = 135°.

Page 76 — 2D Shapes

1 **C** — The shape has no right angles so it can't be a right-angled triangle. It has no equal sides so it can't be equilateral or isosceles. All the sides and angles in a scalene triangle are different, so the answer is C.

2 **A** — First, rule out the shapes that can't go in that row. A square, an equilateral triangle and a rhombus have all equal side lengths, so you can rule out B, D and E. Next, rule out the shapes that can't go in that column. A rectangle has all equal angles, so you can rule out C. The answer must be A — a trapezium.

3 **Isosceles triangle** — The shape has no obtuse angles, so all the angles inside the shape must be 90° or less — this means the shape can only be a square, a rectangle or a triangle. The next clue says that it has no right angles, so it can't be a square or a rectangle — it must be a triangle. The final clue says that two of its sides are equal in length. A right-angled triangle or an isosceles triangle can have two equal side lengths, but this shape doesn't have any right angles. The shape is an isosceles triangle.

4 **9 cm** — The diameter of the circle is 18 cm, so the radius is 18 ÷ 2 = 9 cm.

Page 80 — 2D Shapes — Area and Perimeter

1 **7.5 cm** — The perimeter of the shape is made up of 10 equal length sides. The length of each side is 75 ÷ 10 = 7.5 cm. So, side Z is 7.5 cm.

2 **C** — Split the shape into two rectangles as shown in the diagram. Work out the length of the missing sides — the horizontal side is 13 − 5 − 5 = 3 cm and the vertical side is 8 − 4 = 4 cm.

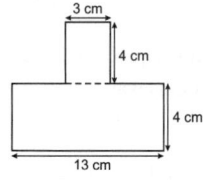

Then work out the area of each rectangle. The smaller rectangle is 3 × 4 = 12 cm². The larger rectangle is 13 × 4 = 52 cm². The total area of the shape is 52 + 12 = 64 cm².

Page 82 — Symmetry

1 **A** — The shape is a trapezium. The diagram shows the reflected shape.

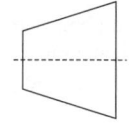

2 **5** — The star has 5 lines of symmetry, as shown on the diagram.

Page 86 — 3D Shapes

1 **B** — Option B is the only net that will not fold up to make a cube — two of its faces would overlap. The diagram below shows which faces would overlap if you folded it up.

2 **64** — The number of vegetable stock cubes that will fit along the length of the box is 4 cm ÷ 1 cm = 4. The number that will fit along the width of the box is 8 cm ÷ 1 cm = 8. The number that will fit up the height of the box is 2 cm ÷ 1 cm = 2. The total number of cubes is 4 × 8 × 2 = 64 stock cubes.

3 **Cuboid** — The net has 4 rectangular faces in a line, then 2 squares at the top and bottom — it will fold up to make a cuboid.

Page 89 — Shape Problems

1 **C** — When you look at the logo from the back of the window it will be flipped over, so you need to look for the option that's a reflection of the original logo. Option C is a reflection of the original logo.

Page 91 — Coordinates

1 **D** — Go through the options one by one. Imagine plotting each point on the grid. A parallelogram is a shape with two pairs of equal length, parallel sides, a pair of equal obtuse angles and a pair of equal acute angles. Only the coordinates for option D make a parallelogram with the existing points on the grid.

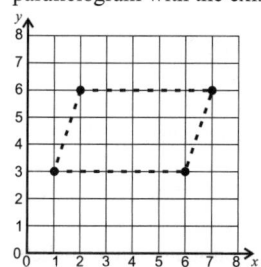

2 **(4, 4)** — Read off the coordinates of the campsite (7, 7) and the car park (1, 1). Halfway between the two x-axis coordinates (1 and 7) is 4. Halfway between the two y-axis coordinates (1 and 7) is also 4. So the coordinates of the farmhouse are (4, 4).

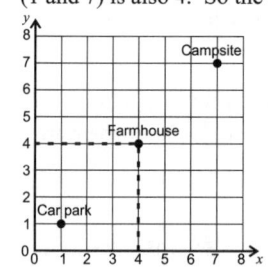

Page 93 — Transformations

1 **(6, 4)** — The diagram shows the shape after it has been reflected in the mirror line. The coordinates of corner Y are now (6, 4).

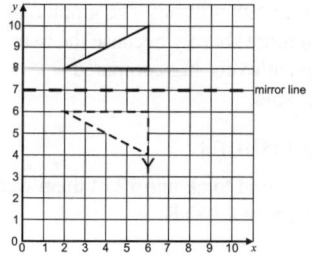

2 **(−1, 4)** — Read off the original coordinates of point Z (5, 7). The new coordinates will have an *x* value that is 6 less than the original *x* coordinate (5 − 6 = −1), and a *y* value that is 3 less than the original *y* coordinate (7 − 3 = 4). The new coordinates of point Z are (−1, 4).

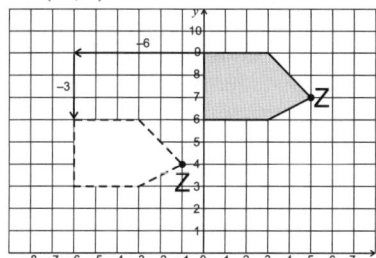

Pages 94-99 — Practice Questions

1 **B** — Angle *w* is smaller than a right angle but larger than half of a right angle (90° ÷ 2 = 45°), so it must be 60° — option B.

2 **131°** — Angles on a straight line add up to 180°, so S = 180° − 49° = 131°.

3 **302°** — Angles in a triangle add up to 180°, so the missing angle in this triangle is 180° − 38° − 84° = 58°. This angle is around a point with angle *x*, so these two angles must add up to 360°. So angle *x* is 360° − 58° = 302°.

4 **D** — Obtuse angles measure more than 90° but less than 180°, so three obtuse angles together must measure more than 90° × 3 = 270°. Angles around a point add up to 360°, so angle *k* must measure less than 360° − 270° = 90°. The only option less than 90° is D — 73°.

5 **44°** — First, look at the quadrilateral made up of the outside edges of the diagram. The angles in a quadrilateral add up to 360°, so the top angle must be 360° − 68° − 122° − 51° = 119°. This angle is made up of angle *y* and a 75° angle, so angle *y* is 119° − 75° = 44°.

6 **C** — The shape has six sides, so it is a hexagon.

7 **D** — She would need at least six sticks to make a rectangle, since the smallest rectangle would have two sides made up of one stick each and two sides made up of two sticks each — 1 + 1 + 2 + 2 = 6. The diagram below shows how she could make the other shapes.

8 **B** — The outside edge of a circle is called the circumference.

9 **1** — A kite has 2 pairs of equal sides and 2 equal angles, so it has 1 pair of equal angles.

10 **120 mm** — The diameter is twice the radius, so the radius is 240 ÷ 2 = 120 mm.

11 **76°** — The angles in a triangle add up to 180°, so the two missing angles must add up to 180° − 28° = 152°. The triangle is isosceles, so these two angles are equal. So each of them is 152° ÷ 2 = 76°.

12 **120°** — Angle *b* is around a point with four angles in equilateral triangles. Each angle in an equilateral triangle is 60°, so these four angles add up to 60° × 4 = 240°. Angles around a point add up to 360°, so angle *b* is 360° − 240° = 120°.

13 **C** — A square has four equal sides and four equal angles, so it is a regular quadrilateral. All of the other options have at least one side or angle that is different in size, so they are irregular quadrilaterals.

14 **12 cm** — A regular heptagon has seven equal sides, so each side is 84 ÷ 7 = 12 cm long.

15 **4** — First, find the perimeter of the pitch. 70 + 130 + 70 + 130 = 400 m, so he needs to paint 400 m of lines. So he needs 400 ÷ 100 = 4 cans.

16 **21 cm** — A regular pentagon has five sides of equal length, so the length of each side is 35 ÷ 5 = 7 cm. Each of the three sides of the triangle in the centre is also a side of a pentagon, so the perimeter of the triangle is 7 × 3 = 21 cm.

17 **80 m** — The original fence around field A was 60 + 50 + 60 + 50 = 220 m long. The fence around the combined fields is 60 + 50 + (60 − 40) + 40 + 40 + 40 + 50 = 300 m long. So the new fence is 300 − 220 = 80 m longer.

18 **D** — The area of a rectangle = length × width, so divide the area by the width to find the length. So the length is 56 ÷ 7 = 8 cm.

19 **5 m²** — The area of a triangle = ½ × base × height. So the area of this triangle = ½ × 2 × 5 = 1 × 5 = 5 m².

20 **47 m²** — Split the shape into two rectangles as shown in the diagram. The missing side in the smaller rectangle is 8 − 2 − 1 = 5 m.

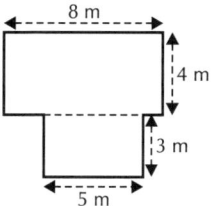

Work out the area of each rectangle. The area of the smaller rectangle is 5 × 3 = 15 m². The area of the larger rectangle is 8 × 4 = 32 m². So the total area of the shape is 15 + 32 = 47 m².

21 **A** — A regular pentagon has 5 lines of symmetry, which is more than the 3 lines of an equilateral triangle, the 4 lines of a square and the 2 lines of a rhombus. All of these lines are shown in the diagrams below.

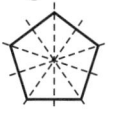

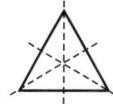

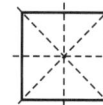

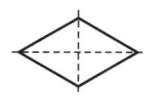

22 **2** — The shape has 2 lines of symmetry, shown on the diagram on the right.

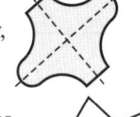

23 **D** — The reflected shape has seven sides, so it is a heptagon.

24 **E** — There are two end faces, so there are 7 − 2 = 5 side faces on the prism. The number of side faces is equal to the number of sides on the end face (e.g. a triangle has three sides, so a triangular prism has three side faces), so the end faces have 5 sides, meaning they are pentagons.

25 **4** — Vertices are corners. A triangle-based pyramid has 4 vertices.

26 **B** — The net has one square and four triangles. The net will fold so that each triangle shares a side with the square and the four triangles meet at a point, so the shape will be a square-based pyramid.

27 **72** — The number of sugar cubes that will fit along the length of the container is 12 ÷ 2 = 6 cubes. The number of cubes that will fit along the width of the container is 8 ÷ 2 = 4 cubes. The number of cubes that will fit up the height of the container is 6 ÷ 2 = 3 cubes. Multiply the number of cubes that will fit along the length, width and height to find the total number that will fit in the container. 6 × 4 × 3 = 24 × 3 = 72 cubes.

28 **D** — Option D is the only net that will not fold up to make a prism — the shaded faces in the diagram below would overlap.

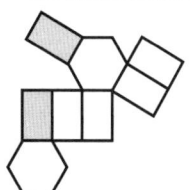

29 **2.5 m** — The planter is a cuboid, so its volume = length × width × height. So 5 = length × 2 × 1 = length × 2. So length = 5 ÷ 2 = 2.5 m.

30 **160 cm³** — First, find the volume of the container. The container is a cuboid, so its volume = length × width × height = 8 × 10 × 7 = 80 × 7 = 560 cm³. This is how much water the container could hold, so he needs to add 560 − 400 = 160 cm³ more to fill the container.

31 **26** — Count all of the faces that would be visible from any angle. There are 12 vertical faces on the bottom layer of the shape, 4 vertical faces on the top layer, 5 horizontal faces on the top and 5 horizontal faces on the bottom.
So she painted 12 + 4 + 5 + 5 = 26 faces.

32 **B** — Each of the original shapes has 5 squares. Since the original shapes do not overlap, the new shape must have 5 + 5 = 10 squares. This leaves only options B and D as possibilities. Option D cannot be made from the original shapes. Option B can be made as shown below.

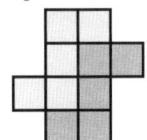

33 **C** — Point Y is 1 square to the right and 3 squares up from point X. This is the halfway point, so go another 1 square right and 3 squares up to find her grandma's house. This gives the coordinates (5, 7) — option C.

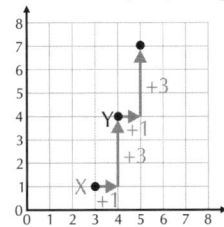

34 **(3, 1)** — Corner H is directly below the corner at (3, 5), so it has the same x-coordinate of 3. The side length of the square is equal to the difference between the x-coordinates of the top corners, so each side is 7 − 3 = 4 units long. The side length is also equal to the difference between the y-coordinates of the top-left corner and corner H, so the y-coordinate of corner H is 5 − 4 = 1.
So the coordinates of corner H are (3, 1).

35 a) **D** — The reflection will not change the y-coordinate of point A, so that is still 7. Point A is 4 units to the right of the mirror line, so it will be 4 units to the left of the mirror line in the reflection. The mirror line is at $x = 2$, so the x-coordinate of the reflected point A is 2 − 4 = −2. So the coordinates of the reflected point A are (−2, 7).

b) **C** — Point B on the original shape is at (5, 4). Translating the shape 2 squares down decreases the y-coordinate by 2, leaving it at 4 − 2 = 2. Translating the shape 8 squares to the left decreases the x-coordinate by 8, leaving it at 5 − 8 = −3. So the coordinates of point B on the translated shape are (−3, 2).

36 **(5, 11)** — Every point is translated by the same amount, so take matching points from the two shapes and work out the translation. Point (7, 1) goes to (3, 3), so the translation was 7 − 3 = 4 squares to the left and 3 − 1 = 2 squares up. Translating point (9, 9) by the same amount leaves the x-coordinate of point T as 9 − 4 = 5 and the y-coordinate as 9 + 2 = 11. So the coordinates of point T are (5, 11).

37 **B** — The point for the statue must be located within the square on the grid. The x-coordinates of the corners of the square are 4 and 8, so the x-coordinate of the statue must be between 4 and 8. The y-coordinates of the corners of the square are 6 and 10, so the y-coordinate of the statue must be between 6 and 10. The only option that fits the criteria for the x- and y-coordinates is (5, 9).

Section Six — Units and Measures

Page 102 — Units

1 **D** — 0.3 g, 3 g and 30 g are all very light — less than the weight of an empty schoolbag, so the answer can't be any of these options. 30 kg is very heavy — about the weight of a child, so this can't be the answer either. The answer must be 3 kg — this is about the weight of 3 bags of sugar, which could easily be carried.

2 **71 servings** — There is originally 28.75 litres = 28.75 × 1000 = 28 750 ml of soup. 350 ml is spilt, so there is 28 750 − 350 = 28 400 ml left. Now you need to divide 28 400 ml by 400 ml to find the number of servings. To simplify the calculation, you could divide both numbers by 100: 28 400 ÷ 400 = 284 ÷ 4. Now use a written method to do the division:
$$4 \overline{)2\,2^{2}8\,4} = 71$$

3 **A** — Each stride is 50 cm so 2 strides will cover 2 × 50 cm = 100 cm. 100 cm = 1 m, so Ashanti takes 2 strides to walk 1 m. 1000 m = 1 km, so in 10 km, there are 10 × 1000 = 10 000 m. To walk 10 000 m, Ashanti must take 10 000 × 2 = 20 000 strides.

Page 105 — Time

1 **Max** — The youngest child must have the latest date of birth. Children born in 2009 must be younger than those born in 2008, so it can't be Jim or Geeta. October is later in 2009 than March and May, so Max must be younger than Meg and Fred.

2 **February** — Keep adding the number of pages she completes each month until you reach 154.
Sep = 30
Sep + Oct = 30 + 31 = 61
Sep + Oct + Nov = 61 + 30 = 91
Sep + Oct + Nov + Dec = 91 + 31 = 122
Sep + Oct + Nov + Dec + Jan = 122 + 31 = 153
There are 153 days between September and the end of January, so she will finish her 154-page book in February.

3 **D** — 4:53 pm + 7 mins = 5 pm, then 5 pm + 2 hours = 7 pm, and 7 pm + 15 mins = 7:15 pm. The total is 7 mins + 2 hours + 15 mins = 2 hours 22 minutes. Watch out — this isn't the same as 2.22 hours. 2.22 hours is 2 hours and 22 hundredths of an hour.

Pages 106-107 — Practice Questions

1 **C** — 17 m, 1.7 km and 0.17 km are far too tall for a car (17 m is the shortest of these options, and this is about the height of a 5-storey building), and 17 cm is far too short (it's about the height of a paperback book). The most likely answer is 1.7 m.

2 **350 ml** — There are 5 divisions between 250 ml and 500 ml, so each division is worth 250 ml ÷ 5 = 50 ml.
The liquid is 3 divisions above 250 ml, which is 250 ml + (3 × 50 ml) = 250 ml + 150 ml = 400 ml.
To get to 750 ml, you need another 750 ml − 400 ml = 350 ml.

3 **D** — Convert all the measurements into the same units:
Sebastian: 340 mm = 340 ÷ 10 = 34 cm,
Khalid: 0.3 m = 0.3 × 100 = 30 cm, Lola: 34.5 cm,
Thea: 0.35 m = 0.35 × 100 = 35 cm. So Thea has knitted the most.

4 a) **13.5 km** — Convert all the distances into km:
600 m = 600 ÷ 1000 = 0.6 km,
4500 m = 4500 ÷ 1000 = 4.5 km.
Now add them up: 0.6 km + 8.4 km + 4.5 km = 13.5 km

b) **£67.50** — There are 2 lots of 500 m in every km, so Priti travels 2 × 13.5 = 27 lots of 500 m in total.
So she gets sponsored 27 × £2.50 = (27 × £2) + (27 × £0.50) = £54 + £13.50 = £67.50.

5 **8** — In 2 bags of lentils there are 2 × 1.6 = 3.2 kg.
3.2 kg = 3.2 × 1000 = 3200 g of lentils. Divide this by the amount of lentils in one batch: 3200 ÷ 400 = 32 ÷ 4 = 8 batches.

6 a) **6** — 2.7 kg = 2.7 × 1000 = 2700 g. 2700 ÷ 450 = 270 ÷ 45 = 30 ÷ 5 = 6. (To make the division easier, we divided everything by 10, then by 9. You can do this in whatever way you prefer.)

b) **18** — She uses 2.4 litres = 2.4 × 1000 = 2400 ml of lemonade. Twice as much as 400 ml is 800 ml, so she uses 800 ml of apple juice. So she makes 2400 ml + 400 ml + 800 ml = 3600 ml of punch. This fills 3600 ÷ 200 = 36 ÷ 2 = 18 cups.

7 **D** — 4 minutes before 16:04 is 16:00, then another 12 − 4 = 8 minutes before that is 15:52, or 3:52 pm in the 12-hour clock.

8 **3 hours 35 minutes** — 9:45 am + 15 minutes = 10:00 am, 10:00 am + 3 hours = 1:00 pm, 1:00 pm + 20 minutes = 1:20 pm. So the tournament lasts for 15 minutes + 3 hours + 20 minutes = 3 hours 35 minutes.

9 **C** — Count back 14 days in July from Isla's birthday. Then count back another 20 − 14 = 6 days. There are 30 days in June, so 6 days before the end of June is 30 − 6 = 24th June.

10 **324 seconds** — There are 5 × 60 = 300 seconds in 5 minutes, so in 5 minutes and 24 seconds there are 300 + 24 = 324 seconds.

11 a) **44 mins** — The first train in the timetable leaves North River at 11:18 and arrives at East Water at 12:02. 11:18 + 2 minutes = 11:20, 11:20 + 40 minutes = 12:00, 12:00 + 2 minutes = 12:02. So the train journey takes 2 + 40 + 2 = 44 minutes.

b) **12:21** — The latest train to arrive in West Mile before 1:30 pm (13:30) gets in at 13:04. This train leaves South Path at 12:21.

c) **13:09** — 35 minutes after 11:15 am is 11:50 am. 15 minutes after 11:50 am is 12:05 pm. The next train from North River after 12:05 pm leaves at 12:25 pm and arrives at East Water at 13:09 (or 1:09 pm).

d) **28 mins** — Mr Adams will arrive at East Water train station at 12:03 pm. The next train leaves at 12:31 pm, so he will have to wait for 31 − 3 = 28 minutes.

Section Seven — Mixed Problems
Page 111 — Mixed Problems

1 **£40** — Work out the volume of the swimming pool. 10 × 10 × 1.6 = 160 m³. If it costs 25p to fill 1 m³ then it will cost £1 to fill 4 m³. 160 ÷ 4 = 40, so it will cost £40 in total.

2 **B** — The pie chart is a circle so all of the angles add up to 360°. A section that is 90° would cover $\frac{1}{4}$ (or 25%) of the pie chart (360 ÷ 4 = 90°). The section for red flowers covers 45°, which is half of 90°. So as a percentage, 45° is 25% ÷ 2 = 12.5%. The correct answer is option B.

Pages 112-113 — Practice Questions

1 **£28** — Area of his garden: 13 × 8 = (10 × 8) + (3 × 8) = 80 + 24 = 104 m². 104 ÷ 30 = 3 remainder 14, so Horace will need 4 bags of fertiliser. So he will have to spend 4 × £7 = £28.

2 **B** — There are 60 seconds in a minute, so in $7\frac{1}{2}$ minutes, there are $7\frac{1}{2}$ × 60 = (7 × 60) + ($\frac{1}{2}$ × 60) = 420 + 30 = 450 seconds. So originally there were 450 × 10 = 4500 g of flour in the sack. Convert this into kilograms: 4500 ÷ 1000 = 4.5 kg.

3 **£210.00** — It costs 300 × 80p = 24 000p = £240 to make 300 cards. $\frac{1}{5}$ of 300 = 300 ÷ 5 = 60, so $\frac{3}{5}$ of 300 = 60 × 3 = 180. He sells 180 cards. 180 × £2.50 = (180 × £2) + (180 × £0.50) = £360 + £90 = £450, so he earns £450 − £240 = £210 in total.

4 **10 cm** — A regular pentagon has 5 equal sides, so the perimeter of the pentagon is 5 × 16 = 80 cm. The regular octagon has 8 equal sides and its perimeter is also 80 cm, so each side is 80 ÷ 8 = 10 cm long.

5 a) **6.0 km** — Read off the graph to find the distance each day, then add them together to find the total distance: 9 + 4 + 8 + 3 + 6 = 30. There are 5 days, so divide by 5 to find the mean: 30 ÷ 5 = 6 km.

b) **30%** — She walks 30 km in total, and she walks 9 km on Monday. $\frac{9}{30}$ is the same as $\frac{3}{10}$, which is 30%.

6 **450 ml** — He makes 2.7 litres = 2.7 × 1000 = 2700 ml of cleaning solution. There are 1 + 8 = 9 parts in total, so one part is 2700 ÷ 9 = 300 ml. He uses 300 ml of bleach, so there is 750 − 300 = 450 ml left.

7 **15** — Write $\frac{3}{4}$ as a percentage: $\frac{1}{4}$ = 25%, so $\frac{3}{4}$ = 3 × 25% = 75%. Work out how many lots of 5% make up 75%: 75 ÷ 5 = 15, so it takes 15 days.

8 **B** — You know (x + 2, y) is 2 units to the right of (x, y), and that (x, y − 6) is 6 units down from (x, y). Do a rough sketch:

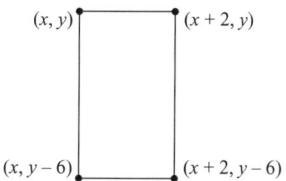

(x, y)   (x + 2, y)

(x, y − 6)   (x + 2, y − 6)

From this, you can see that the shape is a rectangle.

9 **B** — Work out how much she earns in total. For the first 10 km, she is sponsored £5 per km, so she gets £5 × 10 = £50. For the remaining 5 km, she is sponsored £8 per km, so she gets £8 × 5 = £40. So she is sponsored £50 + £40 = £90 in total. So the mean amount is £90 ÷ 15 = £6 per kilometre.

10 a) **72%** — Add up the cost of her items: £1.80 + £1.50 + £2.30 = £5.60. Then write the amount she spent as a fraction of £20: $\frac{5.6}{20}$ is the same as $\frac{56}{200}$ or $\frac{28}{100}$, and $\frac{28}{100}$ is 28%. She spent 28%, so she has 100% − 28% = 72% left.

b) **£5.00** — Work out how much they spent in total: £1.80 + £1.80 + £2.30 + £1.60 = £7.50. The ratio 2 : 1 has 2 + 1 = 3 parts in total, so one part is £7.50 ÷ 3 = £2.50. So Annabel pays £2.50 × 2 = £5.00.

11 **C** — List the prime numbers between 1 and 20: 2, 3, 5, 7, 11, 13, 17, 19. There are 8 prime numbers between 1 and 20, so $\frac{8}{20}$ are prime. This isn't one of the options, so you need to simplify it: $\frac{8}{20}$ is equivalent to $\frac{2}{5}$, so the answer is C.

12 **42°** — The sum of the angles in a quadrilateral is 360°: 65° + 85° + 2p + 3p = 360°, so 5p = 360° − 65° − 85° = 210°. 5p = 210°, so p = 210° ÷ 5 = 42°.

13 **21.8 cm** — Count up to find how many days the flower has been growing for. There are 31 days in May, so it is 26 days to the end of May, then another 16 days of June, so it has been 26 + 16 = 42 days. The flower grows 4 mm each day, so it has grown 42 × 4 = (40 × 4) + (2 × 4) = 160 + 8 = 168 mm. 168 mm = 168 ÷ 10 = 16.8 cm. The flower was 5 cm tall when it was planted, so now the flower is 5 + 16.8 = 21.8 cm tall.

Mixed Practice Tests
Pages 114-115 — Test 1

1 **8** — A regular octagon has 8 equal sides and 8 lines of symmetry.

2 **D** — 4030 ml = 4030 ÷ 1000 = 4.03 litres.

3 **1657** — M = 1000 and IX = 10 − 1 = 9, so MMIX = 1000 + 1000 + 9 = 2009. So the church was built 352 years before 2009. Partition 352 into 300 + 50 + 2 and then subtract from 2009: 2009 − 300 = 1709, then 1709 − 50 = 1659, and 1659 − 2 = 1657.

4 **17:32** — Add the 37 minutes in stages: 4:55 pm + 5 minutes = 5 pm. 37 − 5 = 32, so add another 32 minutes. 5 pm + 32 minutes = 5:32 pm, which is 17:32 in the 24-hour clock.

5 **23 000** — The 3 (in the thousands column) is being rounded. The 4 (in the hundreds column) is less than 5, so 23 486 rounds down to 23 000.

6 **363** — 4 = 12 ÷ 3, so the answer to 1452 ÷ 4 will be three times bigger than 121 (the answer to 1452 ÷ 12): 1452 ÷ 4 = 3 × 121 = (3 × 120) + (3 × 1) = 360 + 3 = 363

7 **105 cm²** — Split the shape into two rectangles and work out any missing lengths:
E.g.

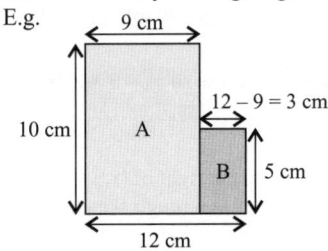

Then work out the two areas separately: the area of A is 9 × 10 = 90 cm² and the area of B is 3 × 5 = 15 cm², so the total area of the shape is 90 cm² + 15 cm² = 105 cm².

8 a) **60%** — 12 cakes were vanilla, so 30 − 12 = 18 cakes weren't vanilla. $^{18}/_{30} = ^{6}/_{10} = 60\%$.

b) **4** — 30 cakes were sold in total and 10 were large cakes, so 30 − 10 = 20 small cakes were sold. 12 vanilla cakes were sold in total and 3 of them were large cakes, so 12 − 3 = 9 small vanilla cakes were sold.
So 20 − 7 − 9 = 4 small lemon cakes were sold.

c) **90°** — Work out the percentage of customers who said tea or coffee: $^{2}/_{5}$ is the same as 40%, so 40% + 35% = 75% said tea or coffee. This means 100% − 75% = 25% = $^{1}/_{4}$ of customers said hot chocolate. Angles in a pie chart add up to 360°, so $^{1}/_{4}$ of the pie chart will have an angle of $^{1}/_{4}$ of 360° = 90°.

d) **E** — 6 × 80p = 480p. Convert £5 into pence: £5 = 5 × 100 = 500p. So he will get 500p − 480p = 20p change.

e) **B** —
A: The number of meals served is odd, and an odd number can't be divided into two equal whole numbers, so A can't be true.
B: If twice as many meals were served with salad, $^{2}/_{3}$ (= 26) of the meals were served with salad and $^{1}/_{3}$ (= 13) of them were served with chips. 39 is a multiple of 3, so B could be true.
C: The total number of meals served is odd, so the sum of the number of meals served with chips and with salad must be an odd number added to an even number. The difference between an odd number and an even number is always odd, so 4 more meals couldn't have been served with chips. C can't be true.
D: $^{3}/_{4}$ of 39 isn't a whole number, so D can't be true.
E: 12 is even, so this can't be true for the same reason as C.

Pages 116-117 — Test 2

1 **E** — A, C and E have a 0 in the ones column, and B and D have a 1 in the ones column, so it can't be B or D.
A has a 9 in the tenths column, C has an 8 in the tenths column and E has a 7 in the tenths column, so E is the smallest.

2 **27** — List the first few multiples of 9: 9, 18, 27, 36, ...
List the first few cube numbers: 1, 8, 27, 64, ...
27 appears in both lists, so it is the answer.

3 **£192** — First find how many boxes of pencils you need: 2400 ÷ 100 = 24 boxes. Each box costs £8, so 2400 pencils will cost 24 × £8 = (20 × £8) + (4 × £8) = £160 + £32 = £192.

4 **426** — First, work out the rule for the sequence. 404 − 393 = 11 and 415 − 404 = 11, so the rule is 'add 11'. So the missing number is 415 + 11 = 426. You can check this by adding 11 again: 426 + 11 = 437, which is the next number in the sequence.

5 **D** — P has been translated 2 units to the right and 1 unit down, so S has also been translated by the same amount. The original coordinates of S are (1, −1), so the new coordinates are (1 + 2, −1 − 1) = (3, −2).

6 **16** — There are 5 + 4 = 9 parts in total, so one part is 36 ÷ 9 = 4 sweets. So Julia gets 4 × 4 = 16 sweets.

7 **D** — The only shape that can be found by rotating Olive's shape is D:

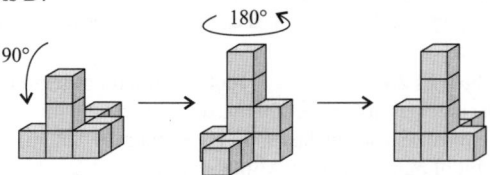

8 a) **2** — There are 3 + 3½ = 6½ circles in total in the France and Spain rows and 4 + 1½ = 5½ circles in total in the UK and USA rows. This is a difference of 1 whole circle, which represents 2 pupils.

b) **E** — From part a), there are 6½ + 5½ = 12 circles in total, so there are 12 × 2 = 24 pupils represented on the pictogram. There are 1½ circles in the USA row so 1½ × 2 = 3 pupils went to the USA on their last holiday. So $^{3}/_{24}$ pupils went to the USA. This isn't one of the options, so simplify it:
$^{3}/_{24}$ is the same as $^{1}/_{8}$.

c) **16 °C** — Count up 4 °C to go from −4 °C to 0 °C, then count up another 12 °C. So it is 4 + 12 = 16 °C warmer in San Francisco.

d) **£90.97** — First add the money she gets for her birthday to the money she has in savings. Partition £34.50 into £34 + £0.50. £271.42 + £34 = £305.42, and then £305.42 + £0.50 = £305.92.
Then subtract the cost of the plane tickets. Partition £214.95 into £200 + £15 − 5p. £305.92 − £200 = £105.92, then £105.92 − £15 = £90.92. Then add the 5p back on: £90.92 + 5p = £90.97.

e) **B** — It costs £5 per hour, so for *H* hours, it would cost 5 × *H* or 5*H*. Then add this to the fixed £8 to get 8 + 5*H*.

Pages 118-119 — Test 3

1 **E** — The only options that have four sides of equal length are a square and a rhombus. A square has four equal right angles, but a rhombus has a pair of equal acute angles and a pair of equal obtuse angles, so the shape must be a rhombus.

2 **12** — 25% is the same as $^{1}/_{4}$, so 25% of 48 = 48 ÷ 4 = 12.

3 **10.43 kg** — Use the column method for addition.
```
    3 . 7 8
 +  2 . 1 5
    4 . 5 0
  1 0 . 4 3
    1 1
```
So the total weight of the parcels is 10.43 kg.

4 **C** — Add the lengths to find the total: 6 + 8 + 9.5 + 5 + 6.5 = 35 Then divide by the number of keys (5): 35 ÷ 5 = 7 cm

5 **7700** — 32 and 68 are both multiplied by 77, so you can work out the answer quicker by adding them together first.
So 32 × 77 + 68 × 77 = (32 + 68) × 77 = 100 × 77 = 7700.

6 **C** — 800 ml is two parts of the ratio, so one part is 800 ml ÷ 2 = 400 ml. There are 3 + 2 = 5 parts in total, so she can make 5 × 400 = 2000 ml of salad dressing.
2000 ml = 2000 ÷ 1000 = 2 litres.

7 **D** —
A: The horizontal axis does go up in even steps, so this isn't true.
B: The graph is only supposed to show data from those years, so this isn't a reason why the graph is misleading.
C: The graph is about ice cream sales in general, so it doesn't matter what flavour the ice cream is.
D: This is misleading because it makes the increase in sales each year look bigger than it actually is. Daily ice cream sales have only increased by 20 in 5 years, but the graph makes it look like they have increased by a lot more than that.
E: The graph is about the average daily sales, so it doesn't matter exactly how many ice creams were sold each day.

155

8 a) **43 minutes** — Look at the times in the first column.
11:25 + 35 mins = 12:00. 12:00 + 8 mins = 12:08.
So the journey takes 35 mins + 8 mins = 43 mins.

b) **12:22** — 2:45 pm is written as 14:45 in the 24-hour clock.
The bus that arrives at 14:56 is too late, so he needs to catch the bus that arrives in Castleton at 13:13. This bus leaves Angelby at 12:34. He needs to leave home at least 12 minutes before this, so the latest time he can leave home is
12:34 – 12 minutes = 12:22.

c) **E** — The logo is made from nine identical small triangles. Three of the triangles are shaded, so $3/9$ of the logo is shaded. This isn't one of the options, so simplify it: $3/9$ is the same as $1/3$, so the answer is E.

d) **D** — The number will be smaller than 15 m, so the answer will have 1 ten and 4 ones. The digit in the tenths column has to be the smallest digit that rounds up, which is 5. 14.5 is smaller than 14.55 and rounds to 15 so the answer is 14.5 m.

e) **6.36 km** — 1000 m = 1 km, so 660 m = 660 ÷ 1000 = 0.66 km.
5.7 + 0.6 = 6.3, and 6.3 + 0.06 = 6.36. So in total,
Nick's journey is 6.36 km long.

Pages 120-121 — Test 4

1 **D** — All of the numbers have a 1 in the thousands column, so look at the hundreds column. Luke's score has a 6 in the hundreds column and Patrick's score has a 7, and the rest have an 8, so neither Luke nor Patrick have the highest score. Look at the tens column — Halima's score has a 2 in the tens column and Jemma's and Suzy's both have a 3, so Halima doesn't have the highest score. Finally look at the ones column — Jemma's score has a 1 in the ones column and Suzy's has a 9, so Suzy's score is the highest.

2 **12.37** — Partition 24.83 into 24 + 0.8 + 0.03.
37.2 – 24 = 13.2, then 13.2 – 0.8 = 12.4, and 12.4 – 0.03 = 12.37.

3 **4** — Add the heights of the bars: 1 + 3 + 2 + 6 + 13 + 11 = 36.
40 pupils voted in total, so 40 – 36 = 4 pupils voted for Thursday.

4 **58.4 cm** — Partition 7.3 into 7 + 0.3.
Then 8 × 7.3 = (8 × 7) + (8 × 0.3) = 56 + 2.4 = 58.4 cm.

5 **A** — Angles on a straight line add up to 180°, so the other angle inside the triangle is 180° – 108° = 72°. Angles in a triangle also add up to 180°, so x = 180° – 32° – 72° = 76°.

6 **E** — The number must be both prime and a factor of 12. The factors of 12 are 1, 2, 3, 4, 6 and 12, so the factors that are also prime are 2 and 3. 3 isn't one of the options, so the answer is E.

7 **16 cm²** — The star is made from the sides of equilateral triangles, so all of the sides of the star are the same length.
There are 8 sides, so each side is 32 ÷ 8 = 4 cm long.
The sides of the square are also sides of the equilateral triangles, so each side of the square is 4 cm long as well.
So the area of the square piece of card is 4 × 4 = 16 cm².

8 a) **17** — Add the masses of the ingredients:
360 g + 180 g + 120 g = 660 g. So she can make
660 ÷ 30 = 66 ÷ 3 = 22 biscuits. She eats 5 biscuits,
so she has 22 – 5 = 17 biscuits left to sell.

b) **3 : 2** — The ratio of butter to sugar is 180 g : 120 g.
Simplify the ratio by dividing both sides in stages:
180 : 120 = 18 : 12 = 3 : 2.

c) **1.8 kg** — 600 g = 120 g × 5, so he has 5 times as much sugar as in the recipe. This means he will need 5 times as much flour as in the recipe to make as many biscuits as he can.
5 × 360 = (5 × 300) + (5 × 60) = 1500 + 300 = 1800 g.
1800 g = 1800 ÷ 1000 = 1.8 kg.

d) **25 cm** — The volume of a cuboid = length × width × height,
so 7500 = 20 × 15 × height = 300 × height.
So the height of the cuboid is 7500 ÷ 300 = 75 ÷ 3 = 25 cm.

e) **9** — Work out how many packs of biscuits Class 6A can make:
72 = 12 × 6, so 729 ÷ 12 = 60 remainder 9. So they can fill 60 packs, and will have 9 biscuits left over.

Pages 122-132 — Test-Style Paper 1

1 a) **Bollenby** — All of the numbers have a 2 in the ten thousands column, so look at the thousands column. Setford's population has an 8 and the others have a 9, so Setford doesn't have the largest population. Then look at the hundreds column — Thekeston's population has a 0 but Pondham and Bollenby both have a 1, so it can't be Thekeston. Then look at the tens column — Bollenby has 7 tens and Pondham has 5, so Bollenby has the largest population.

b) **30 000** — The 2 (in the ten thousands column) is being rounded. The 9 (in the thousands column) is more than 5, so 29 086 rounds up to 30 000.

c) **1714** — M = 1000, D = 500, C = 100, X = 10, IV = 5 – 1 = 4.
So Setford was founded in 1000 + 500 + 100 + 10 + 4 = 1614.
Pondham was founded 100 years later, in 1614 + 100 = 1714.

2 a) **20p** — Three metres of flowery fabric costs
3 × £6.10 = (3 × £6) + (3 × £0.10) = £18 + £0.30 = £18.30.
Then add the cost of the thread: £18.30 + £1.50 = £19.80,
so she gets £20 – £19.80 = 20p change.

b) **30** — Find the answer by working out £45 ÷ £1.50.
£45 ÷ £15 = 3, so £45 ÷ £1.50 = 3 × 10 = 30.

c) **£20.40** — 10% of £24 = £2.40 and 5% of £24 = £1.20,
so he gets £2.40 + £1.20 = £3.60 off.
So his items cost £24 – £3.60 = £20.40 after the discount.

3 a) **38p** — One book costs £3.80 ÷ 10 = £0.38 = 38p.

b) **6000** — One pack contains 10 × 120 = 1200 pages,
so 5 packs contains 5 × 1200 pages.
5 × 12 = 60, so 5 × 1200 = 60 × 100 = 6000 pages.

c) **£114** — 300 exercise books = 300 ÷ 10 = 30 packs.
Each pack costs £3.80, so the total cost is
£3.80 × 30 = (£3 × 30) + (£0.80 × 30) = £90 + £24 = £114.

4 a) **2** — 2 is prime, because it only has 1 and itself as factors.
But 2 is also a factor of 84 (84 = 2 × 42), so it should be in the shaded section.

b) **7** — Factors of 84: 1, 2, 3, 4, 6, 7, 12, 14, 21, 28, 42 and 84.
The biggest number in this list that is also prime is 7.

5 a) **14 minutes** — The paper round took 40 minutes on Friday and 26 minutes on Tuesday, so it took 40 – 26 = 14 minutes longer.

b) **6:39 am** — He took 34 minutes on Wednesday, so count back 34 minutes. 7:13 am – 13 minutes = 7 am. Then count back another 34 – 13 = 21 minutes. 7 am – 21 minutes = 6:39 am.

c) **32 minutes** — Add up the times for each day:
35 + 26 + 34 + 25 + 40 = 160.
Then divide by the number of days (5): 160 ÷ 5 = 32 minutes.

6 a) **(–1, 5)** — The fourth coordinate will have the same x-coordinate as A and the same y-coordinate as C, so the coordinates are (–1, 5).

b) **(1, 1)** — Counter C has the coordinates (3, 5), so after the translation, its coordinates are (3 – 2, 5 – 4) = (1, 1).

7 a) **C** — If you look at the shape directly from the right, you would see this shape.

b) **112 cm³** — All of the edges of a cube are the same length, so the volume of each cube is 2 × 2 × 2 = 8 cm³.
There are 14 cubes in total, so the volume of the shape is
8 × 14 = (8 × 10) + (8 × 4) = 80 + 32 = 112 cm³.

8 **26 cm** — Convert everything into cm:
1.08 m = 1.08 × 100 = 108 cm, 340 mm = 340 ÷ 10 = 34 cm.
First, add up the heights of the first two blocks. Partition 48 into 40 + 8. 34 cm + 40 cm = 74 cm, and 74 cm + 8 cm = 82 cm.
So the height of the third piece is 108 cm – 82 cm = 26 cm.

9 **Pentagon** — The reflected shape has 5 sides, so it's a pentagon.

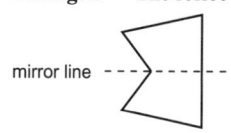

mirror line

Answers

10 a) **350** — Add the tickets she sold in the first three weeks:
$$\begin{array}{r} 339 \\ + 627 \\ \underline{484} \\ 1450 \\ 12 \end{array}$$
Partition 1450 into 1400 + 50, and subtract this from 1800.
1800 − 1400 = 400, then 400 − 50 = 350.
So she sold 350 raffle tickets in Week 4.

b) **£1.50** — £2700 ÷ 1800 = £27 ÷ 18 = £3 ÷ 2 = £1.50.
(Here, we divided both numbers by 100, then by 9, to make the division easier. You can use whichever method you prefer.)

c) **£2530** — Work out the total cost of the prizes:
£95 + (5 × £15) = £95 + £75 = £170.
So she donated £2700 − £170 = £2530.

11 a) **36 minutes** — 11:56 + 4 minutes = 12:00, and 12:00 + 32 minutes = 12:32, so it takes 4 + 32 = 36 minutes.

b) **13:07** — The last train to arrive in Ternslow before 2 pm (14:00) is the one that arrives at 13:47. This leaves Wetherton at 13:21. She needs to leave home at least 14 minutes earlier so the latest she could leave is 13:21 − 14 minutes = 13:07.

c) **90 minutes** — Bert arrives in Wetherton at 13:49.
13:49 + 1 hour = 14:49, 14:49 + 30 minutes = 15:19.
So he cycles for 1 hour 30 minutes = 90 minutes.

d) **45 km** — 1 hour 30 minutes = $1\frac{1}{2}$ hours.
He cycles 30 km each hour, so in $1\frac{1}{2}$ hours, he cycles $1\frac{1}{2} \times 30 = 1 \times 30 + \frac{1}{2} \times 30 = 30 + 15 = 45$ km.

12 a) **18** — 9 + 14 = 23 people like milk in their tea and 2 + 3 = 5 people don't like milk.
So 23 − 5 = 18 more people like milk.

b) **$\frac{1}{2}$** — Work out how many people Rachel asked:
9 + 2 + 14 + 3 = 28 people. 14 like milk and no sugar, so $\frac{14}{28} = \frac{1}{2}$ of people like milk and no sugar.

13 **49** — You're looking for a cube number and a square number that add up to 76. The cube number must be smaller than 76, so the only possible options are 1, 8, 27 and 64. 76 − 1 = 75, 76 − 8 = 68, 76 − 27 = 49, which is square: 49 = 7 × 7 = 7^2.
So there are 27 green marbles and 49 red marbles.

14 a) **Right-angled** — One of the angles in the triangle is also an angle in the rectangle. All angles in a rectangle are 90°, so it is a right-angled triangle.

b) **78°** — The sum of angles in a triangle is 180°, so the other angles in each small triangle are 180° − 90° − 53° = 37°, and 180° − 90° − 25° = 65°. Angles on a straight line also add up to 180°, so x = 180° − 37° − 65° = 78°.

15 a) **7h + 4** — It costs £7 per hour, so for h hours it will cost 7 × h, or 7h. Then add on the £4 fixed cost to get 7h + 4.

b) **£75** — The cost for one person to go ice skating for 2 hours is (7 × 2) + 4 = £18, so it costs 5 × £18 = £90 for five people.
They get £15 off, so the total cost is £90 − £15 = £75.

16 a) **17** — There are 3 symbols in the sparrow row, so she saw 3 × 4 = 12 sparrows. There are $1\frac{1}{4}$ symbols in the blackbird row, so she saw $1\frac{1}{4} \times 4 = 5$ blackbirds. In total, she saw 12 + 5 = 17 sparrows and blackbirds.

b) **1 : 2** — She saw $1\frac{1}{2} \times 4 = 6$ magpies and 3 × 4 = 12 robins, so the ratio is 6 : 12. In its simplest form, this is 1 : 2.

c) **0.9 kg** — She uses 150 g of seed every day for 6 days, so she uses 6 lots of 150 g. 6 × 150 = (6 × 100) + (6 × 50) = 600 + 300 = 900 g. 900 g = 900 ÷ 1000 = 0.9 kg.

17 a) **1800 g** — He needs 1.2 kg = 1.2 × 1000 = 1200 g to make 8 portions. 12 = 8 × $1\frac{1}{2}$, so he needs 1200 × $1\frac{1}{2}$ = 1200 + 600 = 1800 g to make 12 portions.

b) **0.8 kg** — He needs 1.2 kg ÷ 2 = 0.6 kg of onions to make 4 portions. 3 parts = 0.6 kg, so 1 part = 0.6 kg ÷ 3 = 0.2 kg. So 4 parts = 4 × 0.2 kg = 0.8 kg of carrots.

18 **43** — Use BODMAS to do the calculation in the correct order:
$(5 − 2)^3 + 8 \times 2 = 3^3 + 8 \times 2 = 27 + 8 \times 2 = 27 + 16 = 43$

19 a) **135°** — Angles in a pie chart add up to 360°, so the angle for 'bus' is 360° − 120° − 60° − 45° = 180° − 45° = 135°.

b) **$\frac{1}{8}$** — 90° is $\frac{1}{4}$ of a pie chart, so 45° is $\frac{1}{4} \div 2 = \frac{1}{8}$.

c) **72** — The 'walk' sector is 60°. $\frac{60}{360} = \frac{1}{6}$, so this is $\frac{1}{6}$ of the pie chart. $\frac{1}{6}$ of the total pupils walked to school, so he asked 12 × 6 = 72 pupils in total.

d) **6** — From above, there are 72 pupils in total. $\frac{1}{3}$ of them travelled by car — $\frac{1}{3}$ of 72 = 72 ÷ 3 = 24 pupils.
Out of these 24 pupils, 25% of them came in a blue car.
25% of 24 = 24 ÷ 4 = 6 pupils.

20 a) **76** — The numbers in this sequence are all one more than a multiple of 7. Check each of the options:
36 − 1 = 35 = 7 × 5   22 − 1 = 21 = 7 × 3
43 − 1 = 42 = 7 × 6   64 − 1 = 63 = 7 × 9
76 − 1 = 75 isn't a multiple of 7, so isn't in the sequence.

b) **141** — Substitute n = 20 into the sequence.
(7 × 20) + 1 = 140 + 1 = 141

21 a) **144 m²** — Split the shape into two rectangles and work out any missing lengths, e.g.:

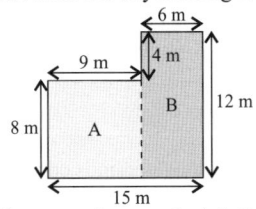

The area of rectangle A is 8 × 9 = 72 m² and the area of rectangle B is 6 × 12 = 72 m², so the total area is 72 + 72 = 144 m².

b) **£432** — The perimeter is 8 + 9 + 4 + 6 + 12 + 15 = 54 m.
54 × £8 = (50 × £8) + (4 × £8) = £400 + £32 = £432.

c) **30 minutes** — There are 5 lots of 0.2 m³ in 1 m³, so there are 6 × 5 = 30 lots of 0.2 m³ in 6 m³. So it takes 30 minutes.

d) **14:05** — 1:35 pm + 30 minutes = 2:05 pm, which is 14:05 in the 24-hour clock.

Pages 133-143 — Test-Style Paper 2

1 a) **12 800 m** — 12.8 km = 12.8 × 1000 = 12 800 m.

b) **5.28 km** — Partition 7.52 into 7 + 0.5 + 0.02.
12.8 − 7 = 5.8, then 5.8 − 0.5 = 5.3, and 5.3 − 0.02 = 5.28.
So he has 5.28 km left to walk.

c) **14:08** — Add 45 minutes to the time he spent walking.
2 hours 43 minutes + 17 minutes = 3 hours. Then add another 45 − 17 = 28 minutes to get 3 hours 28 minutes.
10:40 + 3 hours = 13:40, then 13:40 + 28 minutes = 14:08.

2 a) **Maggie** — All of the guesses have a 3 in the thousands column, so look at the hundreds column. Maggie and Zara's guesses have a 2 in the hundreds column. Jaleel's has a 7 and David's has a 5, so it can't be Jaleel or David. Then look at the tens column. Maggie's guess has a 4 and Zara's guess has a 6, so Maggie's guess is the smallest.

b) **153** — Partition 3519 into 3500 + 10 + 9.
3672 − 3500 = 172, then 172 − 10 = 162 and 162 − 9 = 153.
His guess is 153 jelly beans away from the actual number.

c) **204** — Partition 3672 into 3600 + 72 and divide each part.
3672 ÷ 18 = (3600 ÷ 18) + (72 ÷ 18) = 200 + 4 = 204.

3 a) **2** — The only prime numbers in the set are 5 and 13.

b) **15** — Factors of 60: 1, 2, 3, 4, 5, 6, 10, 12, 15, 20, 30 and 60.
Factors of 90: 1, 2, 3, 5, 6, 9, 10, 15, 18, 30, 45 and 90.
The biggest number in both lists that is also in the set is 15.

c) **3** — 1 is both a square and a cube number (1 = 1^2 and 1 = 1^3).
8 is a cube number (8 = 2^3). 9 is a square number (9 = 3^2).

4 a) **13 °C** — The highest temperature reached was 24 °C at 14:00. The lowest temperature was 11 °C at 07:00, so the difference was 24 °C − 11 °C = 13 °C.

b) **8 hours** — The greenhouse first reached 17 °C at 09:00 and fell below 17 °C at 17:00. 09:00 + 3 hours = 12:00, then 12:00 + 5 hours = 17:00, so the temperature was at least 17 °C for 3 + 5 = 8 hours.

Answers

c) **–4 °C** — 6 pm = 18:00 in the 24-hour clock. On the summer day, it was 15 °C at 18:00 in the greenhouse, so on the winter day, it was 15 °C – 19 °C = –4 °C at 18:00.

5 **⁴⁄₅ of 25** — Work out the value of each expression:
½ of 30 = 30 ÷ 2 = 15   25% of 40 = 40 ÷ 4 = 10
⁴⁄₅ of 25 = 25 ÷ 5 × 4 = 20   50% of 20 = 20 ÷ 2 = 10
¼ of 60 = 60 ÷ 4 = 15

6 a) **3827 g** — Use the column method for addition.
```
   1 4 5 6
 + 2 3 7 1
   ───────
   3 8 2 7
       1
```
So they picked 3827 grams of blackberries.

b) **1.44 kg** — Partition 480 into 400 + 80.
480 × 3 = (400 × 3) + (80 × 3) = 1200 + 240 = 1440 g.
1440 g = 1440 ÷ 1000 = 1.44 kg.

c) **75%** — There are 3 × 8 = 24 slices of pie in total.
2 + 3 + 1 = 6 slices have been eaten, so 24 – 6 = 18 slices are left. ¹⁸⁄₂₄ = ¾ = 75%.

7 a) **21 minutes 30 seconds** — The number will be smaller than 22 minutes, so the answer will have 2 tens and 1 one. The digit in the tenths column has to be the smallest digit that rounds up, which is 5, so the answer is 21.5 minutes. 0.5 × 60 = 30, so 21.5 minutes = 21 minutes 30 seconds.

b) **26 minutes** — Find the total of the times:
26 + 24 + 22 + 32 = 104. Then divide the total by 4 to find the mean: 104 ÷ 4 = 26 minutes.

c) **£16.00** — He gets sponsored £1.20 + £1.30 + £1.50 = £4 for every 250 m, so he gets 4 × £4 = £16 for each kilometre.

d) **20 km** — He gets £16 for each kilometre.
32 = 16 × 2, so £320 ÷ £16 = 20 kilometres.

8 a) **2000 – 80x** — 2 litres = 2 × 1000 = 2000 ml. She pours 80 ml of glue into x pots, so she pours out 80 × x = 80x ml. So the amount left in the bottle is 2000 – 80x.

b) **0.8 litres** — 80 × 15 = (80 × 10) + (80 × 5) = 800 + 400 = 1200 ml. Partition 1200 into 1000 + 200, and then subtract. 2000 – 1000 = 1000, then 1000 – 200 = 800. 800 ml = 800 ÷ 1000 = 0.8 litres.

9 a) **1** — The shape has one horizontal line of symmetry.

b) **(–5, 2)** — Before the reflection, W has coordinates (–5, –2). It is two squares below the x-axis, so after the reflection it will be 2 squares above it. So the coordinates are (–5, 2).

c) **(0, –3)** — Before the translation, Y has coordinates (–2, –5). To get to (3, –4), it is translated 5 squares to the right and 1 square up. X is translated by the same amount. Originally it had coordinates (–5, –4), so the new coordinates of X are (–5 + 5, –4 + 1) = (0, –3).

10 **71** — 10 = 3 + 7, 17 = 7 + 10, 27 = 10 + 17, so to get the next term, you add the previous two terms together. So the sixth term is 17 + 27 = 44, and the seventh term is 27 + 44 = 71.

11 **4326** — 7 = 14 ÷ 2, so the answer to 618 × 7 is 8652 ÷ 2 = 4326.

12 a) **45** — Split 135 into smaller parts that are easier to divide.
135 = 90 + 45. 135 ÷ 3 = (90 ÷ 3) + (45 ÷ 3) = 30 + 15 = 45.

b) **£360** — 1200 = 12 × 100, so 1200 eggs cost £1.80 × 100 = £180. 2400 = 1200 × 2, so 2400 eggs cost £180 × 2 = £360.

c) **£27** — Work out the cost of the order.
(3 × £5) + £5.75 + (3 × £2) = £15 + £5.75 + £6 = £26.75. The 6 (in the ones column) is being rounded. The 7 (in the tenths column) is more than 5, so £26.75 rounds up to £27.

d) **£14** — There are 2 + 1 = 3 parts in total, so one part is £21 ÷ 3 = £7. So Gregor pays 2 × £7 = £14.

13 a) **Rhombus** — There are four sides, so it can't be a pentagon. None of the angles are right angles, so it can't be a square. It has two pairs of parallel sides, and each side of the grey tile is also the side of a regular hexagon, so all four sides are the same length. So the shape is a rhombus.

b) **12 cm** — The design has 16 sides. Each side is the side of a regular hexagon, so the sides are all the same length. So each side is 48 cm ÷ 16 = 3 cm long. The grey tile has four sides, and each one is also the side of a hexagon, so they are 3 cm long as well. So the perimeter of the grey tile is 4 × 3 cm = 12 cm.

c) **£15.60** — A grey tile costs ⅓ of £3.60 = £3.60 ÷ 3 = £1.20.
4 hexagon tiles costs 4 × £3.60 = (4 × £3) + (4 × £0.60) = £12 + £2.40 = £14.40, so the total cost of the design is £14.40 + £1.20 = £15.60.

d) **21** — The first pattern has 3 hexagon tiles, the second pattern has 3 + 3 = 6 tiles and the third pattern has 6 + 4 = 10 tiles. The rule is 'increase the number of tiles added by 1 each time'. So the fourth pattern will have 10 + 5 = 15 tiles, and the fifth pattern will have 15 + 6 = 21 tiles.

14 **4** — The mean is 6, so the total number of acorns is 6 × 5 = 30. Add up the acorns he finds on the other days: 7 + 6 + 5 + 8 = 26, so he found 30 – 26 = 4 acorns on Tuesday.

15 **9** — Do each operation in reverse to find the original number. First subtract 11 from 74 to get 63, then 63 ÷ 7 = 9.

16 a) **120 cm²** — The area of a triangle is ½ × base × height, so each triangle has an area of ½ × 5 × 12 = 30 cm². There are four triangles, so the total area is 4 × 30 = 120 cm².

b) **23°** — Angles on a straight line add up to 180°, so the other angle on the straight line is 180° – 113° = 67°. Angles in a triangle also add up to 180°. The triangles are right-angled, so one of the angles is 90°. So x = 180° – 90° – 67° = 23°.

17 **46** — Each cube has 2 cm long sides, so she can fit 14 ÷ 2 = 7 pieces of toffee along the length, 8 ÷ 2 = 4 pieces along the width and 4 ÷ 2 = 2 pieces up the height. So she can fit 7 × 4 × 2 = 56 pieces of toffee in the box. She removes 10 pieces, so there are 56 – 10 = 46 pieces left.

18 **3a – 15** — 3(a – 5) = 3 × (a – 5) = (3 × a) – (3 × 5) = 3a – 15.

19 a) **⁹⁄₂₀** — Find equivalent fractions so you can add them up:
²⁄₅ = ⁸⁄₂₀, so ²⁄₅ + ³⁄₂₀ = ⁸⁄₂₀ + ³⁄₂₀ = ¹¹⁄₂₀ of the spaces are used. This means 1 – ¹¹⁄₂₀ = ²⁰⁄₂₀ – ¹¹⁄₂₀ = ⁹⁄₂₀ are free.

b) **150** — Work out how many cars were parked at 10 am:
¹¹⁄₂₀ = ¹¹⁰⁄₂₀₀, so there were 110 parked cars at 10 am. There are 40 more cars, so there are 110 + 40 = 150 cars.

c) **21.4 m** — There are 8 parking spaces and 7 gaps between the spaces. 20 cm = 20 ÷ 100 = 0.2 m, so the length of the row is (8 × 2.5) + (7 × 0.2) = 20 + 1.4 = 21.4 m.

20 **C** — The gap between the bars changes from 10 years to 40 years, so it looks like the sales have suddenly increased by a lot, but the increase might have actually been more gradual. The other options aren't correct: The graph is about the UK, so sales in other countries don't matter. The sales before 1960 are not relevant to what the graph is trying to show. Writing the numbers in thousands would not change what the graph is showing. A bar chart is a suitable choice to display this data.

21 a) **60°** — Angles in a pie chart add up to 360°, so the 'three cats' sector is 360° – 90° – 90° – 120° = 60°.

b) **⁷⁄₁₂** — 'Fewer than two cats' is the sum of the 'no cats' sector and the 'one cat' sector. 90° + 120° = 210°, so 210° out of 360° represents 'fewer than two cats'. ²¹⁰⁄₃₆₀ is the same as ²¹⁄₃₆ = ⁷⁄₁₂.

c) **24** — Work out the smallest number that is a multiple of 6 and 8. The first few multiples of 6 are 6, 12, 18, 24, 30... The first few multiples of 8 are 8, 16, 24, 32, ... The smallest number on both lists is 24, so it will be 24 days until they both open a new bag on the same day.

d) **8th July** — Count on 24 days from 14th June. There are 30 days in June, so 14th June + 16 days = 30th June, then add another 24 – 16 = 8 days to get to 8th July.

22 **C** — The nets for options A, B, D and E all result in cubes with the two shaded faces sharing an edge, and not opposite.

Index

2D shapes 73-82
3D shapes 83-86

A
addition 9, 10
algebra 43-46
angles 71-74
area 77-80

B
bar charts 59
BODMAS 21

C
circles 73
converting units 101
coordinates 90, 91
cube numbers 27
cubes 83
cuboids 83

D
data 57-66
decimals 5-8, 37-39
denominator 32, 33
division 13, 14, 18-20

E
elevations 87
equations 44
equilateral triangles 73
equivalent fractions 32
even numbers 27
expressions 43

F
factors 29-31
formulas 44
fractions 32-34, 37-39

I
improper fractions 33
isosceles triangles 73

L
length 100
line graphs 59

M
mass 100
mean 63, 64
misleading data 65, 66
mixed calculations 21, 22
mixed numbers 33
mixed problems 108-111
multiples 29-31
multiplication 13-17

N
negative numbers 27
nets 83
nth term of a sequence 47
numerator 32, 33

O
odd numbers 27
ordering fractions 33

P
percentages 37-39
perimeter 77-80
pictograms 60
pie charts 60
place value 5, 6
plans 87
polygons 74
prime numbers 30, 31
prisms 83
projections 87
proportions 35, 36, 60
pyramids 83

Q
quadrilaterals 71, 73

R
ratio 35, 36
reading scales 100
reflection 81, 92, 93
right-angled triangles 73
Roman numerals 27
rounding 7, 8

S
scalene triangles 73
sequences 47-49
shape problems 87-89
square numbers 27
subtraction 11, 12
symmetry 81, 82

T
tables (data) 57, 58
time 103-105
transformations 92, 93
translation 92, 93
triangles 71, 73

U
units 100-102

V
volume 84, 100

W
word problems 50-53